MANAGEMENT AND LEADERSHII
EDUCATION SERIES

Series Editors: PETER RIBBINS AND JOHN
SAYER

**Radical Educational Policies and
Conservative Secretaries of State**

TITLES IN THE MANAGEMENT
AND LEADERSHIP IN EDUCATION SERIES:

Titles marked * originally appeared as part of the
Education Management series

MIKE BOTTERY:
The Ethics of Educational Management *

HELEN GUNTER:
Rethinking Education: The Consequences of Jurassic Management

MOLLY HATTERSLEY (ED):
The Appraisal of Headteachers*

IAN LAWRENCE (ED.):
Education Tomorrow *

IAN LAWRENCE:
Power and Politics at the Department of Education and Science*

PATRICIA LEIGHTON:
Schools and Employment Law*

PETER RIBBINS AND BRIAN SHERRATT:
Radical Educational Policies and Conservative Secretaries of State

KATHRYN RILEY:
Quality and Equality: Promoting Opportunities in Schools*

JOHN SAYER:
The Future Governance of Education*

DAVID SCOTT (ED.):
Accountability and Control in Educational Settings*

VIVIAN WILLIAMS (ED.):
Towards Self-managing Schools: A Secondary Schools Perspective*

Forthcoming

PETER RIBBINS:
Leaders and Leadership in the School, College and University

CHRISTINE PASCAL AND PETER RIBBINS:
Headship on the Primary School

STEVE RAYNER AND PETER RIBBINS
Leaders and Leadership in Special Education

Radical Educational Policies and Conservative Secretaries of State

PETER RIBBINS AND BRIAN SHERRATT

CASSELL

Cassell

Wellington House   PO Box 605
125 Strand   Herndon
London WC2R 0BB   VA 20172

British Library Cataloguing-in-Publication Data
A catalogue record for this book is available from the British Library.

ISBN   0-304-33906-7 (hardback)
          0-304-33907-5 (paperback)

Typeset by Action Typesetting Ltd, Gloucester
Printed and bound in Great Britain by
Redwood Books, Trowbridge, Wiltshire

Contents

Acknowledgements

A number of people have made this book possible. We are grateful in particular for the unfailing and enthusiastic support which we have received from Martin Brandon Bravo in paving our way to the former and current Secretaries of State for Education who are the subject of this study. Without this, it is unlikely that we would have been able to undertake this project. We are also grateful to Kenneth Baker, Mark Carlisle, Kenneth Clarke, John MacGregor, John Patten and Gillian Shephard for finding the time and patience in impossibly busy lives to speak to us and to check the texts we sent to them. We wish to thank Clyde Chitty for agreeing to construct an 'as if' conversation with the late Sir Keith Joseph and Stephen Ball for his generosity in allowing us free use of a substantial interview which he conducted with Sir Keith. Finally, we are grateful to those who have played a part in the initial transcriptions of the interviews. In this regard, we are not sure what we could have done without the willing and highly professional support of Rosemary Greenway.

Grateful acknowledgement is given to A. P. Watt Ltd on behalf of the National Trust for granting permission to include a quotation from Rudyard Kipling's 'If' on page 118. Source: *The Oxford Dictionary of Quotations* (2nd ed.), 1953.

Abbreviations

ATL	Association of Teachers and Lecturers
BMA	British Medical Association
CLEA	Council for Local Education Authorities
CSE	Certificate of Secondary Education
CTC	City Technology College
DES	Department of Education and Science
DfE	Department for Education
DfEE	Department for Education and Employment
FAS	Funding Agency for Schools
GCSE	General Certificate of Secondary Education
GM	grant-maintained
GMS	grant-maintained school(s)
GNVQs	General National Vocational Qualifications
HMCI	Her Majesty's Chief Inspector
HMI	Her Majesty's Inspectorate
HMIs	Her Majesty's Inspectors
IEA	Institute of Economic Affairs
ILEA	Inner London Education Authority
INSET	in-service training
LEA	Local Education Authority
LMS	Local Management of Schools
MORI	Market and Opinion Research International
MSC	Manpower Services Commission
NAS	National Association of Schoolmasters and Union of Women Teachers
NCC	National Curriculum Council
NHS	National Health Service
NUT	National Union of Teachers
NVQs	National Vocational Qualifications
OFSTED	Office for Standards in Education
SACRES	Standing Advisory Council for Religious Education

SATs	Standard Attainment Targets
SCAA	School Curriculum and Assessment Authority
SEAC	School Examinations and Assessment Council
TEC	Training and Enterprise Council
TTA	Teacher Training Agency
TVEI	Technical and Vocational Education Initiative
WEA	Workers' Educational Association

Conservatives reforming education: conversations with seven Secretaries of State

PETER RIBBINS AND BRIAN SHERRATT

Preface

In the last few months of 1970, Maurice Kogan undertook the series of conversations with first Anthony Crosland and then Edward Boyle which were subsequently reported in *The Politics of Education* (1971). His main purpose was to explore with 'two of the ablest politicians to emerge since the 1939–45 war', who between them had held office for almost all of the five years between July 1962 and August 1967, what they saw as their role as Ministers of Education. These conversations, along with Kogan's substantial introduction to them, have significantly shaped our understanding of the role of the centre in policy-making and the management of education. But they took place at what some have come to see as a high point of the consensus on education and its management which developed in the wake of the 1944 Education Act and which was reflected in the praxis of these two influential ministers. Whether such claims are justified as an accurate description of the time is a matter of growing debate. In developing this and related points Kogan suggests that

> In the 1950s several changes occurred which decisively altered the balance of power between central and local government ... [which] brought the Department from being the holder of the ring between the 'real' forces in education policy making, which had hitherto been the local authorities, the denominations, and the teachers and parents, to being the enforcer of positive controls, based increasingly on knowledge which the Department itself went out to get ... Yet whenever called upon to pronounce, central government dutifully preached the contrary to central control.
>
> (Kogan, 1971, pp. 29–30)

In support of this view, he quotes Crosland's frank admission that 'all who have had to cope with local government are schizophrenic about the extent of central government's control over it' (p. 30). Whether Crosland actually did favour a decisive shift in the nature of the relationship between the central and local government of education is not fully clear. The remark quoted above is located in a passage of conversation in which the former minister explains that

> until there's reorganization you can't give local authorities much more power than they have at the moment ... As far as education is concerned I wasn't conscious at the DES of any great problem or any demands on either side for a major change in the relationship with LEAs.

(p. 171)

Boyle, in some ways, seems more genuinely enthusiastic about the contribution of local government than Crosland. He notes that 'quite a lot of important ideas in education have come up from the local authorities', and speaks with considerable warmth about the work of Bristol, Hertfordshire, Leicestershire, Southampton, the Isle of Wight and the West Riding (pp. 125, 127). Pressed by Kogan, he agrees

> there is and has to be some central framework ... But I'd hope that governments for the most part play along with what local authorities genuinely want to do, rather than to have to impose too many things on them they don't want to do.

(p. 127)

This is not, as we shall see, a view which would find too much favour among contemporary Conservative Education Secretaries. Even so, neither Boyle nor Crosland seriously contest the view which Kogan put to them in one form or another at a number of points in these interviews, that they 'were beneficiaries of the popular mood of the 1960s when few were prepared to argue against stronger government leadership and intervention in education' (p. 20).

To an extent this fits rather uneasily with the many claims that have been made before and after the 1988 Education Reform Act that it represents an unprecedented lurch towards central control. As Jack Straw put it in the debate on the Second Reading of the Bill which took place in December 1987,

> it should be called the 'Education (State Control) Bill'. Under the disguise of fine phrases like 'parental choice' and 'decentralization' the Bill will deny choice and instead centralize power and control over schools, colleges and universities in the hand of the Secretary of State in a manner without parallel in the Western World.

(*Hansard*, 1987, 781)

This view was shared by some Conservatives. Indeed, Edward Heath suggested that

> The Secretary of State has taken more powers under the Bill than any other member of the Cabinet, more than my right hon. Friends the Chancellor of the Exchequer, the Secretary of State of Defence and the Secretary of State for Social Services.

(ibid., 792)

While there may be an element of exaggeration in such claims, we do not expect to hear any Secretary of State in the foreseeable future, of whatever political disposition, repeat the proud boast of George Tomlinson, the longest serving holder of the office in the post-war era, that 'Minister's now't to do with the curriculum' (Smith, 1957, p. 162). Indeed, it could be that no such minister would be likely to admit to sharing fully Anthony Crosland's more modest view that

> the nearer one comes to the professional content of education, the more indirect the minister's influence is. And I am sure that this is right ... generally I didn't regard either myself or my officials as in the slightest degree competent to interfere with the curriculum. We are educational politicians and administrators, not professional educators.
>
> (Kogan, 1971, p. 172)

Whether or not the Boyle and Crosland years represent a final flowering of the post-war consensus on education in general and of the role of the Secretary of State in particular or, as John Patten suggests, the beginning of its demise, is an issue which we will return to briefly later in this chapter. In the book as a whole we have drawn upon the approach, modified as appropriate, which Kogan pioneered, to explore this and related issues in conversations with the seven Conservative Secretaries of State who have held office since 1979. We have asked them questions about the nature of the 'radical' reform agenda for education which has been pushed through in recent years and about their part in determining and delivering it. Unlike Kogan, we were interested in the seven Secretaries of State as people, and have attempted, in a preliminary and tentative way, to consider how their personalities have shaped and been shaped by their experience before, during and after their years in office. In doing so we have built upon the work we have been engaged in which has focused upon other educational leaders. Much of this has been concerned with the life and work of the contemporary headteacher (Ribbins and Marland, 1994) and in this we were influenced not only by Kogan but also by points made by others. First, John Rae (1993), who, in reflecting upon his years at Westminster, complains that too little of what has been written about headship 'tells you much about what it is really like to do the job'. Indeed, he claims that fictional accounts may, in general, be more illuminating, but suggests that even among these, only Auchincloss really gets close to understanding 'how the demands of the role draw out particular aspects of his personality ... What makes the life of a ... headmaster interesting is not just how he did the job but what the job did to him' (ibid., pp. 11–12). We believe much the same might be said of other educational leaders, including Secretaries of State for Education. Second, Peter and Jo Mortimer, who in the context of their study of primary heads and headship claim that 'there are few books which enable heads to speak for themselves' (1991, p. vii). This, as we shall explain, is essentially what we have tried to do in our conversations with the last seven Secretaries of State.

With all this in mind, in the rest of this chapter we will say something about *how the interviews were produced*; *the history and nature of the Conservative reform agenda for education and of the role of our seven interviewees in this, as they see it*; and finally, *the sort of people they are and the kinds of professional lives which they lead*. In attempting the latter we have been influenced by the life-history approaches which have been advanced of late by Peter Gronn and others to examine the careers of individual and cohorts of educational leaders (Gronn and Ribbins, 1996).

The Conversations in Context

Six of the seven chapters which follow report separately upon one-to-one conversations which one or other of us have had with Mark Carlisle, Kenneth Baker, Kenneth Clarke, John MacGregor, John Patten and Gillian Shephard. In these discussions, the first of which took place in May 1994 and the last in March 1996, they respond to a series of questions which touched upon: the influences which shaped their views on education and educational policy; how and why they chose a career in politics; their career in Parliament and how they became a minister and then a cabinet minister; how eager they were to become Secretary of State for Education, and why; how it compares with other cabinet-rank posts; what was Conservative policy on education before 1979, between 1979 and 1988, and after 1988; what were the key influences on the making of educational policy during these years; how important was the 1988 Act; what ideas on educational policy did they bring with them when appointed to the Department; to what extent does this policy contain contradictions and ambiguities; what reservations they might have on any aspect of policy-making during these years; what being Secretary of State was like; is the Department of Education different from other departments, and, if so, how, and what did this entail for them; what particular difficulties did they face, and how did they go about overcoming these, and with what success; what did they achieve, and how satisfied were they with their time in office; how did they learn they were to cease to be Secretary of State, and what was their response to this; are they satisfied with Conservative achievements since 1979; in what ways do they think Conservative policies superior to the alternatives proposed by the other parties; and, what have they done since ceasing to be Secretary of State. Although the questions listed above constituted the core set, each Secretary of State was sent a somewhat amended interview schedule which tried to have regard to his or her particular history and circumstances, in so far as we were aware of them.

After an initial contact had been made, a letter setting out the terms of reference of the project and the particular list of topics we wished to raise was sent to each of our respondents in advance of our discussion with them. In our letter we asked if any of the topics which we wished to raise were not acceptable, and if there were others which we had not identified which needed to be discussed. Only once was a theme identified as unacceptable, and even in this case the respondent, in the event, relented. A great advantage with a face-to-face interview is that it is possible to revise and renegotiate the agenda of discussion as a natural part of an ongoing conversation. In practice this happened a good deal. Each Secretary of State – two of the six were in office at the time of the interview (John Patten and Gillian Shephard) – was interviewed at least once, and two were interviewed twice. The interviews with each respondent in total varied between just over an hour to just under two hours. Each was tape-recorded, transcribed and edited. Each of our respondents was sent a transcript of their interview and invited to propose such revisions or additions as they might wish to see included in the final text. All made some use of this, although not as much as one of the authors has experienced using a similar approach with secondary headteachers (Ribbins and Marland, 1994). There is always a risk that the advantage of allowing respondents to have prior sight of the interview schedule and enabling them to comment subsequently upon a draft script of the conversation might be gained at the cost of spontaneity and authenticity. This was a price we felt we had to pay. In any case, in retrospect we feel that the conversations as reported do not lack colour or veracity.

In this context, perhaps we should also say something about the interview style which we agreed between ourselves to try to use. In this, our approach was to an extent determined by our wish to give our interviewees an opportunity to speak for themselves in the way proposed above. As such, it was not our intention to try to go out of our way to catch them out, or to hector or badger them. As such, our approach in both the face-to-face and the constructed conversations was intended to be much closer in style to that of Cliff Michelmore – an interviewer whose skills, we feel, were much underestimated, not least by some of those to whom he talked – than Jeremy Paxman. We feel that such a strategy can produce accounts which are sometimes much more revealing than those achieved using a more brutal approach. It is for such reasons that we have described these discussions as 'conversations' rather than labelling them as 'interviews'.

In any case, the second 'conversation' was produced using a very different approach. As a result of our initial approach in early 1994 to the current and former office holders, we learnt of the seriousness of Lord Joseph's final illness. Various arrangements were explored which might have made it possible for us to talk to him, but although there was much good will on both sides, this did not in the event prove possible. However, our knowledge of the period, and our conversations with Kenneth Baker, Kenneth Clarke and John Patten, confirmed the significance of the part which Keith Joseph had played in determining the shape of the radical agenda for educational policy constructed after 1979. We felt our book must, in some way, have regard for this. In the event, we decided on an approach which would enable the production of an 'as if' conversation with Sir Keith Joseph. Clyde Chitty agreed to undertake this. In doing so he knew he would be able to draw upon an interview which he had conducted with Joseph in the late 1980s in preparation for his book *Towards a New Education System: The Victory of the New Right* (Chitty, 1989). In addition, he also knew of a substantial interview which Steven Ball had undertaken with Lord Joseph. Although Chitty and Ball had drawn upon their interviewees in others texts, this had been done very selectively and the bulk of both interviews had remained unpublished. We are very grateful to Stephen Ball for his generosity in allowing us to make such use of his interview transcript as we wished. In addition to material from these interviews, Chitty has, as far as possible, sought to use Sir Keith's spoken or written words as these are set out in *Hansard*, in media and other interviews, in books and papers, and in his biography. In producing the text of this 'conversation', Chitty has constructed it with regard as far as reasonably possible to the issues which are identified in the core interview schedule used for the other six conversations amended in the way discussed above. What is apparent is that after 1979, Joseph, and the others, had a great deal to say about the need for radical educational reform, and it is to this notion that we now turn.

A Radical Agenda for Education: Constructive Reform or Crude Revision?

In this section we shall briefly examine aspects of the origins, character and development of the Conservative reform agenda for education before and after the Reform Act of 1988. To set the scene, we shall focus upon the debate on the Order for the Second Reading of the Education Reform Bill which took place in the House of Commons on 1 December 1987. In considering what happened thereafter, we will draw upon a number of other sources. All this is intended to serve as a context for a more detailed discussion contained in that part of the next section entitled 'incumbency' (pp. 29–45), which seeks to explore the role of the seven Secretaries of State for Education who have held office since 1979, as they see it, in shaping, enacting, implementing and developing this agenda for reform.

Opponents and supporters of the 1988 Education Reform Act alike are given to making comparisons between it and the 1944 Act. In the debates on the Education Bill which took place in December 1987, the earlier Act was spoken of with considerable warmth by the opposition. For example, in his opening remarks, Jack Straw, in leading for the opposition, takes Kenneth Baker to task, saying:

> Outside the House the Secretary of State has had the audacity to describe his Bill as the most important since the Education Act 1944. As the right hon. Member for Old Bexley and Sidcup [Mr Heath] said, to compare the Bill 'with what Rab Butler did would make that great man turn in his grave'.
>
> (*Hansard*, 1987, 781)

Giles Radice makes a similar point, but stresses what he sees as the essential difference between 1944 and 1987:

The Secretary of State often compares his Bill, in a self-congratulatory manner, to the Education Act 1944. Let us make that comparison. In 1944 there was a national consensus about what was needed to be done ... There had been authoritative reports that illustrated the need and the way ahead. R. A. Butler, ably supported by Chuter Ede ... was able to build on the national consensus.

(ibid., 795)

This consensus, as Jack Straw observed, had been carefully built:

Not for Butler the contempt for those who might have a different point of view or the mockery of a 10 week consultation period. Butler listened for two years; he learned; he gained agreement. Because of that, his Act stood the test of time. His lasted: the Secretary of State's will not.

(ibid., 781)

It could be that subsequent events have proved Straw both right and wrong. On the one hand there are some signs that a new consensus may slowly be developing; certainly some of the seven believe this to be happening. They make the point forcefully. As John MacGregor, not noted as the most combative of the seven, said:

the Labour party, having opposed so much of what we carried through in the 1980s, have now come around to the recognition that we were right, and will not attempt to reverse most of the reforms. Listening to Tony Blair's speeches recently, I have been struck by the extent to which he is claiming that the Labour party would pursue policies which, when I and other Secretaries of State were taking them through Parliament in the 1980s, were being bitterly opposed by Labour spokesmen ... This is just another example of how the Conservatives won the battle of political ideas in the 1980s, and of how politics have now moved firmly on to our ground.

We spoke to Gillian Shephard both before and after the events which led Tony Blair and Harriet Harman to send their respective children to a grant-maintained and a selective school. In the first of these conversations (October 1994) she said:

I don't believe that the Labour party has had any kind of coherent education policy over the last fifteen years. Indeed it's very difficult to perceive that they have any now. They seem to oppose vehemently all the changes to do with standards, ... accountability to parents, with self-government, with the new curriculum, with the exams, with the testing, with performance tables – they have opposed all of these. Only, a couple of years after each event they come creeping up behind ... It is the Conservative party that has set the pace throughout ...

As far as the Liberal Democrats are concerned, again, it is very difficult to see what they have contributed to the debate. They say they want more spending on education. Well, everybody is always happy with that, but what they don't say is what they would spend it on.

Eighteen months later, she was, if anything, even more dismissive, claiming that

the Labour party ... has now got into a position where its policy is divided, muddled and chaotic. It is not possible [for example] to know where they stand on selection, given that they appear to support it for some members of their front bench, but appear to want to get rid of it for others.

But, in fact, even the Conservative reform agenda has taken some time to work out. It seems probable that members of the opposition parties would regard these judgements as a caricature. It could also be that they would reject or, at best, substantially qualify the idea that a new consensus is in the process of being built on the basis of the Conservative reforms taken as a whole.

Certainly, there was in 1987 little sign of the consensus proposed above. In this respect, at least, things may have been very different in 1944. But if there is a good deal of agreement among commentators that the Education Act of that year was based upon a consensus, some have questioned whether it was in any real sense reformist in intention. Barber (1994) lists various criticisms. One is that it

> was insufficiently radical. It left the Dual system intact; it failed to challenge the role of the independent schools; and it provided for an essentially selective system of secondary education. The view is summarised by Roy Lowe: 'in essence the new order in English education which [the Act] ushered in was, as Simon concludes, "the old order in a new guise"' (Lowe, 1992, 14). On this interpretation, the Act is very much a Tory Act: sufficient to buy off the radical reformers but restricted enough to maintain the interest of Tory voters.
>
> (Barber, 1994, p. 119)

But as Barber acknowledges,

> the problem with this interpretation is that it was not seen as so conservative a measure by commentators, particularly radical ones at the time ... The fact is that after the intense frustrations and bitter disappointments of the 1920s and 1930s, Butler's Act was a tremendous, and radical, breakthrough.
>
> (ibid., p. 120).

Given this, it is unsurprising that the 'leadership of the Labour Party had been amongst his most enthusiastic supporters throughout his period at the Board of Education'. (ibid., p. 120)

If this was true of their position in 1944 (*Hansard*, 12 May), the debates upon the 1987 Education Reform Bill (*Hansard*, 1 December) show that most Labour and other opposition speakers continue to be enthusiastic about the 1944 Act and to talk with appreciation of the achievements of Rab Butler. Conversely, with the exception of Edward Heath, those who spoke from the government side on 1 December 1987 made few enthusiastic references to the 1944 settlement and were conspicuously moderate in their acknowledgement of Butler's legacy. Baker, when opening the debate, set the tone. In moving the Bill he said:

> Our education system has operated over the past 40 years on the basis of the framework laid down by Rab Butler's 1944 Act ... We need to inject a new vitality into that system. It has become producer-dominated. It has not proved sensitive to the demands for change that have become ever more urgent over

the past 10 years ... The need for reform is now urgent ... There is now a growing realization that *radical change* [our emphasis] is necessary.

(Hansard, 1987, 771)

The idea that the proposals contained in the 1987 Bill were radical was repeated by speaker after speaker from the government benches. For example, Alan Amos, in his maiden speech, claims that 'the Bill deserves the support of the House because it is a radical and reforming measure which boldly and imaginatively creates a dynamic framework to our education system fully into the 21st century' (ibid., 815); Michael Heseltine talks of 'the determination of the Secretary of State to bring about a fundamental reform in the provision of education' (ibid., 819); and James Pawsey asserts simply, 'The Bill is radical. It represents a major and necessary reform' (ibid., 830). If this was the government view, it was not shared by any speaker from the opposition benches. They describe the proposals before them as a 'deception' and a 'fraud' (Jack Straw, ibid., 781) and say that, 'In place of Rab Butler's one nation, the Bill will create two nations in education' (ibid., 790); 'the evident fact ... is that the proposals described in the Bill have, in truth, little to do with reforming education or national regeneration' (Terry Lewis, ibid., 828); 'This is not a major reformist Bill. In the history of educational administration it will be seen as crudely revisionist and instrumentalist' (Dafydd Elis Thomas, ibid., 830); and, 'It is a hopeless Bill and in time it will be seen as a reactionary and useless piece of legislation' (Martin Flannery, ibid., 845). Is the Bill appropriately described as 'constructively reformist' or as 'crudely revisionist'?

In introducing the Bill, Kenneth Baker stressed that the need for reform was urgent. In doing so he claimed that

> Lord Callaghan was alive to this more than 10 years ago when, in his Ruskin College speech, he drew attention to the need for change ... The ground has been prepared by the pioneering work of my two predecessors. My noble Friend Lord Carlisle extended the rights of parents with the 1980 Act ... My noble Friend Lord Joseph focused public attention on the central issue of quality and standards.
>
> (ibid., 771)

In concluding, he asserts that

> The proposals which I have outlined to the House today constitute a major change. I would sum up the Bill's 169 pages in three words – *standards, freedom* and *choice*. The purpose of all these measures is to improve the *quality* of education for all our children ...
>
> (our emphasis, ibid., 780).

These four concepts have remained at the heart of Conservative claims for their reforms of education. With the passage of time they have been joined by others, notably 'accountability' and 'diversity'. If such a statement can be taken to represent the views of those who would argue that what was intended was 'constructive reform', it did not go unchallenged in 1987 and has continued to be contested since then. A variety of criticisms were advanced in the debates on the Bill. Most, but not all, of these were made by members of the opposition. Thus, for example, Jack Straw claimed [the Bill] represented no more than 'a few crude ideas and gimmicks' based on 'the prejudices and fantasies of the Conservative right ... [as part of] a constant campaign to instil a sense of distrust in state education and of the competence of the teaching profession'. He also suggested that 'the Bill is not about parents and pupils, but about power' (ibid., 782, 784, 789). Paddy Ashdown argued that 'the truth is that the Bill will achieve none of the aims that the Government's propaganda claims for it' and that this is not surprising given that

> There are hidden, malign threads running though the Bill ... The first of these threads is the further prosecution of his [Baker's] personal vendetta against local government ... Another secret item on the Government's agenda is the unscrupulous, undercover and unacceptable reintroduction of selective education.
>
> (Ashdown, ibid., 805)

Finally, Andrew Smith probably spoke for many in opposition when he concluded that

> As the debate proceeds it becomes ever clearer that the Bill has nothing to do with choice, freedom, standards ... but has everything to do with the application of a toxic mixture of free market ideas and centralism to our education system.
>
> (ibid., 835)

Many of these and other related criticisms were robustly contested by those who spoke from the government benches, but even here the Secretary of State was not without his critics. The most open of these was a former Prime Minister, Edward Heath, who alleges, *inter alia*, that 'Parental choice in the Bill is largely a confidence trick' (ibid., 793), that parental power is 'completely unrealistic' (ibid., 794), that the opting-out proposals will lead to 'a fee-paying system of independent schools of choice', and that this would be 'immensely damaging ... It will be divisive and it will be fatal to the education of a large number of children' (ibid.). If few of the official opposition were as blunt as this, it was also the case that the debate contained coded warnings from other senior conservatives. Norman Tebbit, having described Ted Heath as 'the other Opposition' (ibid., 807) and having noted his support for the idea of a national curriculum, went on to say:

> However, my right hon. Friend must be aware that ... he has to tread a narrow path between the dangers of the national curriculum becoming set in concrete ... and becoming just a matter of fudge and therefore totally ineffective. He is right to have a core curriculum – that is fine – but I counsel him not to overdo it.
>
> (ibid., 810)

Michael Heseltine also commended 'the thrust of this legislation', but never-theless urged

> my right hon. Friend to look again at two specific parts of the Bill. I do this not from any hesitation in supporting what my right hon. Friend seeks to achieve but from precisely the opposite stance. My concern arises from the voluntary nature of some of the proposals.
>
> (ibid., 821)

There was also some recognition, well placed as it turned out, from both sides of the House that the 1988 Act might not be the end of the story. As Tebbit put it, 'I have no doubt that this will not be the last Education Reform Bill of the decade. It is almost inevitable that another Bill will be required to take things forward' (ibid., 808). Perhaps even he did not anticipate the need for three further major Education Bills over the next six years, one of which was to become the 1993 Education Act, which is a hundred thousand words in length. Whatever its other merits, it has the distinction of being the longest piece of legislation in the history of British education.

Much of the above discussion reports on debates which took place in anticipation of the 1988 Education Reform Act. To an extent similar contro-versies have marked the passage of subsequent legislation as successive Conservative Secretaries of State and others have struggled to construct and implement an agenda of reform. How, in retrospect, has this been regarded? Ranson (1992) claims that to understand the developing Conservative agenda for education, it is necessary to see this in its wider social and political context. For him, the post-war world constituted a particular political order, rooted in notions of social democracy and based on the principles of justice, equality of opportunity and the centrality of collective choice informed by the collective interest. This has been chal-lenged by demands for a new political order. How this new order is to be characterized in educational and other contexts has been variously inter-preted. For some it is informed by the precepts implicit in notions of neo-liberal consumer democracy under-determined by the principles of diversity, competition and the primacy of individual choice exercised in the light of the individual interest. To take such a view is to be committed to the idea that the Conservative social, economic and educational reform agenda in recent times has been imbued in theory and in practice by the develop-ment of a unified philosophy or ideology.

Others contest this. They suggest that at best it offers a partial explana-tion of the activities of the Conservatives in office since 1979. Those who take the latter view tend to believe that deep ambiguities lie at the heart of the government's reform agenda, and that these derive from the shifting patterns of influence which the ideas of the various factions of the 'Right', and especially the 'New Right', have had upon its educational and other policies. How these ambiguities are to be depicted is the subject of debate within the literature. In one study of *The Making of Tory Education Policy in Post-War Britain*, Knight (1990) suggests various sets of categories for the classification of 'Conservative educationalists' and their influence over the policy of the party in recent times. Two seem particularly illuminating. The first is drawn from a typology proposed by Dale (1983), which roughly classifies Conservative educationalists into the *Paternalist-Right* and the *Market-Right*. Using the language of the party itself, this might be seen as the conflict being fought out between the *One Nation Tories* and *Enterprise Culture Conservatives*. Whatever concepts are used to describe this contest, at a macro level there may be an underlying coherence to the prescriptions of Conservatives in general and of its various New Right wings in particular. Gamble (1988), for example, argues that the majority of its adherents share a common commitment to the apparently paradoxical doctrine of 'free economy/strong state'. This elegantly expressed view is capable of more than one interpretation, which may explain why it is widely quoted. For some, it means

> New Right philosophy has contradictory policy implications and the ambiguity owes much to a division between those on the one hand who emphasise the merits of a free trade economy, often referred to as the neo-liberals, and those on the other who attach much more importance to a strong state, the so called neo-conservatives.
>
> (Chitty, 1989, p. 212)

The *neo-conservative* view was forcefully expressed by various writers in the early 1980s, and in the 1970s and beyond, and their ideas importantly influenced Keith Joseph's thinking. Brian Cox (1981), for example, advocated a renewed commitment to the notion that education should embody a clear and traditional hierarchy of values which must be expressed in curriculum terms. It followed that

> the aim of all schools should be to keep alive the best values, to transmit to young people high ideals of excellence. Through the humanities, through literature and history, we keep alive all that is best in our traditions; we help the voices of the past to live again in the experience of the student. Through maths and science we train the informed, rational mind ... All these values involve discrimination between good and bad, true and false ... Unless our school system reflects such hierarchies of value it will inevitably degenerate into relativism and impotence.
>
> (Cox, 1981, pp. 22–3)

Roger Scruton (1980) took a similar position in *The Meaning of Conservatism*. Neo-conservative thinking, he argued, is informed by a special reverence for authority, hierarchy and the maintenance of social order, and for the primacy of the rights of the state as against those of individuals. From such a perspective, the market as a means, through the exercise of choice and competition, of maximizing the interest of all must, at best, be regarded as a contingent good. Not surprisingly, those who shared this belief were among the strongest advocates of the need for greater regulation of schooling in the form, *inter alia*, of a National Curriculum, the main purposes and forms of which were to be specified by the state.

In the debates on the Bill in 1987 there were depressingly few references to the views of philosophers or educational theorists. Of these, two touched upon the themes discussed in the last paragraph. In the first, Dafydd Elis Thomas quotes the work of Gordon Kirk on the notion of the core curriculum, to the effect that it 'introduced a state-controlled curriculum and was "the deliberate use of political power to mould the minds of the young". That is how this revisionist measure will be understood in the future' (*Hansard*, 1987, 830). In the second, Derek Fatchett, in rejecting the ideology of the market which he felt dominated the Bill, said:

> I thought it would be useful to have a look at the definition of Conservatism. I went and found somebody who is the architect of the thinking that underpins much of the Bill, Roger Scruton. He said that he would define conservatism as 'faith in arrangements that are known and tested'.
>
> (ibid., 849)

It remains to be determined how far Scruton was an architect of the Bill, but if the argument we present above is correct, he was unlikely to have advocated this aspect of it with the enthusiasm which Fatchett implies.

What is clear is that the neo-conservative view was contested by the neo-liberal wing of the New Right. Stuart Sexton, Director of the Educational Unit of the Institute of Economic Affairs and formerly Keith Joseph's special adviser, has argued that

> The best 'national curriculum' is that resulting from the exercise of true parental choice by parents and children acting collectively, and being provided collectively by governors and teachers in response to that choice. The substitution for that freely adopted curriculum ... of a government-imposed curriculum is a poor second best.
>
> (Sexton, 1987)

What he was advocating was 'a national curriculum dictated by the "market" instead of a nationalised one dictated by the government' (Sexton, 1988). Among those who spoke in the debate in 1987, Norman Tebbit's line was closest to this view. In developing his warning that too great a level of prescription from the centre on the National Curriculum would be undesirable, he suggested that 'enough consumer choice will encourage the professionalism among school teachers ... needed to produce the curricula that will please parents and do well for children' (*Hansard*, 1987, 810). But others, including Edward Heath and Jack Straw, did express concern about the dangers of too great a level of control or prescription from the centre.

From this perspective the free market is not to be seen as just another contingent good, rather it represents the most effective means currently known of organizing social life in order to maximize the private interest and the public good. As such, the key policy task is to create the conditions under which the market can be enabled to operate as effectively as possible. This would, it was argued, entail the privatization of education and its liberation, in particular, from over-government and local government. Both factions of the New Right, then, if for different reasons, were critical of existing forms of local government of education, and both advocated the need for greater institutional autonomy through site-based local management. To understand why, it is necessary to examine the government's agenda for educational reform rather more fully than has been possible above.

Few would deny the scope and complexity of the Conservative educational reform agenda, but whether it is coherent is less clear. Thus, for example, it has been suggested that the National Curriculum, while it has had many builders, has had no architect. However, as the debates in 1987 make clear, the government certainly appears to think that its educational reforms are informed by a coherent and radical philosophy. In 1992 the Department for Education (DfE) published a White Paper entitled *Choice and Diversity: A New Framework for Schools* which attempted to summarize the main features of the government's educational reform agenda, and in doing so identifies 'five great themes [which] run through the story of educational change in England and Wales since 1979: quality, diversity, increased parental choice, greater autonomy for schools and greater accountability' (DfE, 1992, p. 2). As we have noted above, this list, with some marginal change in wording and the significant addition of 'accountability', is similar to that produced by Kenneth Baker in moving the Education Reform Bill of 1987.

Even so, and for a variety of reasons, making sense of this agenda of educational reform is not easy (Ribbins and Thomas, 1993). Firstly, it is both wide-ranging and far-reaching. Thus, for example, the Education Reform Act of 1988 alone includes 238 clauses (many containing two or more sections and sub-sections) and 13 schedules, and gives the Secretary of State numerous new powers. Precisely how many is a matter of dispute. Jack Straw and others in the debate on the Bill suggest about 175, a figure which had risen to over 200 after 1988. In contrast, Angela Rumbold claimed in winding up the discussion on the Bill that

> Many of the powers given to the Secretary of State ... are explicitly fashioned to enable him to push responsibility down to the local level beyond the town hall to the schools and colleges. They are devolutionary powers [as such]. The proposals mean less control, not more, and that was not the case to anything like the same extent in the Education Act 1944, which has been extensively quoted during the debate. It gave over 100 powers to the Minister at the time.
> (*Hansard*, 1987, 855).

As Baker (1993) was later to put it,

> most thoughts on education reform had centred upon increasing the powers of the Department and reducing the powers of the local education authorities. I was deeply suspicious of such a change which merely reflected competition between bureaucracies. I wanted to empower local schools and colleges and thereby give real influence to parents and children – the consumers of education. I started first with the management of schools. The principle which we

argued over was decentralization, and the metaphor I coined and used again and again was the hub and rim of the wheel. I wanted to disperse responsibility away from the hub and down the spokes to the rim. The argument raged over what was the rim ... Some favoured the LEAs ... but for me the rim consisted of the individual schools and colleges. Slowly the Department was won around.

(Baker, 1993, p. 211).

However that may be, the 1988 Act and its successors have allocated many new powers to the centre and spawned numerous regulative instruments and circulars which seek to set out in detail how these are to be interpreted and enacted.

Secondly, the reforms have been both highly complex and continue to some extent to be protean. Since 1988 the agenda within which the reforms have been constituted has been constantly rationalized, reinterpreted and revised as the government sought to produce the 'far reaching proposals [required] to complete the transformation of the education system in England and Wales begun in the 1980s' (DfE, 1992, p. 1).

Thirdly, taken separately, the dimensions of reform which constitute the agenda as a whole appear to be ambiguous or even contradictory. To consider them as a whole requires an examination of their *context*, *content* and *character* in terms of their implications for the *substance* of education, particularly of schooling, and for the *system* as a whole within which the work of educational agencies of all kinds operate. Such a review is beyond the scope of this introductory chapter, and in any case one of us has attempted to undertake it elsewhere (Ribbins and Thomas, 1993). Given this, we will restrict our discussion to a brief sketch of some of the issues entailed.

The 1992 White Paper identifies the *context* of the Conservative reform agenda as a growing concern for the five issues listed above. Writing shortly after this, David Forrester, then Head of Schools Branch at the DfE, placed the pursuit of quality at the centre. What this means, and why it should be so, is less clear. Nick Stuart, drafter of the 1988 Education Reform Act, then a deputy secretary at the DES, writes of a growing conviction in government circles that the economic well-being of the nation 'was being adversely affected by the performance of an educational service that was neither as good as it could be nor as good as it needed to be' (quoted in Ribbins and Thomas, 1993, p. 170. See also Stuart, 1994, p. 8 for a development of these and related points). Such claims need to be located in historical context. Lawton (1994), for example, suggests 'in 1944 the question of improving education was seen largely as a question of *quantity* ... the *content* – the curriculum – was not ... even mentioned in the 1944 Act' (1994, pp. 1–2). He believes that only in the late 1960s did 'parents, employers and eventually politicians [begin] increasingly to ask critical questions about quality of provision' (ibid., 2). Like Stuart, and a number of those who contributed to the debate on the 1987 Bill, he identified a speech 'critical of education' by

James Callagahan, the Labour Prime Minister, at Ruskin College in 1976 as an important turning-point.

Chitty (1989) and others argue that this speech marked the point at which the Labour party, or at least some of its leadership, came to believe that greater centralization of power, particularly over the curriculum and its delivery, was necessary. This, he believes, was a view which came to dominate Conservative thinking during their long years in office. But this did not happen overnight. Chitty argues that 'for at least the first seven years of its existence, the new Conservative government was prepared to operate largely within the terms of the educational consensus constructed by the Labour leadership in 1976' (Chitty, 1989, p. 172). This is an issue which we took up in our conversations with the seven Education Secretaries since 1979, and while they seek to explain and qualify it in various ways, it seemed to us that they did not seriously contest this view. As Kenneth Clarke put it,

> I think you are right. I think that's a fair criticism. It always rather surprised me that Margaret Thatcher, who had been an Education Secretary herself, did not give higher priority to education in the earlier years than she did. I think she decided that the key issues that she was facing in the first two Parliaments when she was Prime Minister were the economic issues. The third Parliament was when she embarked on social reform ... We turned to education reform and then reform of the National Health Service ... Before that we had not made a high priority of it. It was not just the Conservative party, I don't think the Labour party had much of an education policy before that either.

The impetus for radical change, and along with it a much greater concern for content, when it came, was signalled by the appointment in 1986 of a new Secretary of State, Kenneth Baker. The years that followed have been characterized by a stream of reforms, and of reforms of reforms.

Taken as a whole, the reform agenda seems to contain a number of fundamental ambiguities which, as we have suggested elsewhere, turn upon a search for centralization and uniformity on the one hand and for decentralization and diversity on the other (Ribbins and Thomas, 1993). Various more or less persuasive attempts have been made to deny (as do several, but not all, of the Education Secretaries to whom we have talked) or to account for these apparent contradictions. For some they are deep and serious, and can therefore only be explained; for others they are superficial and trivial, and can accordingly be resolved.

Those who take the former view usually seek to explain their existence as a result of shifting and conflicting patterns of influence and power within the different factions, especially of the 'New Right', which constitute the Conservative party. In the making of educational policy, three New Right groups seem to have been especially important: the Institute of Economic Affairs (the source of much neo-liberal thinking), the Centre for Policy Studies, and the Hillgate Group (the source of much neo-conservative thinking). Albeit for quite different reasons, both wings shared a belief in the need for decentralization at the system level and for the development of market conditions for education and its provision. Where they disagreed, as we have argued earlier, was over the need for the kind of centralization entailed by the introduction of a national curriculum. On this, as Ranson (1988) has observed, in the decision to legislate for a national curriculum, the Hillgate Group's view that the curriculum provides a means of incorporating a statement of the nation's culture and values – and therefore that a degree of central prescription was necessary – was, for a time anyway, to be more influential on Conservative policy-makers than the views of the IEA that the content of the curriculum should be resolved by the choices which pupils and parents and teachers and schools make within the educational market-place.

Those who believe that ambiguities in Conservative educational policy-making are superficial tend to claim that it is possible to identify one or more common strands informing its centralizing and decentralizing impulses. In one such strand, both centralization and decentralization, it is proposed, can be seen as a challenge to the dominant role hitherto enjoyed by producer groups within the educational establishment in schools, colleges, universities, local authorities and even the civil service over policy-making. For Thomas (1989), it is this challenge to the 'producer interest' that has led to sets of reforms that simultaneously seek to centralize and decentralize control over educational policy and practice. By centralizing control over the school curriculum, the reforms attempt to reduce the control of professional educators. By devolving control over human and physical resources to the governing bodies of schools, the reforms both reduce the power of educational administrators within local government and require school-level managers, particularly headteachers, to work more closely with governors. Moreover, at the level of the school in particular, decentralization, it is assumed, will foster greater and more open competition in a market-place in which parents will be given the information and will have the opportunity to make informed choices based upon their judgement of the quality and type of service apparently on offer. From such a perspective, the centralizing and decentralizing dimensions of these reforms can be explained as complementary aspects of a policy designed to restrict 'producer control' and diminish 'professional power'. It is not yet clear if practice matches theory in this or other aspects of the policies for education which the government has put in place since 1979. Fascinating as these speculations may be, they are not the main theme of our enquiry. Rather, we have set out to understand the identification and implementation of these policies from the perspective of those who have held the office of Secretary of State during the long years of their evolution. In doing so we have hoped to be able to say something about the sort of people they are, how they have sought to interpret the role, and with what consequences for others and for themselves. These are the themes of the rest of this introductory chapter.

Seven Lives and Careers

A central debate within social and organizational theory turns upon different conceptions of the link between human agency and social structure. Gronn and Ribbins (1996) have argued that, remarkably, studies of leadership have, to date largely ignored these debates. But they will not do so for much longer. A concern for this connection will loom increasingly large in post-positivist approaches to the study of educational management and policy in general, and to leadership in particular. In this context, given the remarkable degree of emphasis on agency and voluntarism in theories of leadership (at times to a crudely naive extent) as the very basis of their popular appeal, leadership commentators will have little choice but to engage with such questions if their views are to remain credible. Certainly, issues such as the relationship between levels of social analysis, their link with structure and agency, structuration, cultural dynamics and analytical dualism have increasingly preoccupied such eminent social theorists as Archer (1988) and Giddens (1979).

Despite the recent work of some leadership theorists (Mouzelis, 1991) and organizational theorists (House et al., 1995), Gronn and Ribbins (1996) claim that the significance of context continues to be badly under-theorized in most studies of leadership. In contrast, they propose that, reconceptualized as the sum of the situational, cultural and historical circumstances which constrain leadership and give it meaning, the concept of context offers a powerful instrument for enabling an understanding of the agency of particular leaders in practice. They advocate, following Kets de Vries (1990, 1993) and others, more use of a *life-history* approach to researching leadership. Such an approach, as English (1995), following Smith (1994), notes, can take various forms, including 'diaries and journals, memoirs, profiles, sketches, portraits and portrayals, and the three most advanced forms (biography, autobiography and prosopography)' (English, 1995, p. 208).

What might a life-history approach to leadership look like? Gronn and Ribbins (1996) suggest three ways in which life-histories can facilitate theorizing about leadership. Firstly, as detailed case histories they may be inspected for evidence of the development and learning of leadership attributes. Secondly, they provide analytical balance sheets on the ends to which leaders, singly and collectively, have directed their attributes throughout their careers within the shifting demands on and options available to them. Thirdly, a comparative analysis of the career paths of leaders as revealed in life-histories can answer broader institutional-level questions such as whether particular sets of leaders, sanctioned by their societies and organizations as worthy to lead within them, share common attributes and whether or not those same societies and organizations screen their leadership cohorts in particular ways to guarantee conformity to preferred cultural types or models.

The relative lack of such studies has important consequences. There is, for example, an absence of any comprehensive and systematic understanding in the literature of how individuals get to be leaders, of how prospective leaders get to be leaders, and of why some leaders progress further than others. In addition, our understanding of cultural diversity and its significance in the definition of different patterns of leadership is slight. Nowhere, it seems, is there anything like a satisfactory answer to Kets de Vries' question, 'What determines who will become a leader and who will not?' (1993, p. 3). One possible antidote would be to devise a framework for ordering understanding of the biographical detail of leaders' lives. This, in its fullest form, would permit the comparative analysis of individuals over and against the systems and/or cultural traditions which have nurtured them.

Gronn (1993) has suggested that *career* is an appropriate construct upon which to build such a framework. In its fullest form this would entail a longitudinal comparative analysis of the careers of leaders which would synthesize biographical and institutional perspectives on leadership in the way proposed many years ago by Gerth and Mills (1953). As such, it would focus upon the dialectical interplay between a leader's own sense of agency (fashioned in part *by* her or him) and the social structure (enabling or constraining possibilities *for* her or him) in which that agency is embedded. From this perspective, what might a leader's career comprise?

Various attempts have been made to suggest what this might look like. Day and Bakioglu (1996), reporting on their study of 'headteachers development in post and the effects of this on their school leadership', identify four main phases, labelled *initiation, development, autonomy* and *disenchantment*. While this template might well have considerable potential merit in examining the careers of ministers over time as they move from their first appointment in government to their last, we have found the wider scope offered in a framework proposed by Gronn (1993) more appealing. In it, he argues that leadership may be thought of as four broad career stages or phases, including *formation, accession, incumbency* and *divestiture*. In examining the careers of the seven Education Secretaries who constitute our study, we will preface our discussion with a brief account of each of these phases.

Formation

Prior to the assumption of leadership roles, there is a preparatory stage in which candidates shape themselves and/or are shaped for prospective office. As part of this general process of formation they are socialized into various societal and institutional norms and values – e.g., codes of taste, morality, beliefs and authority – by three key agencies; family, school and reference groups. Sometimes the individual experiences consistent influences and conditioning within and between these agencies; on other occasions inconsistency and/or contradiction. Taken as a whole, these groups and agencies shape a prospective leader's character by generating a conception of self, and the rudiments of a work-style and outlook. A comprehensive examination of the particular and collective influence of all these agencies upon the seven very busy people who are the subject of this book was beyond the scope of our study. Instead, we chose to focus upon their educational experience and their early career as formative influences in shaping their leadership careers. Several also pointed to the influence of members of their family upon them, and where possible we have tried to build upon this.

A criticism which is frequently advanced against Conservative Education Secretaries is that they are charged with responsibility for a system of state education which few of them have attended and to which few send their own children. Carlisle took a robust line on this, saying roundly:

> I had no direct personal knowledge of the state sector either as a pupil or as a parent – my daughter attended a private school. And I had been ... to an independent school myself [...] I see absolutely nothing incompatible about supporting state education and sending your own children to a private school. For my own part, I always argued that I was lessening pressure on the state school system by educating my daughter privately.

This was not an issue much addressed by others among the seven. In fact, taken as a set, they may be untypical, since only Joseph and Carlisle had no direct personal experience of state schooling. The rest attended state primary schools, and three, Baker, Patten and Shephard, then transferred to state secondary schools. Baker was subsequently moved to St Paul's, where he spent the last five of his school years. Clarke, after attending a state primary school, won an LEA scholarship to Nottingham High School.

Having researched the views of other educational leaders (Ribbins and Marland, 1994), we were a little surprised to hear how positive, or at least how uncritical, this group were about their own schooling and about their teachers. On the former, Joseph has commented, 'I was happy at school though I felt under no great pressure to excel on the academic side.' Carlisle, talking of Radley, says, 'I enjoyed school; I enjoyed the games; I enjoyed the work ... I enjoyed it, and enjoyed the general friendship of the place.' Others echo these sentiments, but several also stress the traditional nature of the primary and secondary schooling which they received. Baker recalls his primary school, Holy Trinity, as providing

> a conventional education of a rather old-fashioned sort which was really rather effective ... I remember those days very vividly. The essence of that type of education was to embed in you the very basic, simple skills of reading and writing and arithmetic. I remember chanting mathematics tables by heart, learning poetry by heart, doing a lot of writing, spelling [and] punctuation ... It was a good education, I have no doubt about that at all.

Patten uses much the same language: '[My] education was formal, old-fashioned ... in two tough – both intellectually and in terms of discipline, behaviour and ethos – voluntary aided Roman Catholic schools.' The schooling he received at Wimbledon College was also 'very formal', which only in the Sixth Form 'became less formal, more civilized'.

One of the few clearly critical comments came from Shephard, who said:

> I am conscious of the limitations of the state system ... I am very conscious now of having been to schools which were extremely small, where I would probably have greatly benefited from having had much stiffer competition early in my school career. I am also conscious of the limitations of the curriculum provided by a small girls' grammar school. For example, there was only one modern language offered, there was only one classical language offered.

But even Shephard stresses, 'It was the fault of no one. The teachers were marvellous.' She recalled many of them with warmth, and willingly acknowledges their influence upon her. In talking about the headmistress of her primary school, Shephard's affection is evident: 'She had the gift of making everything interesting to children because she herself was enthusiastic about natural history, about local history, about language, everything.' But whatever her reservations about the lack of size, competition and opportunity at her secondary school, she recalls

> many of my teachers ... with great affection and gratitude because they put so much time and effort into all of us ... You couldn't have a more dedicated set of teachers, and it does give me a certain view of the potential role of teachers in the way they influence children.

Sentiments of this kind are echoed by others of the seven. For the most part they had little difficulty in remembering teachers from their primary, secondary and university days, who they remember with the same kind of affection and gratitude. Some remembered with pleasure making contact with one or more of their former teachers. Baker recalls when, holding a surgery, in 1986,

> a small and elderly lady came in and asked me, 'Were you the Kenneth Baker I taught at Holy Trinity?' I remembered her as a young teacher – Miss Makin. Shortly afterwards, as Education Secretary, I had the pleasure of taking her with me on a nostalgic visit to our old school.

And Patten is still in contact with the head of one of his primary schools: 'Mother Mary-Anna ... is still alive and now living in retirement ... We correspond at Christmas time and on those sort of occasions. She wrote to me after some years.'

All but one attest to the importance of their schooling in shaping their values and their views on educational policy. Clarke was the exception. As far as he was concerned

> There is an excessive concentration ... in the debate on educational policy, on everybody's own experience of schooling ... I don't think I was ever guilty of that. My views on education were not determined by my own experience of education.

He has little else to say other than

> my own experience of education, for what it's worth, was state infant and junior school, followed by 11-plus sending me to an independent day school that took about a third of its pupils from the local authorities paid for by scholarship.

Baker's view is more typical. As he puts it, 'Politicians usually have decided views on education. In this they are much like those who work in education … One's own education, I think, is very important.' Patten takes a somewhat different view, saying, 'I've never been one for introverted self-examination of the influences on my life'. Even so, he acknowledges that both his schools 'taught me the importance of working hard, competitiveness with oneself rather than particularly with other children … Tough, demanding, long hours, don't mess about, get on with it.'

The clearest and fullest statement on this issue came from John MacGregor. As he says,

> one has to go back to one's own education. There are three aspects I would pick out.
>
> First, although I was heavily involved academically, the school I was at [Merchiston Castle] put great stress upon a very wide range of sporting and extramural activities. The fact that the school offered so many alternatives to the academic life was one of the formative influences of my life. We were expected and encouraged to live every single day to the full. That expectation has been with me ever since: it has always been a part of my approach to education …
>
> Second, and on the purely educational side, I have always believed in everyone striving for excellence to the limit of his or her abilities. That was also inculcated in me at school, and it remains important today …
>
> Thirdly, and in purely educational terms, perhaps the most important formative influence has been related to my studies at university. I had originally wanted to be a Scottish advocate … I went to St Andrew's, where you had to take five subjects in your first two years. I did not know what fifth subject to study. I decided to take 'Political Economy', and that decision changed my life. It meant … I did not become a Scottish advocate. Ever since, I have felt that the English system encourages a narrow specialization too early. When I was Secretary of State I wished to see what I could do to change this.

MacGregor was one of only two or three who identified the influence of parents and other family members as significant in shaping his views on education, and his values and aspirations more generally. His father was a doctor in a coal-mining village called Shotts, half-way between Glasgow and Edinburgh, who sent him to boarding school with some reluctance and 'was very worried about whether he could afford this'. Curiously, Baker says of the decision to send him to St Paul's:

> My father did this because he felt he could, by then, just about afford it. Even so, as a middle-ranking civil servant, I think it was a very big sacrifice for him. We lived modestly, but both my parents felt that the really important thing was to give my sister and myself the best opportunities in life that they could.

He also stresses the importance of the grandmother he never met:

[She] was an Irish girl who came over in the 1880s and trained at Wandsworth
Teachers' Training College ... She ingrained in my father ... the importance
of education ... [My] great-aunt Ida ... ran education in South Wales for the
Catholic Church before the turn of the century. So there has been a tradition
in my family ... of there being lots of teachers around. My wife, Mary, had also
been a teacher ... When I met her, Mary was teaching in a remedial class in one
of the first comprehensive schools in London ... All this has meant I have
always had a very high regard for the teaching profession, and have been fully
aware of its importance.

Unlike others of the seven who had taught (Shephard in further education,
Patten in higher education, and Carlisle, for a term, in a school), he had
never considered teaching as a serious option. Rather, 'I wanted to go into
business and politics principally, and that is what I did.'

Although only three of the seven had significant experience within the
educational profession (Joseph as a Fellow of All Souls, Patten as a Fellow of
Hertford and Shephard as an administrator and inspector in Norfolk), few of
the rest might be wholly appropriately described as career politicians from
the outset. Several were barristers (Carlisle, Clarke, Joseph), others worked
as journalists (MacGregor, Patten), in management (Baker), in the City
(MacGregor), and in the Forces (Carlisle, Baker). Some, especially the barristers, continued to practise after being elected to Parliament. It may be a sign
of our times that only one went out of his way to stress unequivocally the
value of this and of having a career before entering politics. As Carlisle put it:

I had an active life outside politics. In fact, and I would not want this to be
misunderstood, I am not a mad enthusiast for what I might call 'full-time party
politicians'. I think, if possible, back-bench MPs ought to have other jobs as well.
I kept on with my work at the Bar to some extent. I think today, sadly, thirty
years later, it's probably impossible to do so ... [A]t the time there were very few
people who came straight from Central Office into the House of Commons
without having done anything else. This kind of full-time party politician is a
more recent invention. My own view is that those of us who had other jobs and
other interests in fact often were able to make a more significant contribution
from the back benches because of it.

How he, and the others, succeeded in moving from the back benches, and
how this took them in time to the office of Secretary of State for Education,
is the subject of the next section.

Accession

Following an initial period of preparation, candidates for leadership during
this phase in their career life-cycle develop, rehearse and test their capacity
by comparison with existing office holders and the field of prospective
rivals. As such, accession is a developmental period geared to the accom-
plishment of two crucial tasks: the construction of oneself as a credible
candidate for office, and the acquisition of a marketable performance
routine to convince talent-spotters, panels and selectors. As leadership

positions become available, candidates learn to present and position themselves or 'jockey' with one another for preferment. In doing so they rely increasingly on networks of peers, patrons and sponsors while awaiting a 'call' for office (Gronn and Ribbins, 1996). In applying these ideas to an analysis of this aspect of the careers of our interviewees, we shall focus specifically upon how they came to take up a life in politics and how they came to be offered the post of Secretary of State for Education.

Asked why he chose politics as a career, Joseph was characteristically blunt:

> I didn't want to run Bovis, the family firm, and I had no wish to teach law at Oxford. And politics seemed to me to be the ideal way of getting things done. I started off in local politics in London, and then I became MP for Leeds North East.

In some respects, at least, Patten's experience mirrors this, while in others it is very different. As a very young don at Hertford College, Oxford, he received a letter from the bursar which told him about his pension arrangements, and he recalls thinking:

> good heavens above, am I really going to be doing this for all of my life? I always wanted to be an academic ... I wasn't active in the Union ... or seriously in the Cambridge University Conservative Association ... [but] I got dragged in ... to local politics ... And one thing led to another and I was invited to put myself up to stand in the 1973 local elections in Oxford and I was elected for the North Ward of Oxford City ... Two Labour people got in, and then I got in by one vote over a Liberal ... I suspect that if I hadn't got in I might have thought, 'Well, that was fun, but it was a bit like hard work', and I might well not have gone on, because I wasn't at all fixed at that stage. But one thing led to another ... And I fought and won [a parliamentary seat in] the 1979 [general] election.

These two sets of comments indicate that the careers of successful politicians may vary a good deal in terms of initial commitment and subsequent planning.

Joseph seems to have discovered he had a political vocation early on. In this he is like several others among the seven. Asked if he was an 'early developer', Carlisle responded:

> I was, I was. I was active in politics at university – I was chairman of the University Conservative Association, and I was chairman of the Federation of University Conservatives for all the universities; so I was already very active even at that stage.

As such he was thinking, even then, of a career in politics, saying: 'You have got to realize (and I am sure Kenneth Clarke would say the same) that reading law naturally leads you into being interested in politics.' We did not explore this last issue with Clarke, but it was clear that he too was an 'early developer' along with a group of others during his years at Cambridge:

> there were a whole lot of us who were contemporaries who were personal friends and all actively engaged in politics. The Cambridge Mafia is the nick-

name given to the ones who became professional politicians – large numbers, actually, of Conservative MPs; six of them became, or have so far, become, cabinet ministers.

At the time, he held many of the same kinds of posts listed by Carlisle:

> I was Chairman of the Conservative Association, I was President of the Union, I was Chairman of the Federation of University Conservative and Union Associations, which was the National Body, and I went straight down to go on to the Conservative candidates list.

Both MacGregor and Carlisle held many of the same roles. Both were aware of the importance of the kind of positioning and networking discussed above. Carlisle being Chairman of the Federation of University Conservatives, for example, 'meant for that year being on the National Executive [Committee] of the Conservative party'. This left him positioned to run for a seat when it became available. Initially, this was in a by-election for the unwinnable seat in St Helens, which he then contested again in the general election.

This looks like a case of careful and successful career planning for a life in politics. But serendipity soon took over. As Carlisle tells it:

> I got married and said to myself, 'Right, that is it, I have had my amusement. I must now be a serious barrister.' I had my name taken off the list of candidates. And then I happened to be watching television one evening ... there was going to be a vacancy at the forthcoming election for the seat of Runcorn ... It was the neighbouring seat to the one I lived in. My wife looked across at me and said, 'Well, what are you going to do?' and I said, 'I have always said that if Runcorn became free it is the one seat I would really like to fight.' I knew the Chairman very well, and that would help ... She said, 'You must have a go. If you don't, for the rest of your life you will blame me for the fact that you did not have a go.' ... So I rang up the Chairman and asked if we could meet for lunch. We did, and shortly afterwards I got selected as the Conservative candidate for Runcorn. I was very, very lucky.

Whether this is best described as an example of luck, or of an ability to respond decisively to an opportunity when it occurs, or of careful preparation and networking, is debatable. What is clear is that most of the seven believe, with John MacGregor, that 'I don't think anyone can "carefully plan" a career in politics.' In his case, after contemplating a career in law, he worked in journalism and in the City before an opportunity arose which finally directed him into politics. As he describes it:

> I got a telephone call from Michael Fraser, ... who was then the head of the Conservative Research Department, inviting me to lunch. He was looking for a second special assistant ... to Sir Alec Douglas-Home, who was then Prime Minister – Nigel Lawson being the first special assistant. It was a most fascinating period, and it got me into politics ... I became fascinated by the challenge and the variety of being at the centre. And so after Sir Alec ... ceased to be Leader of the Party, I went to work in opposition for Ted Heath, as the head of his private office. That brought me into the centre of politics in a big way.

So when the opportunity came to contest the seat in South Norfolk, he found that, whatever his initial reservations, his mind had been made up, and, 'having decided he might have to wait for five years, he 'was extremely fortunate to win a constituency almost at my first attempt ... In a sense I got into Parliament much earlier than I had expected.' Again the notion of luck, but as famous sporting stars often claim, the better prepared they are the luckier they seem to get. What part does luck, preparation and planning and the rest play in climbing the slippery pole of politics in Parliament?

Some, initially, made rather slow progress. In his case, Patten felt there were good reasons for this. As he puts it, much of his early career was on the back benches:

> Because I wasn't so up to speed politically, I didn't say very much around my first year. It was full of my contemporaries who had been long involved in politics. My old friend Chris Patten ... William Waldegrave; a certain John Major, and others. We all came in in the 1979 intake, and for the first year or so I was very quiet, very much trying to catch up with my contemporaries who'd been much more involved in ... politics.

He did, of course, catch up, but it could be that this relatively slow start may to some extent explain why, unlike all but Carlisle, although he spent many years as a junior minister in a number of departments, he was to hold only one post of cabinet rank. That post was one, as we shall see, he had not expected. In thinking about how Patten and the others came to be appointed as Education Secretary, we shall consider the extent to which they expected this appointment, how and why they came to get it, how well prepared they felt for it, and how they reacted when first offered the post.

Patten was among those who had not expected to be offered the post of Education Secretary. As he recalls it:

> I was successively in the Northern Ireland Office, the Health Department and the Home Office for a very long stint. Obviously, the one job for which I might have thought myself suited was this one, and I never, therefore, thought that I would ever be appointed to this job because it's axiomatic in government that you don't normally appoint 'specialists'. Even though I was by that stage rather a post-dated specialist. So I hadn't thought much about it.

Carlisle was another who had not expected to get it. As he explains:

> I never expected to be made Secretary of State for Education. My interests politically had always been in the Home Office, and professionally I was a barrister, therefore when I was asked to be Secretary of State for Education (or, rather, Shadow Secretary of State) in 1977 ... it came as somewhat of a shock.

Asked how and why he came to be offered the post of (Shadow) Education Secretary, Carlisle points to the influence of the kind of patron or sponsor identified above. As he recalls it:

> the *full* story, I am pretty sure, is this. Tragically, Airey Neave was killed. Somebody had to move over to become Shadow Secretary of State for Northern

Ireland, and this left a vacancy in the Shadow Cabinet; and my guess is that Willie Whitelaw said it was his turn to nominate somebody. I don't think I would have been Margaret's first choice, whereas I think I probably would have been Willy's first choice. I had worked with him on Home Affairs matters in opposition.

John MacGregor was another who seems to have benefited from the support of a powerful sponsor at key points in his cabinet career. We have already referred to his early contact with Nigel Lawson as special assistants to Alec Douglas-Home when he was Prime Minister. Later, as another Prime Minister, Margaret Thatcher confirms in her memoirs *The Downing Street Years*, in the reshuffle of September 1985, 'At Nigel's request, I replaced (as Chief Secretary to the Treasury) Peter Rees with John MacGregor' (Thatcher, 1993, p. 420). Lawson's backing might also have had some influence in getting MacGregor the post of Education Secretary. We know from *The View From Number 11*, that Lawson believed his colleague had 'a long standing interest in education and had thought a good deal about it' (Lawson, 1992, p. 606) and that the appointment was 'a particularly appropriate one' (ibid., p. 610). Helpful as it to have friends in high places, MacGregor's answer when asked how he became a cabinet minister offers a timely reminder. As he says, 'I was asked!' Ultimately, of course, it is the Prime Minister who does the asking. In his case, as with others of those whom she appointed, we have some idea why Margaret Thatcher came to this decision: 'I was happy to appoint John MacGregor, with his Scottish devotion to Education, as the right person to deal with the nuts and bolts of making our education reforms work' (Thatcher, 1993, p. 598). In one case, at least, the Prime Minister was both sponsor and selector. As she recalls, regarding the reshuffle of September 1981:

> Keith Joseph had told me that he wished to move from Industry. With his belief that there was an anti-enterprise culture which had harmed Britain's economic performance over the years, it was natural that Keith should now wish to go to Education where the culture had taken deep roots. Accordingly, I sent Keith to my old department to replace Mark Carlisle.
>
> (ibid., p. 151)

MacGregor was happy to be asked to be Education Secretary. This was so, even though

> if initially I had ever contemplated a ministerial career, I would have thought Chief Secretary was the job that most suited me. But if I'd ever asked myself the question, 'What is the ideal job that I'd want to do after that?' Education would certainly have been one of them. Education has had a very high priority in my life. I'm a Scot, and I have a Scottish attitude towards education ... I have always had very strong views about the importance of education. My father believed that, like most doctors, he was unlikely to be able to leave us very much in the material sense but that, if he could leave us with a good education, that was the most important thing. That is exactly the attitude I have taken towards my own children. I feel the same very strongly for the nation as a whole ... So when the opportunity came to do something about this, I was absolutely delighted.

Others were also happy to be offered the chance to be Education Secretary. Talking of the way in which his thinking on education had been shaped by his predecessors in office, Patten, having had the call to go to the Department, recalls his 'surprise and delight at the news'. Not all were quite so delighted. Those in this category, like Baker, Clarke and, to some extent, even Shephard, already held posts of cabinet rank. They respond, with some variation in emphasis, in rather similar ways. None seem to have been overwhelmed at the prospect of the move to Education, but all then emphasize their commitment to education.

Clarke, asked if he really wanted to be Education Secretary, responded:

> Yes, although it is true I didn't immediately. It was the one reshuffle where I resisted the proposed move and tried to persuade Margaret not to move me ... [until] the health reforms came into effect – I thought she was moving me at the wrong time ...

He was to say much the same about his move from Education eighteen months later. Furthermore, he qualifies his apparent reluctance by insisting that

> I very much wanted to be Secretary of State for Education, which is one of the jobs I had always found attractive in government, but I didn't want to be Secretary of State for Education just yet. You know, if she had asked me again in five months' time, I wouldn't have argued.

Shephard was more phlegmatic than we expected. Asked, 'If the photographs tell the truth, you were obviously delighted when you were appointed Secretary of State for Education,' her response was matter-of-fact: 'In the Cabinet the reality is that you accept what the Prime Minister asks you to do or you resign ...' Having stressed that she had 'enjoyed the other two cabinet jobs that I have done enormously', she did note, shortly after her appointment, that her past experience meant 'I have a rather antique but nevertheless relevant professional background, which I hope will enable me to make a sound contribution'. Warming to her theme, she went on to acknowledge that

> of course it also has to be said that education, in my view, is one of the most important issues at any time in a country's history ... it is about our future; it is about our competitiveness; it is about our cultural inheritance. It's about all our young people, and our children – all their aspirations and their parents' aspirations. I don't think you could have a more important agenda than that.

This may be so, but Baker did not seem to regard his transfer to Education as a promotion. As he puts it:

> I don't believe that at the time Education had a high place in the batting order of government departments ... my previous department, Environment, had a much greater influence within the government as a whole than the Department of Education and Science; particularly during the 1970s and 1980s.

Later in our conversation, he seemed to qualify this, and concluded that

> In summing up my views and attitudes towards education, I would stress that education was the way in which the Baker family had moved on in society ... My grandfather had been a docker – a wonderful man – and education had been our ladder. I am not just well disposed towards education – I worship it.

Whether the seven felt anything like as well disposed to their experience of being Secretary of State for Education is an issue to which we shall now turn.

Incumbency

Upon appointment to their first leadership post, successful candidates undergo either immediate formal or informal induction into their new institutional role. Each subsequent role switch, and in particular those entailing promotion of some kind, requires further induction into organizational and workplace norms. Regardless of level, institutional roles comprise at least three main elements: constraints, demands and opportunities (Stewart, 1989). The precise mix shapes the fine detail of the expression of the new role incumbent's sense of style, self and outlook. The performance of institutional leadership roles entails exercising the responsibility of office and facilitates expression of the leader's potency, ambition and vision. Incumbency can be regarded as the exercise of leadership within a single role (*role incumbency*) or across a whole career of successive roles (*career incumbency*). It follows that during incumbency, as used in the latter sense at least, leaders may occupy a number of roles, each varying in respect of status and significance.

Applied to the role of the Secretary of State for Education, the development components of incumbency can be said to include, *inter alia*, a period of informal induction within the Department in which the incoming Secretary of State establishes working relationships with officials and ministers; adapting to the institutional culture of the Department, working within the constraints, overcoming the demands and capitalizing on potential opportunities; clarifying the extent to which the Secretary of State is seen to have the support of the Prime Minister; establishing a public stance *vis-à-vis* the teaching profession in schools, further and higher education; exercise of the role of office of Secretary of State in which the incumbent is seen to have the vision, drive and ambition to develop and/or implement policy.

In this section examples of the various components as described by the seven Secretaries of State are given along with examples of how they have viewed their role and the relaxation and other interests which they have pursued while in post.

Relations with the Department, civil servants and junior ministers

Carlisle describes his time at the DES (May 1977 to September 1981) as one in which you 'had all the responsibility and no power'. This, he feels, is particularly true of the relationship between the DES and the LEAs. Unlike some of his successors, he is not necessarily convinced DES officials had an agenda of their own, but he did find 'that as a minister you did not have a powerful administrative machine of the kind which I had become used to at the Home Office behind you'.

When Kenneth Baker moved from the Department of the Environment in May 1986 to the Department of Education and Science at Elizabeth House, it was like 'moving from the manager's job at Arsenal to Charlton. You crossed the River Thames and dropped down two divisions' (Baker, 1993, p. 166). Morale was low. The DES had the strongest 'in-house ideology' (ibid., p. 168), he claims, of all Whitehall Departments with a 1960s ethos and agenda. In consequence, he found it difficult to drive 'distinctively Conservative policies past powerful civil servants in opposition'.

Baker could rely on support from Sir David Hancock, his Permanent Secretary; he nevertheless describes him as 'the nominal Head of Department', and considered the intellectually formidable Deputy Secretary, Walter Ulrich, at the time at Schools Branch – who was 'no particular fan of Government policies' – to be the real force to be reckoned with. Baker had to make it clear to Ulrich that 'there was only room for one boss in my department'. In taking this line, he recalled Bob Dunn complaining that when ministers in Keith Joseph's time

> eventually reached a political decision about a policy matter, Walter, if he didn't like it, would unpick it by sending a dissenting minute and then re-argue the issue face to face with Keith. Bob felt that both Keith and Chris Patten would end up admiring Walter's fine Wykehamist mind and concede the intellectual point rather than persist with the political argument.

Halcrow offers a colourful description of these events:

> Sir Keith, Fellow of All Souls, would sit, with coat off, displaying his elegant braces, at the centre of a long table, on which landed the mass of paper generated by the Department and at which he presided over discussion after discussion with officials and outside experts. The gatherings were often large and the discussions long ... Everyone usually agreed that it was stimulating; it was no way to run a revolution, which was what the zealots wanted.
>
> (Halcrow, 1989, p. 173)

Bob Dunn was not alone in being irked by such events: 'Rhodes Boyson [also] often found it more constructive to find other things to do when these meetings took place' (ibid.).

Lord Carlisle may also have found Ulrich rather difficult to work with, describing him as 'that strange – perhaps "strange" is the wrong word – bright man'. In addition, he recalls some 'middle ranking civil servants who had strongly hostile views on things like the Assisted Places Scheme'.

John MacGregor was struck by the 'insularity' of the DES, and 'was fairly constantly frustrated at the slowness with which things happened in the Department on the one hand, and the over-burdensomeness and lack of worldly realism which existed on the other'. Concerned with the amount of paperwork produced by officials 'to justify their existence', he measured it by 'putting each publication going out to schools from the Department on my window-sill in order to see how that pile was growing, and growing'. Even so, he felt most officials were 'dedicated to a desire to make the reforms work'. Likewise, Shephard, who is quite prepared to 'bang the table', finds 'an enormous amount of enthusiasm in the Department' for government policies. However, in our first conversation she describes the DfE as quite unlike her previous post at Agriculture, where the work was 'terrifically "hands on"'. Indeed, she finds it 'more "hands off" than some of my earlier tasks' because it is the LEAs and the GM sector who are carrying out the policies. Reflecting on the merger of Education and Employment, she says:

> there is a very different culture, you would expect it to be so because education has always been run by others, not by Government, and therefore the Department for Education had a policy role and a regulatory role, but not a hands-on role. That has changed a little over the years, but that has been its role, whereas of course the Employment Department has always had a hands-on role: it runs the Employment Service; it runs training schemes; it has an active role in the regions, and therefore you can immediately see that the two heritages of the Departments fit them to play different roles. Therefore, there has had to be some adjustment ... for both sides.

Whereas DES officials may have been helpful to Kenneth Baker in respect of City Technology Colleges, 'they were not at all helpful over grant-maintained schools'. This experience is shared by John MacGregor, who complains that 'it is true that there were people in the DES who didn't favour this reform, and who were always trying to squeeze it out'. Similarly, Kenneth Clarke found the DES officialdom an impediment to pushing forward Conservative reforms: 'There was a battle royal going on in the Department ... They didn't like grant-maintained schools and they didn't like CTCs. They were trying to minimize the policy. So I took it as an issue and ran with it.' Moreover, Clarke faced an additional problem – 'the fact that not everybody in the Government was as keen on CTCs as I was'. Where the curriculum reforms were concerned, Clarke 'took the officials head on'. In the context of education policy prior to 1986, Patten refers to 'a very strong view among civil servants, understandably', and, with tongue in cheek, to the fact that 'civil servants aren't to blame for anything because they just do as they're told' by ministers.

John Patten describes his way of working with civil servants as 'trying to be as corporate as possible', and talks of his daily departmental meeting which was known colloquially as 'morning prayers'. He is fulsome in his praise of his junior ministers, especially Baroness Blatch – 'she is the most elegant and stylish engine room that any Secretary of State could imagine' – and Eric Forth. Since he is good friends with all his ministers, 'we don't have to spend too long talking because we know each other's minds'.

Carlisle recalls, when referring to Rhodes Boyson, that they were a 'largely united', 'fairly successful' and 'happy team'. Although Kenneth Clarke worked closely with HMI and took seriously the opinions of the Chief Inspector, Eric Bolton, he considered that HMI 'varied a lot', and 'I had a very different opinion, personally, of the respective quality of the different parts of it' – further education, secondary education, primary education. In addition, of course, he set up OFSTED.

Relations with the Prime Minister and other cabinet ministers
In some ways, Joseph had the easiest time of it with a formidable prime minister. After all, in her memoirs, Thatcher herself has described him as her 'oldest political friend and ally, even mentor' (Thatcher, 1993, p. 562). Even so, as his biographer notes, she was not above interrupting him if she felt he was going on too long in Cabinet, and on one famous occasion he even had to be rescued from her by Nigel Lawson (Halcrow, 1989). If even he found it difficult sometimes, what hope was there for the others?

Carlisle's time at the DES was not 'made any easier', he maintains, by the fact that Margaret Thatcher 'didn't much like teachers' or the 'civil servants she encountered at the DES'. He admits that he 'found the pressures very hard, very exacting'. Clarke, while obviously valued by the Prime Minister, when she wished to move him from Health, 'tried to persuade Margaret not to ... I didn't want to be Secretary of State for Education just yet ... if she'd asked me again in five months time I wouldn't have argued'. However, as Shephard observes: 'In the Cabinet the reality is that you accept what the Prime Minister asks you to do or you resign.'

Ultimately, once the DES officials realized that Baker was determined to carry out his proposed reforms,

> They helped me because ... I kept on saying, 'You know, the Prime Minister will support me.' It was a great thing to say that. In fact I didn't discuss it [the CTCs] with her very much at that stage. But it's always a good argument.

Similarly, Shephard finds that she receives considerable support from John Major:

> What is so splendid about this job is that its importance is fully recognized by the Prime Minister, with all that that means. It means that there is a support for this Department, an interest in everything that we do, an active engagement in the discussion of policy which not all colleagues have the benefit of in other Departments. And I have of course been in five Departments, so that I am in a position to make comparisons.

John MacGregor's apparent popularity with the teaching profession led to the view that he was not popular with Margaret Thatcher, who moved him from the DES to be Leader of the House following Sir Geoffrey Howe's (later Lord Howe) resignation. Whereas Mrs Thatcher considered Kenneth Baker to be a good communicator of policy, she thought of John MacGregor as a good implementer. While MacGregor makes the point that he had no 'fiery debates with Margaret on education', and that she supported what he was doing in higher education, such as the introduction of the student loans scheme, he nevertheless wonders whether 'she perhaps misunderstood what I was doing' when she saw the final History Working Group report in March 1990. Indeed, there is reason to question whether she fully understood the implications of the National Curriculum, particularly of the detail in the 'foundation' subject syllabuses. It is not clear whether she envisaged it as a set of guidelines within which teachers could operate with flexibility without stifling professional individuality, or whether she supported Kenneth Baker's original notion of a uniform national standard.

John Patten suggests that he and the Prime Minister saw eye to eye on the need for the parental ballot as the route to grant-maintained status for schools: 'The Prime Minister and myself regard grant-maintained as the natural model, but we also believe in choice – we're Tories – and freedom of choice.' Shephard also emphasizes what she and John Major share in common:

> the Prime Minister and I come from similar social backgrounds. Very different in terms of environment, but similar social backgrounds which have given us very similar attitudes towards the importance of education as an enabler and a ladder for children. Which means that we start from the same position without having to describe it to one another.

Mark Carlisle's view of the success of his team – both ministers and civil servants – was not shared by Margaret Thatcher, who considered that, leaning to the left, he 'had not been a very effective Education Secretary' (Thatcher, 1993, p. 151). The Prime Minister, he recounts, never told him exactly what she was unhappy about, and never came to the Department while he was there. If Nigel Lawson is correct, it seems she did not hesitate to make her views clear to Kenneth Baker:

> The Cabinet Sub-Committee on Education Reform proceeded in a way unlike any other on which I have served. The process would start by Margaret putting forward various ideas ... there would be a general discussion ... Margaret would sum up and give Kenneth his marching orders. He would then return to the next meeting with a worked out proposal which bore little resemblance to what everyone else recalled as having been agreed at the previous meeting ... After receiving a metaphorical handbagging for his pains, he would then come back with something that corresponded more closely to her ideas ...
>
> (Lawson, 1992, p. 619)

Needless to say, this was not how Baker remembered these events. Even so, when asked, he did not deny that there were some important policy differences between them in so far as she appeared to want a more restrictive National Curriculum, a simpler form of assessment, and many more grant-maintained schools than Baker envisaged. As Baker says of the last of these:

> the pace of opting out became another area of difference between Margaret and

myself. In an interview she gave to Peter Jenkins in September 1987 ... Margaret said, 'I think most schools will opt out'. This contrasted with my refusal to predict the number of schools that would opt out ... since the whole thrust of our policy was to extend parental choice, it would be parents, not the Government, who decided the pace of change.

(Baker, 1993, p. 220)

This dispute came back to haunt him in the debates on the Bill in 1987 when Giles Radice recalled

a radio programme that I shared with him was delayed for half an hour while the Secretary of State communicated with the right hon. Member for Chingford [Tebbit], who relayed to him what the Prime Minister was saying at her press conference. The Secretary of State's face grew paler and paler as he spoke ... It was very embarrassing for [him], and I felt extremely sorry for him.

(*Hansard*, 1987, p. 797)

One could also feel sorry for John MacGregor. In her book, the Prime Minister notes that during his term of office she 'had become thoroughly exasperated with the way in which the national curriculum proposals were being diverted from their original purpose. I made my reservations known in an interview I gave to the *Sunday Telegraph*' (Thatcher, 1993, p. 596). MacGregor responded to our questions on this with the comment, 'I think she perhaps misunderstood what I was doing – I did try to explain to her from time to time.'

On the whole, we learnt less from these conversations about the role of the Cabinet, cabinet committees and of other cabinet ministers in policy-making in education than we did about the Prime Minister. Carlisle, asked if he spoke much to the Prime Minister on policy issues, offers one reason for not doing more of this. He claims:

It is very difficult to get over to those who have not experienced it, the enormous pressure at which government today works. There is rarely time for such discussions. The Cabinet cannot devote much time to any but the most extraordinary issues.

Even so, he talks of 'taking a lot of the issues on expenditure to Cabinet' and of his battles with the Treasury and with Number 10. As it happens, there is at least one case discussed in the conversations of a very busy and senior cabinet minister who did, it seems, find the time to involve himself to a significant degree in policy-making in education. This focused upon Nigel Lawson's claim that as Chancellor he suggested to the Prime Minister that he put some ideas on educational reform to her. Once she had agreed, his response on returning to the Treasury was to call

a meeting with John MacGregor [and others]. I ... warned them that they were not to breathe a word to anyone in the DES: not only would they be unhelpful, but I had little doubt that Kenneth would be more inclined to embrace an initiative which he believed had emerged from Margaret than he would one that emanated from me. (Lawson, 1992, p. 607).

Relations with teachers
Baker maintains that he 'made a big point of never attacking the profession of teaching' and of drawing a distinction between teacher unions and teachers. Nevertheless, he acknowledges that he was not popular with teachers: 'We took away their negotiating rights but set up a system which assured that teachers got better rewards than they had ever been awarded in the history of the profession.' Before him, Carlisle, who had 'inherited a situation in which the NUT were about to go on strike because of Shirley Williams' proposals', bemoans the fact that although he 'got on alright with Fred Jarvis' he was at loggerheads with the rank and file simply because 'I was a Conservative minister'. Similarly, Patten fell foul of the teacher unions who boycotted classroom tests. Following Patten, Gillian Shephard quickly established a working relationship with the teacher unions, and remembers her own teachers: 'with great affection and gratitude'.

Frustrated by the fact that whenever he paid tribute to teachers in recorded interviews the tribute would always be edited out, John MacGregor made sure they knew he valued them by visiting schools and meeting them. Reacting to the suggestion that he was one of the more popular of Conservative Secretaries of State, in that he appeared to be more producer-orientated, MacGregor declares, 'I did not know about my relative popularity. Nobody told me at the time, only afterwards!' However, he takes the view that 'you don't achieve results unless you carry the people who must implement them with you'.

Kenneth Baker's first hurdle as Secretary of State was settlement of a long-running teachers' dispute. The teacher unions had made themselves thoroughly unpopular, he argues. 'We were able to appeal to the parents over the heads of the teacher unions – they had not experienced that from any minister before.' Settlement of the dispute cost 'an absolute fortune'; it required fighting 'every inch of the way' to ensure that the bills were met.

> The fact that I was able to settle an industrial dispute that had gone on for so long greatly enhanced my reputation amongst my colleagues. I was seen as someone who could resolve things in education and who therefore had to be listened to.

Never enjoying universal acclaim among teachers, Kenneth Clarke recounts how he took notice of a primary school head who 'sat me down and gave me a most ferocious lecture about these SATs, and why they had created chaos in her school'.

Pressing ahead with the radical reform agenda
Mark Carlisle, looking back, is proud of introducing the Assisted Places Scheme and the integration of 'special education with the rest of education' (the 1980 Act, which Gillian Shephard describes as 'epoch-making'), as recommended by the Warnock Committee which had been set up by Shirley Williams. He mentions that 'rightly, or maybe wrongly, we accepted the

GCSE in principle during that period' and 'put in train the idea of a National Curriculum' while working through LEAs. Like Shephard, who speaks of the need for 'a period of consolidation and stability' in which the reforms can be 'thoroughly bedded in and refined', he also observes that 'When I was appointed I thought there was a need for a period of stability, and during my period of office I tried to achieve this.'

Reflecting on the 1988 Education Reform Act, Lord Carlisle concludes, 'there was a heck of a lot in it', and expresses concern for 'the children that are left over' in the push for grant-maintained schools. On the other hand, he may have been more radical: 'if one was going down the line of grant-maintained schools ... perhaps we ought to have gone the whole 100 per cent hog'.

Keith Joseph, having served four years and nine months there, spent much longer at Education than did any of his six contemporary colleagues. He was characteristically ambiguous about what he saw as his key achievements, contenting himself when asked with such gnomic observations as, 'I think what I can claim to have achieved is to have shifted the emphasis from quantity to quality'; 'I am entitled to feel that I failed. Not that it would have been possible to transform the quality and effectiveness of education in a mere five years'; and 'I have put in place the building bricks from which a change in effectiveness may emerge ... What would I like to be remembered for? Drawing attention to the 40 per cent who get little benefit from education, perhaps, I don't know.' His time at the department saw some important successes (GCSE, TVEI), but also some spectacular failures (Education Vouchers, Student Loans). Furthermore, as he himself acknowledges, 'when I was at the DES, there was that awful pay dispute [with teachers] going on all the time. That soured relationships. I was in conflict in one way or another with all the teachers' unions over pay and conditions.' This conflict undermined him as a man and as a politician. Joseph's biographer notes that 'the behaviour of militant teachers distressed him in a way that militant students and steelworkers had not done' (Halcrow, 1989, p. 186), and he was 'particularly outraged that the unions had found methods of disruption short of complete strikes, so that the teachers still drew their salaries' (Halcrow, 1989, p. 174). But he also believed 'teachers should be well paid, although he regarded some of the demands as absurd; what was more important was that good teachers should be paid more than the less good' (ibid.). But because

> to a degree perhaps unique among ministers, he declined to 'play the Whitehall game' against the Treasury ... several times during his years at Education the Treasury were astonished when he accepted a *No* which other ministers would have regarded only as a first stage in a negotiation process. The Education budget lost out at a time when it perhaps ought to have fared better than other departments.
>
> (p. 175).

In this regard, the only other distinguished Education Secretary who has been accused of similar financial rectitude in recent times is Shirley Williams. Carlisle comments:

> I followed Shirley Williams as Secretary of State for Education. Shirley Williams, as far as I know, was the only Labour minister who attempted, with any degree of success, to implement Denis Healey's request that the load of expenditure which was carried by the central government should be reduced.

Most of those to whom we have spoken in these conversations attach considerable importance to the legacy in education which Keith Joseph has left the Conservative party. Of these, the most unequivocal is John Patten. Even he, however, began by telling us the tale that

> Keith Joseph was apparently, in the old DES, given to wandering around the corridors when he first came and saying, 'Please show me the levers; I can't find any levers.' And he did most of the ground-clearing thinking, I think, which underpinned much of Ken Baker's work ... It may have taken Joseph several years to begin to find the levers, but he began to switch the whole ethos of government educational policy from inputs towards outputs ... He was trying to rethink the whole way in which the government looked at education, and that took him a long time against massive vested interests ... both inside and outside the Department ... I'm busily trying to refurbish [his reputation] because he was a most cerebral man. And I don't think we would have got anywhere without him having gone through the horrors of all of that.

Those less inclined to accord him this prominence include, perhaps, Joseph himself, and Carlisle, who told us simply, 'I am not quite sure what he actually did.' Shephard believes both that 'Keith Joseph was certainly the force behind the education policy that we now have' and that 'the sheer strength, determination and bounciness of Kenneth Baker in pushing the stuff through the Commons was essential to get the whole thing up and running'. Perhaps, not surprisingly, Baker's view is similar:

> after 1979, Keith's role in shaping our policies on education and beyond is very important. He was certainly the most intellectually distinguished of all Margaret's ministers. He had very clear ideas and views of startling simplicity ... Where Keith was not successful was he found it difficult, I think, to deal with the actual administrative consequences of that understanding ... [But] by making quality the centre of the education debate, he made possible the other later changes we were able to introduce.

Kenneth Baker, having dealt with the teachers' dispute, began 'fashioning ... all the other policies, including the curriculum policy' in which role he characterizes himself as 'a very hands on minister'. Convinced that the key to raising educational standards was a national curriculum, and supported by Margaret Thatcher, the Prime Minister, he took a gamble in announcing his proposals for a national curriculum on the Sunday television programme *Weekend World*, without reference to colleagues. With regard to the effectiveness of the National Curriculum implementation, he was conscious that the hours taught by teachers in the English education system are significantly less than those of our competitors in Europe, America and Japan:

> the big thing that I regret is not pressing harder for more teaching hours. The lack of hours was the source of many of the problems we had with regard to the National Curriculum. It meant that we had to make unnecessarily difficult decisions.

However, Baker felt that he was unable to lengthen the school day because the teachers' strike had only just been resolved on the basis of a 1,265 hours-a-year commitment. An extra forty-minute period a day would have helped him in resolving the time problem.

Baker's first policy initiative was to set up City Technology Colleges (CTCs) as a vehicle for increasing choice, diversity and standards, and for shifting the locus of power towards parents as consumers in the education market-place. They were to be 'beacons of excellence' (Baker, 1993, p. 178) to show what could be achieved and to make it happen. 'We wanted CTCs to be testbeds for new teaching methods and new school management methods which could be used in other schools' (ibid., 178). These new colleges in a sense spearheaded the reforms of the 1988 Act in so far as they were seen to embody such key principles as parental choice, *per capita* funding and local, autonomous, managerial control as opposed to LEA control. They could be used as a 'tin-opener' to achieve his other goals as set out in the reforms that followed: 'we had very interesting discussion because it [the CTC concept] raised all the major issues which subsequently found their way into the Bill'. Had he concentrated on the whole range of problems with which he was faced, and attempted to tackle them on a broad front, he feels that he would have made no progress. Rather, 'In order to crystallize change, in order to create the circumstances that make change possible, I believe very strongly that you have to set up something as quickly as you can to demonstrate how it can be done.' Having created the circumstances, change came rapidly.

Appalled by the arbitrary closure by LEAs of schools that he considered to be good, Baker wanted to give local parents a voice. 'From that idea, in part, came the development of the CTCs, and they, in turn, were the genesis of the grant-maintained schools movement.' Seeing a need to 'release the energy into the system', Baker believed it was not possible to do this 'by going through the local education authorities'. Although, as he confirms, other organizations such as the No Turning Back Group and the Adam Smith Institute have claimed to have been the first to suggest the concept of the grant-maintained school, Baker maintains that 'the idea ... owed more to me, I think, than to anyone else'.

Baker is clearly proud of his achievements as Secretary of State, and feels that subsequent developments have not capitalized fully upon the potential for success implicit in his reforms: 'I was very proud of what emerged from the National Curriculum discussions; but it proved very difficult to produce in practice. Some of my successors have messed around with it rather too much.' Speaking of his curriculum reforms in general, he remarks that 'This is one clock that will not be turned back. Much of the clock will not be turned back.'

On reflection, Kenneth Baker accepts that 'we might have given, in fact we probably did give, rather too much [power] to the governing body and not enough to the headteacher', and John MacGregor confirms that some governors 'were finding it difficult to adjust, and some began to complain about the burden of responsibility which they carried. I was never very sympathetic.'

John MacGregor followed Kenneth Baker as Secretary of State in July 1989. He 'came to the view very quickly that Kenneth Baker had carried through the major reforms, particularly in the school sector ... and that my job was to make them work'. To this end he set about gaining the confidence of disaffected teachers who were concerned with the speed of change. 'My task was not to achieve one of those great creative drives forward in policy change, but rather to make a big change in policy actually working.' He tackled 'detailed aspects' of the curriculum policy that were 'clearly over-complex and perhaps moving in the wrong direction. Furthermore, I wasn't always happy about some of the people who had been entrusted with achieving this. It was a big challenge to get this side of things right.' MacGregor was considered 'probably an appropriate person to do it'.

Where post-16 and higher education were concerned, 'there was a great deal to do both in policy and in implementation'. Finding this fascinating, John MacGregor considers his time 'was a creative period for developments in this area: polytechnics became universities; necessary financial reforms were introduced in higher education; and a huge expansion was taking place in higher education'. During this time his policy on student loans came to fruition, 'but the student loan scheme was only one part of the many changes that we were taking through'.

MacGregor maintains:

> On grant-maintained schools, I was much more enthusiastic than Kenneth Baker. I was very impressed by the enthusiasm and rejuvenation in morale that was being achieved by the early GM schools. I organized the first conference of grant-maintained schools at which we had present the chairmen and head-teachers of the first 20 schools.

Kenneth Clarke felt that by the time he arrived at the DES in November 1990 – in his view prematurely, because the Health Reforms had not yet come into effect – 'things were going reasonably well', but that the outline of the reforms was better than the detail. 'I thought the reform programme was better than its implementation ... the devil is in the detail of delivering any of these ... public services'. Believing there was a danger of the implementation programme running out of steam, he 'tried to bring to the job a new sense of urgency' by tackling the detail.

Inheriting problems associated with what he considered to be an over-loaded curriculum, Clarke does not hide his frustration: 'I never did get round to doing what I really wanted to with the curriculum, which I think has only been done since by John Patten and Sir Ron Dearing.' In addition, as a 'fervent believer in testing', he tried to make some sense of 'those wretched SATs'. The NCC and SEAC were both a cause of frustration to Kenneth Clarke in his attempt to go about 'the job of delivering on the ground what we wanted in the right way'. Clarke admits that he had 'trouble with them from the start' and that he never really had the impression 'that they were wholly committed to the policy which they had agreed to deliver by accepting service on the bodies'. Indeed, there was a danger that they would 'deliver things that weren't actually what we wanted at all'.

On GM schools, Clarke maintains that his 'predecessors had been much more cautious' than he had been over grant-maintained status. Believing GMS to be 'the natural corollary of the local management of schools', he claims to have given 'a whole new impetus to the grant-maintained school system', making 'a deliberate point of seeking to drive up the number of schools opting for grant-maintained status as rapidly as possible ... and insisting that we got on with the job of vetting the applications'. Clarke confesses that 'If I'd been Secretary of State in 1988, I would not have put in this balloting system', because, in his experience, 'it produces quite extraordinary local political campaigning of intense bitterness'. He had resisted Health Authority ballots while consulting on Trust Status for the hospitals. This had resulted in nearly 100 per cent NHS Trust Status for hospitals, and Clarke thinks that 'if we hadn't had the ballots on grant-maintained schools we'd have reached the same outcome'.

Referring to the setting up of OFSTED (the Office for Standards in Education), which John Patten regards as 'a very great achievement', Kenneth Clarke maintains that

> the government was entitled to define a curriculum and to give an indication of the way in which it wants to see standards raised. You couldn't do that unless you had some powerful independent body which was respected which could monitor standards being achieved on the ground, report on them openly to the general public, and to parents in particular, and be of support to schools in the delivery of what we wanted.

Clarke also addressed the issue of school-based teacher training which, 'with twenty-twenty hindsight', John Patten believes should have been the starting-point for the Conservative reforms: 'now, fifteen years later', he remarks, 'we are doing it, and I think the Teacher Training Agency will be very important'.

John Patten sees the 1988 Education Reform Act and the subsequent Acts of the 1990s taken together 'as a bundle of reforms' as being important and radical. Like the 1944 Act, they usher in a new 'settlement', in this case characterized by 'choice and diversity', in which 'outputs are more important than inputs'.

Believing that since 1944 there has been a damaging drift to uniformity in educational provision, Patten wanted to 'give schools a much wider range of opportunities to develop their particular strengths', and encouraged schools 'to specialize in technology, science and mathematics by becoming technology colleges'. This was an attempt on his part to reverse a trend – 'our failure to take technical and vocational education seriously'.

Whereas Kenneth Clarke recollects that 'we introduced the first league tables with a minimum of fuss', Patten recalls the difficulties associated with the introduction of the 1992 performance tables 'against quite strong advice … from a lot of people', because, in line with the Citizen's Charter, he was determined to make sure parents knew what was happening in schools: 'What I hadn't realized', Patten admits, 'was just what a powerful lever … the simple publication of information has been', and he alludes to its 'electrifying effect in a lot of schools'. The publication of information is, he believes, 'one of the most important post-war levers for levering up standards'. Referring to the Baker reforms, he questions whether 'if implementation hadn't happened rather quickly, would anything have happened at all?' This, he argues, is the 'classic dilemma of the reformer. Do you try to get everything right, or do you actually drive it on?'

John Patten, who kept a card on his desk with the latest statistics on the number of schools operating as grant-maintained, and details of ballot outcomes and pending ballots, insists that 'We're bound by our election manifesto – parental choice drives the process.' Responsible for the setting up of the Funding Agency for Schools as 'a conduit for state funds for grant-maintained schools', Patten saw the move towards grant-maintained status as an 'irreversible change' and proclaimed that 'I will eat my academic hat garnished if by the time of the next election we haven't got more than half of England's secondary schools grant-maintained'.

In any event, observes Patten, LEAs will be 'mutating, changing, diminishing', and 'No one has to have an LEA … any more after the 1993 Act'. He goes further, in claiming that,

> If I was a chief education officer, I would be proud of the fact that my schools were running at such a high level of delegation that it was no longer necessary for me to be in existence any more. But I guess there aren't many people like me as chief officers of local education authorities.

Gillian Shephard came to the Department with a number of objectives:

> the introduction of full-scale nursery education; a thorough and fundamental review of higher education; an emphasis on the importance of vocational education, and overall a very strong emphasis on standards. I am delighted to have been in the position to have introduced a qualification for headteachers.

The merger of Education and Employment, she notes, 'brings other opportunities and certainly enriches the chances we have of improving vocational education'. She regards her introduction of nursery vouchers as a 'seminal' part of a strategy for putting parents at the centre of the system. For far too long people have been emphasizing the interest of the 'institution', and indeed the debate surrounding the introduction of vouchers shows that we haven't got very far along the road of separating out the interests of providers from those of the customer, which is very regrettable. The debate over nursery vouchers has certainly focused attention on that. It is quite clear that the opposition and many local education authorities are still utterly absorbed by the interest of providers in institutions. Now the world has moved on entirely from that in every other respect, in every other sphere, and why not education?

Shephard is convinced that both teachers and the public agree with her that what is now needed is consolidation and stability in schools, and rules out further legislation during her time as Secretary of State. In the higher education sector, however, she believes the time is right 'to look at what a degree is, what we mean by a degree now'. At the other end of the spectrum, she is 'keen to tackle' education in the early years. The correct use of English is also one of her concerns. Her mind is particularly exercised by a need for 'very convincing vocational education'. Critical of an education system that relegates vocational education to a second-class status, she claims with conviction that 'Doctors, after all, have been trained vocationally, so have lawyers, and I don't think they would take kindly to being described as dim.' Nevertheless, she maintains that 'what is essential is that the rigour is retained in A level. Indeed that A level is retained. But that we give the opportunity to broaden what can be offered at the same time. But rigour is all important – we cannot leave it.' She is also a supporter of selection.

Commenting on the speed with which the reforms were introduced, Gillian Shephard maintains that 'Politicians travel hopefully. They have to. You always feel there isn't time.' Acknowledging that the introduction of the National Curriculum has not been without its difficulties, she accepts that 'schools have felt very over-loaded in terms of the requirements of the changes'. She intends to 'refine and make less onerous the demands of the National Curriculum'.

Regarding one of the main successes of the grant-maintained schools initiative as 'the impact they have had on LEA performance', she does not

> for a minute believe that LEAs would have moved so far or so fast without the GM spur. The key to making any supplier responsive is to give the customer a choice. That is what GM status does. LEAs knew that if they did not shape up, they would lose their schools.

Gillian Shephard claims to see GM status as providing great opportunities for schools to exercise their autonomy, and is actively promoting further opportunities for autonomy:

> The Bill currently before Parliament will allow GM schools to borrow commercially. The popular Seed Money Scheme, the Public Finance Initiative and the new rules on asset disposal will all put GM schools even more firmly into the driving seat.

She believes that

> Schools are best placed to judge how they should develop to meet local needs.
> That has to be within some national framework which can balance conflicting
> interests. But within those limits, I want the national controls to be as light and
> flexible as possible. I want schools to feel that it is for them to shape their future.
> Without needing to keep seeking permission. Without having to jump through
> endless hoops.

While acknowledging that the Labour and Liberal Democrat parties seem
to be totally opposed to the creation of GM schools, Gillian Shephard nevertheless expects there to be 'many, many more GM schools' before the next
general election: 'I think any group of politicians, whatever party they were
in, would give themselves cause for thought if they were faced with
2,000,000 parents spread right across the country.'

What is it like to be Secretary of State?

Mark Carlisle states that 'my strongest memory of my time as Secretary of
State is that it was very hard work', which he nevertheless enjoyed as the
high point of his political career, even though it 'was not an easy time to be
in charge of a major spending department' when the government was
determined to 're-establish control of public expenditure'. He observes that
'it was the one cabinet job which the Prime Minister herself had done'.

Speaking of the general nature of the role of the politician, Baker believes
that once it 'gets into your blood it's hard to escape'. A life in politics, he
maintains, is attractive 'if you want to change things. I wanted to change
things for the better. I still do.' Of the role of Secretary of State for
Education and Science in particular, and the equanimity with which he
seemed to cope with it, he maintains that he enjoyed the responsibilities –
'You had to be very cool about it.'

John MacGregor talks at some length of the cost of commitment:

> It has its attractions. It offers a very, very full life. Its one real penalty lies in
> what this means for family life. You don't get enough time ... particularly when
> the children are young, to be with them, because you are so heavily involved in
> Parliament during the week and in your constituency at the weekends. I hope
> it hasn't done my children any real harm. But I do regret not having been with
> them as much as most other fathers could have been. That is one disadvantage.
> The other lies in the sheer work and hours that it entails, although I have never
> minded that as much as some.

Despite this, he has clearly enjoyed 'the sheer mental stimulus of it all', the
demands of running a large department, dealing with 'political and policy
changes', using the media, speaking in the House of Commons and at
'endless functions'. And working with busy, 'stimulating and intelligent
people' means that 'you don't get tired', whereas 'When I am on holiday I
can fall asleep in front of the television at 10 o'clock as well as anyone else.'

Kenneth Clarke admits he works hard and that it is something to do with
temperament: 'I like working hard.' He has been told he does not 'seem to
be a worrier', and considers himself fortunate that he is 'determined', has 'a

retentive memory', can 'work very quickly' and can 'absorb information
well'. Going to a new Department holds no terrors for him, since 'There's
nothing much new to me within Whitehall because I've been at it for so
long, really.' Furthermore, he sees himself as 'a pretty active politician' who
has been appointed to his various posts 'to make big changes'. At the DES it
was 'very combative' and a matter of working 'under very high pressure' to
'keep the show on the road'.

For Patten, being Secretary of State for Education is 'high profile' and
'extremely hard work, like all cabinet jobs'. He feels that he has succeeded
in making the national education debate 'more interesting', although by no
means 'always in ways that I found particularly comfortable, particularly ...
in the row over the National Curriculum and testing'. Patten admits that 'I
found it in my first two years quite the most demanding job I've ever had,
but also quite the most rewarding ...' He goes on to reveal that 'there are
some times I feel a bit like a foot soldier in the Second Battle of the Somme.
You know, in a shell hole sometimes (as I was last year over testing); sometimes trudging through the mud towards the wire'.

Despite the fact that her workload 'has doubled' since the merger of the
Departments of Education and Employment, Shephard maintains that her
present post must be 'one of the most interesting jobs to have in government'.

Other interests
As Secretary of State, Mark Carlisle confessed to greatly enjoying debating
with Neil Kinnock on the floor of the House of Commons: 'Neil Kinnock
was always short on details. He did not do his homework. I used to quite
relish Question Times with Neil Kinnock.' For recreation he plays golf. We
know relatively little of the interests, outside politics, of Keith Joseph. In his
youth he had a great passion for cricket, which, it seems, to some extent he
retained later in life.

Kenneth Baker's relaxation interests are essentially literary. He is an avid
collector of books and has assembled a splendid collection of original political cartoons. In addition to his autobiography, *The Turbulent Years*, he has
edited a number of publications, including *I Have No Gun But I Can Spit*
(1980), *London Lines* (1982), *The Faber Book of English History in Verse* (1988),
Unauthorized Versions: Poems and their parodies (1990), *The Faber Book of
Conservatism* (1993), *The Prime Ministers: An irreverent political history in
cartoons* (1995), *The Kings and Queens: An irreverent cartoon history of the British
Monarchy* (1996). He has also found time to produce and present television
programmes, including *The Prime Ministers*, as seen through his cartoon
collection. He is a practising Anglican of the High Church tradition and
worships at St Mary's Bourne Street.

John MacGregor talks of his 'great passion for music' which was stimulated by one of his masters at secondary school. 'I began to love it then, and
it has lived with me ever since.' His recreational activities also include

conjuring (he has been a member of the Magic Circle since 1989), and he likes reading and gardening. Some of the others, including Patten and Shephard, also like gardening. We do not know if Kenneth Clarke shares this passion. His media image is that of a night-owl and a beer-swilling bruiser, but he denied he was anything of the kind. 'If I go to a party ... I enjoy it – but I don't go to many parties ... But yes, I do enjoy life, and I like a pint every now and again, and I don't hide the fact. I like smoking, so sometimes I'm photographed smoking.' A supporter of Nottingham Forest and Nottingham City football clubs, he also likes cricket, modern jazz music and bird-watching.

John Patten, a devout Roman Catholic, is very much the devoted family man. The Pattens live in London *en famille* during the week – his daughter Marie-Claire attends a London state primary school – and at their country home near Abingdon at the weekends. Louise Patten is a successful business woman. They try never to be apart for long: 'we have breakfast in the morning and I shall see them all tonight: so that's my kind of major plea-sure'. The family includes two Burmese cats who travel backwards and forwards with them. Patten's interests include waterside plants at their Oxfordshire home and two splendid Bristol motor cars. Once every six weeks the Pattens try to go to France, 'leaving Emily [Blatch] in charge, which she does wonderfully well'. Gillian Shephard finds her work in the constituency 'a tremendous relief and support'. Norfolk, as she observes, is 'a long way from London'. She finds relaxation in walking – when possible, she walks to the Department – swimming, gardening, cooking and, like Baker, MacGregor and Patten, she enjoys a 'big, rich life at home which is completely separate from work'.

Divestiture

At some point in a role incumbency, a leader will end her or his term of office and perhaps take up another. At some point in a career incumbency, due to factors associated with ageing, illness or incapacity, or, for politicians, due to the result of an election, leaders divest themselves of leadership. Whether at the end of a role incumbency or a career incumbency, divesti-ture may be voluntary or involuntary, planned or unplanned, and may be experienced by the leader and the organization as either smooth or trau-matic. With voluntary and planned divestiture, the leader decides (e.g., by resignation or retirement) to relinquish an appointment. With involuntary and unplanned divestiture (due, for example, to the abolition of the office, dismissal, a coup, illness or death), the decision is made for, rather than by, the leader. Except in cases where divestiture is the prelude to a sideways or upward move, loss of office (and its trappings) almost always means a loss of influence, loss of the fruits of office and the modification of one's heritage of leadership at the hands of successors.

For all but one (at the date of publication Shephard is still in post), divestiture was involuntary and unplanned, with the decision being made by the Prime Minister. Two (Baker and Clarke) had the consolation of promotion, one (MacGregor) moved sideways, two never held another cabinet post (Carlisle and Joseph), and one, John Patten, may never do so.

Mark Carlisle would have liked to have stayed longer at the DES. Some would claim, he suggests, that 'I was complacent in 1979 and that is why I did not do anything worthwhile. I don't accept that view.' He acknowledges there is 'some truth' in the criticism that 'I was not disposed to be as radical as some wanted', and he was 'not the slightest bit surprised when I was asked to give up my office'. While admitting his disappointment, he was 'in no way embittered', because he could see that Margaret Thatcher would need to 'mould the Cabinet more in her own image' if she was going to achieve the changes she wanted. He left the Cabinet, as the Prime Minister put it, 'with courtesy and good humour' (Thatcher, 1993, p. 151). Considering it to have been 'a great honour to be in the Cabinet for two and a half years', he still does not know 'what it was within the Department … that had caused any displeasure'. What he resented was the implication in the press – whether leaked from No.10 by the Prime Minister or her Press Secretaries 'isn't for me to say' – throughout July and August 1981 that he might be dropped in the reshuffle for having 'failed' and for making 'no worthwhile contribution'. He feels that his contribution was considerable, and that 'legacies of my days in office' are still to be found in schools.

Lord Carlisle believes that had we been able to interview Lord Joseph he would have been 'kind enough to say I had made a contribution'. Joseph had written to him saying 'he had no idea until he went into the Department how much we had achieved in those two and a half years'. They were not easy years: 'People would say, "This or that is not up to scratch. Well, that's Mark Carlisle's fault. He isn't up to it".'

Reflecting on the stability he believes he created, he concludes: 'In the years that followed, it is that stability which I think has been lost.' Nor is he convinced standards have improved: 'What I do know is there has been a lot of disruption over the last few years.' In his maiden speech in the House of Lords in 1987 he expressed reservations on the education reforms because he was uncertain 'how successful the changes proposed would be in improving provision for the less able'. This was the year in which he began building up his law practice again. Since then he has been Chairman of the Parole Review Committee (1987–88) and is currently chairing the Criminal Injuries Compensation Board and the Prime Minister's Advisory Committee on Business Appointments. He is also a Judge of the Courts of Appeal of Jersey and Guernsey.

Keith Joseph, as in so many other things, is an exception within the group. In her memoirs, the Prime Minister makes it clear that the initiative to go came from him. She knew for some time before he resigned that he 'was thinking of retirement' and that, indeed, he had to be persuaded to stay 'a little longer' than he may have really wanted to (Thatcher, 1993,

p. 420). Eventually, he made it clear that 'he wished to leave the Cabinet. The departure of my oldest political friend and ally, indeed mentor, saddened me. He was irreplaceable; somehow politics would never be the same again' (ibid., 562). Joseph himself may not have seen it like this. Halcrow reports that a few days before he resigned

> he gave an interview to a teachers' union magazine ... As reported it was an interview in the classic Joseph's style: 'I asked Sir Keith if he looked back over his period at Elizabeth House with a sense of achievement. "No", he replied. "Not at all?" "Even my worst critic would admit that education is now at the top of the agenda ... I welcome it but I don't think it's due to me". Sir Keith's Press Officer, silent up to that point, weighed in ... Sir Keith would have none of it.'
>
> (1989, p. 187)

He seemed ready to go. As Kenneth Baker remembers it, 'When I met Keith ... in his room at the House of Commons, he started by saying "I have no bitterness. I have been wanting to go since Christmas"' (Baker, 1993, p. 161). Baker concludes by saying that this

> confirmed my belief that it is better for politicians to decide for themselves when they want to leave the centre stage rather than wait to be pushed off it. It allows them to make the necessary changes in their own minds and attitudes in a measured and considered way rather than having to react to a painful crisis.
>
> (ibid.)

What of Baker himself?

Kenneth Baker left Education to become Chairman of the Conservative Party in July 1989. In retrospect he would have liked to have stayed longer at the DES, 'to have embedded the reforms of 1988 a bit further'. With reference to the Dearing proposals, he hopes that too much ground will not have been lost: 'if it has been, that will be a great pity, because the curriculum which I set out to develop was a real attempt to try to introduce a standardized system'. He fears that there could be a return to too much flexibility. Like Angela Rumbold, he does not believe, given the nature of the 1988 Education Reform Act, that it would have been possible 'to get such a major piece of legislation perfect the first time'. He foresaw the need for development and did not intend that the changes he made should be 'set in aspic': 'I would have liked to have been able to take the development of the curriculum a bit further and to have sorted out the problems that have developed over testing at an earlier stage.' On testing, he regrets that 'things have got ragged on this over the last couple of years and the failure to grasp the mistakes in the English test have led to the abandonment of lots of other things which should not have been lost'. He makes no bones about putting this down to 'carelessness', mistakes that were avoidable. While acknowledging that teacher training has been 'much improved' by his successors, he regrets that a wider range of CTCs were not developed more quickly. He is delighted that the staying-on rate at 16 has risen significantly, and believes that this is 'as a result of cumulative change which stems from the 1988 Education Act ... This may be the most important educational change which has taken place over the last ten years. I'm rather proud of this because, I think, I had a hand in making it happen.'

Convinced that the 1988 Education Reform Act was 'the biggest single measure of social reform ... undertaken in the Thatcher years ... the most comprehensive measure of its kind', Baker believes that history will conclude that this was the most important of his achievements over a long period in politics. He enjoyed being Education Secretary, 'eggs and all', but declines to make an overall judgement on the reforms: 'I was too close to them.'

John MacGregor, having survived the salmonella-in-eggs scare as Minister of Agriculture, was moved to Education to bring stability after the introduction of the 1988 Education Reform Act. He quickly won a reputation as a pragmatist. Describing his time at the DES as 'exciting', he confesses that 'It is the one regret of my political life that I did not stay at Education longer.' He feels that ministers need about three years to implement what they set out to achieve, and in his case he was asked to leave 'at the moment when I was getting ... things moving'. Bringing a practical mind to the task, he wanted to find 'workable solutions' to some of the problems generated by the National Curriculum, and feels that in part he was successful. In particular, he had wanted to 'look closely at teacher training'. Following the 1989 reshuffle, Margaret Thatcher had said that 'This is the Cabinet with which we shall now go through to the election.' However, the unforeseen resignation of Sir Geoffrey Howe had meant that she needed a new Leader of the House. While unhappy about leaving Education, MacGregor was pleased to be asked to fill the vacancy.

Concluding that he 'left certainly no more than half way through the job, and probably less even than that', MacGregor nevertheless speaks of his achievements in pressing ahead with the reforms on the Local Management of Schools (LMS), grant-maintained schools, the City Technology Colleges (CTCs) and higher education. He hopes that he had started to gain support from 'the good teachers in the profession', and adds that he had attempted to explain to Margaret Thatcher, presumably without much success, why it was so important to regain their confidence. He fears that she might not have realized that he was in fact 'driving ahead with the reforms'. Thatcher had wanted Norman Tebbit back in the Cabinet as Education Secretary, and felt that 'John MacGregor's limitations as a public spokesman were costing us dear in an area of great importance'. Understandably, MacGregor disagrees with this analysis – 'Look, if Geoffrey Howe had not resigned there wouldn't have been a change anyway, and I would have been able to complete the second half of what I wanted ... But I *strongly* disagree with the notion that this was quote "costing us dear" unquote.' He considers his willingness and ability to speak to teachers as a strength, not a weakness, and finds it 'interesting' that Thatcher's comments 'focus almost exclusively on the National Curriculum'. The CTCs were taking up much of his time, and he regrets that 'that's just another example of an area that

Margaret did not mention'. Across the range of reforms, he maintains, there was no disagreement between himself and the Prime Minister, because 'these reforms were happening and they were working'. Leader of the House of Commons from 1990 to 1992, for which post, according to Downing Street, he 'pretty well selected himself', John MacGregor was Secretary of State for Transport from 1992 to 1994.

Kenneth Clarke, while clearly an ambitious politician, nevertheless expresses regret at the very start of our interview with him 'that I didn't stay longer at Education, just as I greatly regret that I didn't stay longer as Home Secretary'. Enjoying his time, and exhibiting considerable zeal at the DES, where he appears to have quickly got to grips with the problem of the education establishment attempting to block the Conservative reforms, he expected to stay at Education after the election to see through 'a good solid stint of policy-making of the kind that I had had at Health'. Having worked quite closely with John Major on education policy before the general election, Clarke had convinced himself that he would be asked to stay on at the Department for a year or so longer. However, when the call came, he did not argue, since the post of Home Secretary is 'a senior job and you might never be offered it again'. In 1993 he became Chancellor of the Exchequer. Even so, he remembers vividly his last few days in office when he was attempting to get the Royal Assent to the (1992) Education Bill before the dissolution of Parliament – 'in the nick of time'.

Believing strongly that 'education wasn't up to standard' and that children were being 'short-changed' he hopes that he will be remembered for putting education 'back on the road towards higher standards', for 'sorting out the difficulties with the curriculum and testing' and for making SEAC and the NCC work for him 'rather than for the Department'.

John Patten's experience of divestiture was probably the most traumatic of this group. The focus of persistent criticism from the time he joined the Cabinet, John Patten escaped the 1993 reshuffle, but his eventual relegation to the back benches was perhaps inevitable. Some of his parliamentary colleagues considered it possible he might be moved to another department, such as National Heritage. Others saw his demotion as central to John Major's strategy to improve the government's image. His two years in Cabinet were not without policy retreats and mishaps which in themselves might explain his downfall, but what must have been for him a miserable two years was in some measure the product of his determination to change the culture of education policy-making. In this he may to some extent have succeeded in that he not only stood his ground with the teacher unions but also saw off a surprising number of officials and advisers at the Department. It is of course too early to judge, because the time-lag between cause and effect in education is so long: no Secretary of State for Education is ever in post to take responsibility for their own policies. In this sense, the problems of an in-coming Secretary of State may not be those instigated by his or her immediate predecessor, but by earlier Education Secretaries no longer in the Cabinet. It has been suggested by several of his colleagues that the late Keith Joseph, much admired by Thatcher, was the cerebral force behind Conservative education reforms, and it is perhaps in his vision for the future of education, variously accommodated and interpreted by successive Secretaries of State, that the strengths and weaknesses of Conservative education policies have their origins. The strength lies in the ideas, the weakness in the implementation.

What are the tangible factors that led to Patten's departure in the July 1994 shake-up? One of his sayings is that 'politics is a rough old trade'. If it is true that no Secretary of State for Education remains to see their policies come to fruition, then perhaps the role of Education Secretary is more to do with morale than policy. John Patten failed to provide the Prime Minister with the right kind of political returns. Although his policies may not have been seen as wrong, he failed to convince parents, teachers and other voters that he was right. In this respect Patten shares much in common with Norman Lamont as Chancellor. Above all, he exhibited the kind of intellectual clarity and honesty that, not unlike Keith Joseph, makes him an uneasy figure in the world of politics. Politics may need its Pattens and its Josephs, even though it is not always kind to them. As John Patten told us, 'it's never too good to have too many ambitions'.

Patten dismissed criticisms of government education policy by parents' groups as 'Neanderthal', and at times exhibited a self-destructive tendency to get involved in controversial matters which took him away from the central policy issues. Effectively it was the national boycott by teacher unions of classroom tests that sealed his fate, although the last nail in the coffin was most probably the fact that he had to agree to pay libel damages to Tim Brighouse, Birmingham's chief education officer, in June 1994, whom he described as a 'nutter' and a 'madman'. The undisclosed damages were believed to be in excess of £25,000, with legal costs of more than £80,000. Returning from illness, the offending remarks were made at a fringe meeting of the 1993 Conservative Party Conference. Mr Patten admitted that he had made 'untrue and highly damaging' comments concerning Professor Brighouse which in court his solicitor withdrew unreservedly. Ann Taylor, Labour spokeswoman on education at the time, commented that 'The case is a fitting end to his tenure of office, the hallmark of which has been confrontation and insult of parents, of teachers, of chief education officers and anyone with whom he has disagreed.'

When we asked him to reflect upon how history might judge him as Secretary of State for Education, John Patten maintained he had no idea, but went on to say that his time at Sanctuary Buildings would be regarded as

> a bit tumultuous; and he led with his chin a bit too much there; and he might not have been as diplomatic as he could have been over here; but my word, he made education something of national interest; he made people for the first time ever aware of what went on in our schools, through the performance tables and the regular school inspections, and he helped us begin the long process of catching up with our competitors.

The irony of the situation was that whereas at the time Labour had increased its already impressive lead in the polls for having the best policies on unemployment, housing, the health service, trade unions, pensions, and public transport, the notable exception was that area of policy-making for which John Patten was responsible: 'amazingly enough, whereas the Labour party has already overtaken us in every single area except defence, where we just cling on to our lead as the most competent party, in only one area has the Labour party actually fallen back since the 1992 general election, and it is in education'.

Whereas other cabinet members who left the government in the June 1994 reshuffle along with Patten – John MacGregor (Transport Secretary), Peter Brooke (Heritage Secretary) and Lord Wakeham (Leader of the Lords) – were to be made lucrative offers elsewhere, the former Education Secretary's prospects were not so financially attractive. As a former Oxford don and Fellow of Hertford College, it is possible that he will eventually return to academia, and already he has expanded his writing and journalistic career. On returning to the back benches he chose for his debut the Foreign Affairs debate on the Queen's Speech.

Along with his three cabinet colleagues, John Patten knew his fate on the night of Tuesday 19 July 1994 when John Major, to spare the sacked ministers the embarrassment of media attention on the Wednesday, asked to see them between 9 p.m. and 11 p.m. After the meeting, which lasted five minutes, John Patten was said to be 'pretty devastated'. John Major wrote to him, praising his performance as Secretary of State for Education:

> For the last two years you have led one of the Departments of State in the vanguard of this Government's reforms: reforms that are vital to the future of our children and, indeed, the future of our country.
>
> The benefits of our changes are already feeding through and, I am sure, will continue to be felt for many years to come. I know that there have been some tough times but these did not prevent you resolutely taking forward our policies ... You have developed our reforms on grant-maintained schools, the national curriculum, testing, inspections, league tables and much more.
>
> Norma and I send you and Louise our best wishes.

A Major loyalist, John Patten nevertheless chose not to observe the usual courtesies by confining his letter of resignation to two sentences:

> My dear Prime Minister,
>
> When we met last night, you explained that you no longer wished me to remain as Secretary of State for Education, and I am writing to say how glad I have been to serve in Her Majesty's Government.
>
> With my best wishes for the future,
>
> Yours ever,
>
> John

Happily, John Patten is not one to dwell long on the hurt of personal criticism: 'I no longer much care what anyone writes about me, save for my dear wife in her diary and the recording angel in his.' His response to someone who had attacked the government was, 'I'm just a simple back-bencher, squire.'

A Postscript

In this introduction to the text, we have tried to say something about the seven fascinating people who have been 'responsible' for Education since 1979. In doing so, we have tried to consider them as individuals and as 'Conservative' holders of a key office of state engaged in an ongoing and demanding struggle to devise and implement a coherent and radical policy for education. Our intention has always been to enable them to speak for themselves about their life and times as Secretary of State for Education. Our conversations with each of them, with Mark Carlisle, Keith Joseph, Kenneth Baker, John MacGregor, Kenneth Clarke, John Patten and Gillian Shephard, are reported in the seven chapters that follow. We hope they speak to you.

References

Archer, M. (1988) *Culture and Agency*. Cambridge: Cambridge University Press.

Baker, K. (1993) *The Turbulent Years: My Life in Politics*. London: Faber and Faber.

Barber, M. (1994) *The Making of the 1944 Education Act*. London: Cassell.

Chitty, C. (1989) *Towards a New Education System: The Victory of the New Right*. Lewes: Falmer.

Cox, B. (1980) *Education: The Next Decade*. London: CPC.

Dale, R. (1983) Thatcherism and education. In Ahier, J. and Flude, M. (eds) *Contemporary Education Policy*. Beckenham: Croom Helm.

Day, C. and Bakioglu, A. (1996) Development and disenchantment in the professional lives of headteachers. In Goodson, I. and Hargreaves, A. (eds) *Teachers' Professional Lives*. London: Falmer (forthcoming).

DfE (1992) *Choice and Diversity: A New Framework for Schools*. London: HMSO.

English, F. (1995) Towards a reconsideration of biography and other forms of life writing as a focus for teaching educational administration. *Educational Administration Quarterly*. 31(2), 203–23

Gamble, A. (1988) *The Free Economy and the Strong State*. London: Macmillan.

Gerth, H. and Mills, C. (1953) *Character and Social Structure: The Psychology of Social Institutions*. New York: Harcourt, Brace & World.

Giddens, A. (1979) *Central Problems in Social Theory*. London: Macmillan.

Gronn, P. (1993) Psychobiography on the couch: character, biography and the comparative study of leaders. *Journal of Applied Behavioural Science*. 29(3), 343–58.

Gronn, P. and Ribbins, P. (1996) Leaders in context: post-positivist approaches to understanding educational leadership. *Educational Administration Quarterly*. 32(3), 452–74.

Halcrow, M. (1989) *Keith Joseph: A Single Mind*. London: Macmillan.

Hansard (1987) *The Education Reform Bill*. London: HMSO, 1st December, 769–860.

House, R., Rousseau, D. and Thomas-Hunt, M. (1995) The meso paradigm: a framework for the integration of micro and macro-organizational behaviour. In Cummings, L. and Staw, B. (eds) *Research in Organizational Behaviour.* 17, Connecticut: Jai Press.

Kets de Vries, M. (1990) Leaders on the couch. *Journal of Applied Behavioural Science.* 29(3), 423–31.

Kets de Vries, M. (1993) *Leaders, Fools and Impostors: Essays on the Psychology of Leadership.* San Francisco: Jossey-Bass.

Knight, C. (1990) *The Making of Tory Educational Policy in Post-War Britain.* Lewes: Falmer.

Kogan, M. (1971) *The Politics of Education: Edward Boyle and Anthony Crosland.* Harmondsworth: Penguin.

Lawson, N. (1992) *The View from No 11: Memoirs of a Tory Radical.* London: Corgi Books.

Lawton, D. (1994) Defining quality. In Ribbins, P. and Burridge, E. (eds) *Improving Education: The Issue is Quality.* London: Cassell.

Lowe, R. (1992) *Education and the Second World War.* London: Falmer.

Mortimer, J. and Mortimer, P. (1991) *The Primary School Head: Roles, Responsibilities and Reflections.* London: Paul Chapman.

Mouzelis, N. (1991) *Back to Sociological Theory: The Construction of Social Orders.* New York: St Martin's Press.

OFSTED (1994) *Taught Time.* London: OFSTED.

Rae, J. (1993) *Delusions of Grandeur: A Headmaster's Life.* London: HarperCollins.

Ranson, S. (1988) From 1944 to 1984: education, citizenship and democracy. *Local Government Studies.* 14(1), 1–12.

Ranson, S. (1992) Towards the learning society. *Educational Management and Administration.* 20(2), 68–80.

Ribbins, P. and Marland, M. (1994) *Headship Matters: Conversations with Seven Secondary School Headteachers.* London: Longman.

Ribbins, P. and Thomas, H. (1993) Pursuit of school quality in England and Wales. In Jacobson, S. and Berne, R. (eds) *Reforming Education.* California: Corwin Press.

Scruton, R. (1980) *The Meaning of Conservatism.* Harmondsworth: Penguin.

Sexton, S. (1987) Letter. *The Independent.* 19th November.

Sexton, S. (1988) No nationalised curriculum. *The Times,* 4th June.

Simon, B. (1991) *Education and the Social Order 1940–90.* London: Lawrence and Wishart

Smith, L. (1994) Biographical method. In Denzin, N. and Lincoln, Y. (eds) *Handbook of Qualitative Research.* Newbury Park, CA: Sage.

Smith, W. (1957) *Education: An Introductory Survey.* Harmondsworth: Penguin.

Stewart, R. (1989) Studies of managerial jobs and behaviour: the way forward. *Journal of Management Studies.* 26(1), 1–10.

Stuart, N (1994) Quality in education. In Ribbins, P. and Burridge, E. (eds) *Improving Education: The Issue is Quality.* London: Cassell.

Thatcher, M. (1993) *The Downing Street Years.* London: HarperCollins.

Thomas, H. (1989) Who will control the secondary school in the 1990s? In Lowe, R. (ed.) *The Changing Secondary School.* Lewes: Falmer.

CHAPTER 2

Mark Carlisle

WITH PETER RIBBINS

Mark Carlisle was born in 1929. He was educated at Radley and Manchester University, where he studied Law. He did his National Service as a Lieutenant in the Royal Army Education Corps during 1948–50. On being called to the Bar, he practised in Manchester from 1954 and became a QC in 1971. He contested St Helens in 1958 and 1959, and was member for Runcorn (1964–83) and Warrington South (1983–87). After serving in a number of junior ministerial positions in the Home Office, he was appointed first Shadow Secretary and then Secretary of State for Education, which office he held between 1979 and 1981. He has served on a number of important committees including, since 1989 as Chairman of the Criminal Injuries Compensation Board. He was raised to the peerage as Baron Carlisle of Bucklow in 1987.

22 June 1994

PR   I would like to begin by asking you about the influences which have shaped your views on education and educational policy, and in what ways they shaped what you tried to do when you became Secretary of State.

MC   I find that question very difficult to answer in a way, because I never expected to be made Secretary of State for Education. My interests politically had always been in the Home Office, and professionally I was a barrister, therefore when I was asked to be Secretary of State for Education (or, rather, Shadow Secretary of State for Education) in 1977, after the death of Airey Neave, it came as somewhat of a shock. Of course, I had always taken an interest within my own constituency in the schools. I had a view in general terms about education. I had looked a bit at what happened within the Cheshire Education Authority, I had visited a fair number of schools. As a

Member of Parliament I had opened schools for the Cheshire Education Authority. I think I can say I am genuinely interested in people and in children.

I had no direct personal knowledge of the state sector either as a pupil or as a parent – my daughter attended a private school. And I had been to university and to an independent school [public school] myself.

PR   Can you say something more about your own education?

MC   I was at Radley College, and after that I went to Manchester University, where I read law.

PR   Did you enjoy your own schooling?

MC   Yes, I did.

PR   How would you describe Radley?

MC   I think it is a very good school. I think it has probably got a lot better in recent years. It is clearly one of the 'in' schools. Although I would have to say that at the time I was there it did not have, perhaps, quite the reputation which it enjoyed when Dennis Silk later became its head. I enjoyed school; I enjoyed the games; I enjoyed the work; I was, I suppose, a reasonable student – if not a particularly bright one. But I enjoyed it, and I enjoyed the general friendship of the place.

PR   What else do you remember about it? Was it an academic school: a place where you were expected to work hard? What were its most important values?

MC   Those who started it would have said that it had a strong Christian ethos and background. The chapel was quite a central part of the school: all the wardens, I think, had been ordained, including Vaughan Wilkes, who was the headmaster or the warden, as we called him, when I was there. His wife was the daughter of the Dean of Durham. There was quite a strong church connection, there is no doubt about that. It had equally quite a strong games side to it. I mean, rowing was the big sport there, not that I rowed. Academically I would have thought that it held its own with others. It was a purely boarding school and was located right near Oxford in very lovely grounds.

PR   What about your primary school?

MC   I was at primary school during the war. I went to a primary school in Cheshire which was called Morland House, which was immediately moved to Wales by the time I got to it. I therefore spent some time in two different buildings in Wales. I really can't say that it had a great impact on me. Again, my recollection is of a perfectly normal and ordinary place. I knew quite a lot of people there, people who lived locally. It was a friendly school, a reasonable, middle-of-the-road school.

PR   John Patten and Kenneth Baker both talked with some warmth about their primary schools. They still remember them and some of their teachers with real affection.

MC   Oh, I certainly remember one or two teachers. I remember a man called A. W. Black who had written a whole history of England in verse for the purpose of getting through to some students who could learn doggerel but were no good at history. I think, although I am not sure, that he'd done this when teaching at the Dragon Prep School. He used to teach Latin in a kind of verse to us, and he would make up card games in Latin and things like that to help us learn. I remember him. I remember some of the other masters there as well. I remember the headmaster. I suppose the masters I would remember best and most easily came from those days rather than in my later years. But then it was a small school with only forty (or perhaps sixty) pupils. It was also easier to remember because of the move to Wales during the evacuation.

PR   Do you remember any of the masters with affection from your early days?

MC   I certainly remember, as I say, masters from my prep school days – and at Radley there was Pop Crowson, who taught us history. And I remember my house master, who later went to Peter House in South Africa. I certainly remember them, but I cannot say that they were outstanding figures in my life.

PR   You then went to university?

MC   No. I did my National Service and then went to university. I was going to go to Cambridge, but the fact is I failed the scholarship. I could have gone if I had been willing to wait a year, since I had been offered a place in Trinity Hall. But since I'd decided by that stage that I wanted to be a barrister it seemed rather pointless to wait. Funnily enough (I'm sorry, I should have said this, because this is relevant), I went back to teach for a term at my old prep school at Morland House, so I taught for a term before going to university.

PR   Was that your only experience of teaching?

MC   That was my only teaching.

PR   Were you active in politics at or before university? Some of the people we have talked to, such as Kenneth Clarke, were clear that the possibility of a career in politics was something which attracted them quite early on in their lives, and they prepared for it actively while at university. Others, such as John Patten, who described himself as a 'late developer', came to this decision much later on. Were you an 'early developer'?

MC   I was, I was. I was active in politics at university – I was chairman of the University Conservative Association, and I was chairman of the Federation of University Conservatives for all the universities; so I was already very active even at that stage.

PR   Were you already beginning to think of a career in politics?

MC   Yes, I was. You have got to realize (and I am sure Kenneth Clarke would say the same) that reading law naturally leads you into being interested in politics. You will know, because you are from the academic world: that law and politics are very closely linked.

PR   I fear I must be something of an exception. I read politics and it completely put me off any thought of becoming a politician. [*MC laughs*]

MC   Well, that may be so. But what I'm trying to say is that if you are going to be a barrister – if that's your intention – you are foolish if you don't take some opportunity to get involved in Union life. One of the things you need to learn is the confidence to speak on your feet. In fact, presumably it is partly because you feel that you have the ability to speak on your feet that makes you want to become a barrister. Therefore you start taking an active part in the Union, and the Union in all universities tends to be dominated by political debate and by those who have a leaning towards or who are reading law; particularly those who are going to the Bar. The Bar and politics go hand in hand; or at least they did in those days. So, certainly, I was active in politics at that time. This was true of others. You have mentioned Kenneth Clarke, but it was also true of the people of my generation. For example, Geoffrey Howe was active at Cambridge and David Waddington at Oxford. It was true of all sorts of people. I seem to remember that at the time Norman St John Stevas had just been president of both the Unions.

PR   So those were your contemporaries?

MC   They slightly overlapped. Then, I became Chairman of the Federation of University Conservatives, and from then onwards I became increasingly involved in politics.

PR   What happened once you graduated?

MC   I went to the Bar in Manchester. I had always intended to practise at the Bar, and I had always intended to practise in Manchester – this was the real reason why I went to Manchester University rather than waiting around for a year to go to Cambridge. I was a pupil in Manchester and I spent the first nine years of my working life at the Bar in Manchester.

PR   Did you enjoy it as a barrister?

MC   I loved it – and I still do. But having got involved in politics, having been Chairman of the Federation of University Conservatives, which meant for that year being on the National Executive of the Conservative party, I naturally carried on my interest in the Young Conservative movement. I was Area Vice-Chairman when the St Helens by-election came up when Hartley Shawcross resigned the seat. I decided to have a go and was the Conservative candidate. Well, St Helens was, of course, a hopeless seat. There was little chance of winning it, but even so I am conceited enough to say that

I had rather a good election. This election took place when things were just beginning to swing back for us after a fairly disastrous period for the Conservatives. I got some quite nice write-ups in the press. This by-election took place shortly before the 1959 general election, and so I stayed on, of course, as the parliamentary candidate for the general election.

Shortly after that I got married and said to myself, 'Right, that is it, I have had my amusement. I must now be a serious barrister.' I had my name taken off the Conservative party list of candidates. And then in 1963 I happened to be watching television one evening when it was announced that Dennis Vosper, who was the MP for Runcorn, had been made chairman of the body that ran Social Security (it was, at this time, called the National Assistance Board) and was going to the House of Lords as Lord Runcorn. Therefore there was going to be a vacancy at the forthcoming election for the seat of Runcorn. This happened just before the election. It was the neighbouring seat to the one I lived in. I sat up, and my wife looked across at me and said, 'Well, what are you going to do?' and I said – 'I have always said that if Runcorn became free it is the one seat I really would like to fight.' I knew the chairman very well, and that would help. But I went on to say to myself, 'No, I have got married and I have also said that I had had enough of that – it's silly, we can't afford it.' She said, 'You must have a go. If you don't, for the rest of your life you will blame me for the fact that you did not have a go. I am not prepared to live with you blaming me all the time for the fact that you did not take this chance to get back into politics.' So I rang up the chairman and asked if we could meet for lunch. We did, and shortly afterwards I got selected as the Conservative candidate for Runcorn. I was very, very lucky. The seat was not as competitive as it might have been in other circumstances. Even so, one of the other two people on the final short-list was Nicholas Scott. It was only two or three months before the general election that the announcement about Vosper's impending move was made. There was no by-election. It was announced that the seat would become vacant at the general election. By then the competition for the seat was nowhere near as strong as it might have been – Geoffrey Howe, Christopher Chattaway, Jeffrey Johnson Smith and John Biffin had all already got prospective seats elsewhere. So I got Runcorn and stayed from 1964 to 1987: twenty-three years in all.

PR   What attracted you to politics?

MC   I was interested in people; I really was interested in people.

PR   You would have seen plenty of people had you settled for a career in law.

MC   I know. My aunt always said if I hadn't been a barrister I ought to have been a vicar or a teacher – her late husband was a vicar. I don't know. But I do know that in those days there was an infectious enthusiasm in politics, there was an excitement about it. The adrenalin ran. It was fun arguing a case from a platform. In the St Helens by-election I remember that we actually stood on the roofs of motor cars to talk to people, and we addressed crowds leaving rugger matches ...

PR   There are not too many modern motor cars on whose roofs you could stand.

MC   No. But I remember we spoke from the back of lorries all decked up, and held open-air meetings.

PR   So it was the fun that attracted you – that is a remarkably refreshing admission.

MC   I think that was partly it; it was the excitement of it all.

PR   In my experience, politicians tend to be terribly worthy when they answer that question – they usually say they want to do as much good for as many ...

MC   Well, yes, but as I have already said, I was interested in people. Obviously wanting to be able to help people is a real consideration. But, let us be honest, the excitement and the interest which are so much a part of a life in politics are also important.

PR   What was your first experience of Parliament? What did you feel about it in the first weeks and months that you were there? Were you reticent initially, or did you try and make a mark early on? Were you ambitious?

MC   I think I was probably ambitious. I, perhaps slightly surprisingly, made my maiden speech in favour of the abolition of capital punishment, which, in my party, isn't the sort of subject you would choose if you wanted a totally quiet life.

PR   Nor one designed to endear you to some of your constituents ...

MC   As you say, not necessarily designed to endear me to some of my constituents or to the Conservative party, but I reckoned that I had enough support in the constituency not to have to worry too much about that.

PR   Even so, it was a brave thing to do.

MC   And, yes, I think I can say that from the outset I played an active part and that I had an active life outside politics. In fact, and I would not want this to be misunderstood, I am not a mad enthusiast for what I might call 'full-time party politicians'. I think, if possible, back-bench MPs ought to have other jobs as well. I kept on with my work at the Bar to some extent. I think today, sadly, thirty years later, it's probably impossible to do so. But in the sixties it was still possible. In any case, as you know, at the time there were very few people who came straight from Central Office into the House of Commons without having done anything else. This kind of full-time party politician is a more recent invention. My own view is that those of us who had other jobs and other interests in fact often were able to make a more significant contribution from the back benches because of it.

In my case, I became quite active quite quickly. I soon became Secretary of the Conservative Home Affairs group, and Selwyn Lloyd made me become Secretary of the North-West Area MPs – he said it would keep me in order – anyway, I took an active part. But I was also still practising at the Bar.

PR   You would defend that as something worth doing?

MC   I would: I think the House wants and needs a mixture, but I think it is more and more difficult to do it. In those days you didn't have so many meetings and you did not have to spend so much time at the House. Of course, if you were appointed on to a committee for a Bill, then you had to be there during the day-time. But because you didn't have all these select committees taking up all the time which they do now, and because you didn't have all these pressure groups that you have to cope with these days, there was time to do other worthwhile things.

PR   The hours are pretty insane now, aren't they?

MC   Yes, they are. But, you see, in those days the hours really started at 4.30 or 5.00 o'clock unless you wanted to be in at Question Time. You could get in at 4.00 and take part in a debate. So it was possible to be at court for much of the day and still be active in the House. In any case, much of the business took place late in the evening. I remember getting quite a lot of publicity within the Tory party for a speech which I made late at night in a packed House. That still happens, but probably the constituents today wouldn't wear people doing other things to the extent which was possible then. Although, I don't believe that any constituent I represented was inadequately represented because I was not totally full-time.

PR   What was your first governmental post?

MC   I was Parliamentary Secretary in the Home Office and then Minister of State in the Home Office from 1970 to 1974 in Heath's government.

PR   Do I recall you saying that had you had the choice, the thing you would most like to have been was Home Secretary?

MC   I suppose my final ambition was to have been Home Secretary. Almost all my early political involvement had been with Home Office matters. I had been secretary of the Conservative backbench Home Affairs Committee; I was appointed very early on to a committee chaired by Peter Thorneycroft, who wrote a book for the party on crime; I was also a member on a committee, with Geoffrey Howe and various other people, chaired by Cripps on Equal Rights for Women within the Law. I then was on the Home Office Advisory Committee on the penal system, set up by Roy Jenkins, before I became a minister. Following that I was a minister, and after that I was chairman of the Conservative Home Affairs Committee. So really that is the side on which I have always been most active. Perhaps if you make your maiden speech on the kind of subject which I did, then you tend to draw that kind of attention to yourself – I don't know.

PR   How did you come to be Shadow Secretary of State for Education?

MC   The *full* story? Well, the *full* story, I am pretty sure, is this. Tragically, Airey Neave was killed. Somebody had to move over to become Shadow Secretary of State for Northern Ireland, and this left a vacancy in the Shadow Cabinet; and my guess is that Willie Whitelaw said it was his turn to nominate someone. I don't think I would have been Margaret's first choice, whereas I think I probably would have been Willy's first choice. I had worked with him on Home Office matters in opposition.

PR   What do you regard as the most important pieces of legislation for which you were responsible during your two and a half years at the DES?

MC   There were three. Firstly, we had the 1979 Act, which restored to local authorities the power to make their own decisions upon comprehensive reorganization. Secondly, we had the major Education Act of 1980. This was controversial. It dealt, among other things, with the Assisted Places Scheme. Thirdly, we had the Education Special Needs Act in 1981 – I must confess I am not very good on the detail of that piece of legislation. By that time Rhodes Boyson must have taken over as Minister for Schools. Or rather he was spokesman for schools in the Commons. Janet Young was responsible for schools throughout my time. But Rhodes, as spokesman on schools in the Commons, took that Bill through. The Education Act itself I took through committee myself.

What else did we do? Well, we recognized the Professional Association of Teachers. I said, when I was dropped, that if I was asked to identify the two things which I had done which I believed would have the greatest long-term benefit – one would be introducing the Assisted Places Scheme, and the other would be recognizing the Professional Association of Teachers. But I gather it is not doing quite as well at the moment as it was at the time.

PR   No, it probably isn't. I think it is losing rather than gaining members.

MC   They had a dynamic general secretary in those early days – his name for the moment escapes me.

PR   The Warnock Committee, set up by Shirley Williams, reported in your time? In effect, you accepted much of it and many of its recommendations?

MC   Oh yes.

PR   It seems quite an important epitaph. I am rather surprised that you seem to rate it no higher than third in importance among the things you did. Many people within the education establishment would, I suspect, rate it by far the most important.

MC   I do not deny its importance, and I hope it is succeeding – I think it probably is – it was based on an attempt to integrate special education with the rest of education. I suppose that I referred to the other two because they were controversial. When I ceased to be Secretary of State for Education, Keith Joseph took over the job; I got a letter from him in which he said that he did not realize how much had in fact been done during those two and a half years. This is sometimes forgotten. We actually did do a lot.

PR   Actually, to be fair, Kenneth Baker said something similar. Do you think your achievements as Secretary of State have been underestimated?

MC   Yes, I do. I think in some ways one can look at these years as a period of relative peace in the educational world. But people forget that I inherited a situation in which there was a strong possibility of a strike. I inherited a situation in which the NUT were about to go on strike because of Shirley Williams' proposals. I managed to carry through a pay agreement which stopped the strike, and we had two and a half years without disruption in the classrooms. That doesn't mean to say my relationship with the teachers was an easy one – it certainly was not. My relationship with the NUT certainly was not easy, but my relationship with the NAS always remained very good. My relationship at a personal level remained good enough with the leaders of the NUT, but with the rank and file I was very unpopular. I suspect that was because I was a Conservative minister. I have always said that whatever a Conservative minister said, the NUT would say the reverse. But I got on all right with Fred Jarvis.

   We did get quite a lot done during those years. For example, rightly or maybe wrongly, we accepted the GCSE in principle during that period. We put in train the idea of a National Curriculum. Actually, I saved our budget very well in the face of considerable pressure to reduce it. I came out unscathed from Cabinet with a lot more of my budget than I expected; partly because I took practically every battle which I had to fight to Cabinet. Quite a few of the issues over public expenditure which were discussed in Cabinet at that stage were issues to do with the education budget. I did lose some battles. For example, I had to accept the total abolition of support for fees for overseas students. At the end of the day, although I was very concerned about it at the time, I'm no longer sure if this was such a bad thing. In fact, subsequently quite a bit of the tab was picked up by the Foreign Office, by first Lord Carrington and then Francis Pym. This meant that we were better able to target the aid going where it should go, rather than giving it indiscriminately to everybody.

PR   Was there anything you tried which was not successful?

MC   Our attempt to charge for school transport was one thing – we were defeated in the Lords on this.

PR   What about your attempts to free the polytechnics from local government?

MC   Did we try that at that stage? I do remember that we made several attempts to resolve the business of school meals and school transport – and were presented for our pains as the wicked Conservative government trying to do away with traditional rights and free education. In the event we failed on school transport but succeeded in giving greater freedom over charging for school meals to local authorities. I think this was reasonable. I said unashamedly at the time that I saw nothing wrong in voluntary support for local schools by those parents who wished and were able to do so. It seemed to me that if parents wanted – provided the state ensured that no school was inadequately funded – voluntarily to raise money to make things available which the state could not make universally available, good luck to them. That has always been my philosophy. Just as I've always said that the duty of the state is to provide an education for everyone who wishes to avail themselves of it. Whether individuals take up this opportunity should be up to them. I see absolutely nothing incompatible about supporting state education and sending your own children to a private school. For my own part, I always argued that I was lessening pressure on the state school system by educating my daughter privately. I think that it is not the state's duty to educate; rather it is the parent's duty to educate. The state's duty is to provide the framework within which such education can be carried out.

PR   Were you content with the kind of broad settlement which controlled policy and practice in education? At the time there was much talk about the educational system being controlled by a triumvirate of power made up of the central government, local government and organized teachers. There was also a feeling that ministers were not and should not be too interested in management and policy-making on the curriculum.

MC   I did say at one stage that the Secretary of State for Education was the reverse of the harlot throughout the ages – you had all the responsibility and no power. That was particularly true with regard to our relations with the local authorities – we had very little power over them. We could not dictate how they spent money. All we could do was to say that in the grants we made to them such and such an amount of money had been earmarked for education. Our lack of power over this used to lead me into a good deal of dispute with some of my colleagues. I would always emphasize what we had given the local authorities for education; what we had earmarked for education. Local authorities used to try to emphasize the costs of the services they provided as a whole, and of the ways in which they spent their resources to pay for this.

PR   What was being Secretary of State for Education like in your time? Did you enjoy it? What sort of Secretary of State were you? I remember, for example, Kenneth Baker saying that what he used to like was large meetings of his senior political and administrative staff in which they would thrash out a policy and then get on with it. Other ministers seem to prefer to make policy in much smaller groups.

MC   My approach was more like that of Kenneth Baker's than the alternative. But I do remember that being Secretary of State was very hard and difficult work. I say this without rancour but it is a fact, which I think should be recorded; it was the one cabinet job which the Prime Minister had herself done.

PR   I was going to ask you about that. She seems to feel that she was stitched up by the educational establishment. That she was fooled into agreeing to the demise of more grammar schools than any other Secretary of State before or since. Both the available evidence, and what we have heard from others, seems to suggest that she did not remember her time at the DES with much satisfaction or affection.

MC   No, she didn't. She didn't much like teachers, and she didn't seem to like civil servants she encountered at the DES. This did not make it any easier for me. I found the pressures very hard, very exacting.

PR   How did they manifest themselves? What kinds of pressures? From whom?

MC   'Pressures' may be the wrong word. I think there was a good deal of pressure on the educational budget from No. 10, without a full awareness of what had happened during the years we were in opposition. The fact is that I followed Shirley Williams as Secretary of State for Education. Shirley Williams, as far as I know, was the only Labour minister who had attempted, with any degree of success, to implement Denis Healey's request that the load of expenditure which was carried by the central government should be reduced. When I took over the Department of Education, it already had fewer civil servants than it had when Margaret Thatcher had left it, and it was spending less in real terms than it had been during her years in office. In contradistinction, in practically every other government department there had been an expansion of numbers and an expansion of everything else, including expenditure. This tended to be forgotten when we started talking about going for a global figure of $X\%$ savings in total expenditure and working out what implications this should have for the budgets of each and every department. It was not always understood when I resisted, and it was not always appreciated when I did so at the level of the Cabinet.

Against this, there were aspects of the job which I very much liked. I enjoyed visiting schools. I enjoyed the House of Commons. I quite liked the debates. I enjoyed Neil Kinnock as an opponent – if I could have chosen an opponent I could not have chosen better than Neil Kinnock. He never worried me as an opponent, because, when it came down to it, Neil Kinnock was always short on details. He did not do his homework. I used to quite relish Question Times with Neil Kinnock ...

PR   One of your colleagues told me he tended to be long on words and short on detail.

MC   Oh yes, he was long on words and short on details. Let me illustrate this with an example. There was an awful time, from his point of view, when he stated, 'Was I not aware that there were schools which', due to our vicious policy, 'had no books at all?' I asked him to name them, and there was a deadly silence. So I enjoyed the Commons; I enjoyed taking the Bills through; I enjoyed the debates.

PR   You took a lot to Cabinet?

MC   I took a lot of the issues on expenditure to Cabinet. But I would not wish you to misunderstand. I have to say that, at the time, those two years were dominated by the government, under Mrs Thatcher, quite rightly and quite properly, seeing it as absolutely essential in the public interest to re-establish control of public expenditure and public finance. This meant that it was not easy to run a spending department, particularly a spending department which, as I have said, had been pretty prudent in its expenditure – Shirley Williams had been a prudent Secretary of State for Education in so far as expenditure was concerned – in which further expenditure cuts were being looked for. So during much of my time as Secretary of State I was occupied in defending my corner on expenditure. But, I repeat, on the two finance rounds that I was involved in I think we did pretty well, and the Department felt that I had fought hard and done well for them. I look back on this with a degree of satisfaction.

PR   The DES has been described as a rogue department; one which is unusually difficult to manage. It is depicted as having an unusually strong sense of its own history and a powerful and on-going agenda which transcends the vagaries of the results of particular elections. Kenneth Baker, for example, claims that

> Of all the Whitehall Departments, the DES was amongst those with the strongest in-house ideology. There was a clear 1960s ethos and a very clear agenda which permeated virtually all the civil servants ... The DES represented perfectly the theory of 'producer capture', whereby the interest of the producer prevail over the interests of the consumer. Not only was the

Department in league with the teacher unions, University Departments of Education, teacher-training theories, and local authorities, it also acted as their protector against any threats which Ministers might pose ... Lest this analysis be dismissed as typical Tory prejudice, I would refer to Bernard Donoughue's book on his experiences as the head of James Callaghan's Policy Unit in the Labour Government. One of Callaghan's first speeches as Prime Minister in 1976 was on education ... He called for more vigorous educational standards, greater monitoring and accountability of teachers and greater concentration on the basic skills of literacy and numeracy. But, as Donoughue writes, 'The NUT was furious. The Department of Education was shocked'. The Green Paper which followed Callaghan's speech was 'sparse in content and complacent in tone'. The officials at the DES and the education establishment had seen to that. This was 'Whitehall at its self-satisfied, condescending and unimaginative worst'.

(1993, p. 168)

What is your view?

MC   I would say two things. Firstly, I am not sure that the DES has had a 'powerful agenda'. In fact, I wonder if the reverse is true. And as for being 'powerful', in some ways the reverse is true. It had very little power compared with that of the local education authorities. Secondly, and conversely, I think there may be more truth in the claim that some of its members do have a particular political commitment. In thinking about the DES, I was struck by a different point. I found that as a minister you did not have a powerful administrative machine of the kind which I had become used to at the Home Office behind you.

PR   Were there civil servants and HMIs, perhaps, that you remember as making a special contribution in the time you were there?

MC   Jim Hamilton was my Permanent Secretary. I had a very good Private Secretary in Peter Shaw. Edward Simpson was the Deputy Secretary in charge of teachers, who I thought was very good. There was that strange, perhaps 'strange' is the wrong word, bright man, Walter Ulrich, who was in charge of higher education. I also remember one or two very good middle-ranking civil servants who had strongly hostile views on things like the Assisted Places Scheme, but who, being good civil servants, having expressed their doubts, then did their best to carry these policies through.

We were, I think – but you will have to ask others like Rhodes Boyson – a happy team; we were a largely united and fairly successful team. But this does not appear to have been a view which the Prime Minister shared.

PR   She describes you in her book as someone who 'leaned to the left', 'who had not been a very effective Education Secretary' (Thatcher, 1993, p. 151). But she does not explain why she held either view.

MC   I never understood what it was that she was unhappy about. For example, I took one or two decisions which, I accept, clearly did not enamour me to the Tory party. The first was to allow Thameside in the end to go comprehensive. Despite the row there had been, and despite their earlier and successful action in the courts to stop them from doing so. The second was to refuse to allow a school in Edward Heath's constituency, Bromley, to revert to its former status as a grammar school. Such decisions were not of the kind which were going to make the Secretary of State for Education necessarily pin-up boy of the month within the party. But, you know, I still believe they were both right.

PR   Did you slow the number of grammar schools being ...

MC   I enabled many of them to remain, but I turned down this one application for a new grammar school. I was not satisfied with the plans I had been presented describing what was going to happen to the children who didn't go there. I allowed Thameside to go totally comprehensive. Two or three elections had been fought which high-lighted the issue at local level. The local people had supported the Labour party. This was a case in which a Labour local authority had twice put the issue of comprehensive reform at the top of their agenda and had twice been elected. If you remember, before this, when Thameside was under Conservative control, the LEA had refused to accept the edict from Mrs Williams to go comprehensive and had won their case in the courts. But they had then lost control in the local elections, and I had to take account of that.

I accept that my decision was controversial. But I believe, and I have said this a number of times, that I think that the Secretary of State for Education must remember, firstly, that it is the job of the government, or the Department, to provide a framework within which education can take place rather than to claim a duty to educate – that is the responsibility of the parents. Secondly, it is their duty to provide for all, even if not all use it. It is not good enough to claim for a particular framework – this is an ideal system for 80 per cent, too bad about the rest. It is for this reason that I was worried about the arguments advanced in favour of the abolition of ILEA. In practice, on this, I may have been proved wrong. Even so, I must say I was a bit surprised the other day to read that the Conservative party were taking great credit for the fact that since the abolition of ILEA the standard of education in Chelsea, Westminster and Wandsworth was far higher than it used to be in the Labour-controlled councils – well of course it is. I expect it was in the days of ILEA as well. You have to take account of the back-ground from which your pupils are coming if you are to make fair comparisons.

PR   You've mentioned the Prime Minister – did you feel you had her support as Secretary of State? Did you speak often to her about educational issues?

MC   Not a great deal. But you should not misunderstand this. It is very difficult to get over, to those who have not experienced it, the enormous pressure at which government today works. There is rarely time for such discussions. The Cabinet cannot devote much time to any but the most extraordinary issues. But the Prime Minister never did come to the Department while I was there. She was planning to come at one stage, but something went wrong and the visit fell through. I had my battles with the Treasury and with No. 10, but I was confident on the major expenditure battles that, if I took them to Cabinet, there were a good many people around that table who I knew would support me. I was proved right several times.

But I was not the slightest bit surprised when I was asked to give up my office, and I was in no way embittered by that fact. Obviously one is disappointed when asked to do so, but I could quite see, from the Prime Minister's point of view, the need to mould the Cabinet more in her own image. She had started with a Cabinet which I think fairly reflected all aspects of the Conservative party. But I can understand her wish at that stage to mould it more in her own image. She would need to do this if she was going to be able achieve what she believed was right for the country. To do that meant she had to make some changes. Once I had appreciated that, then my departure, among others, did not surprise me in any way.

PR   It has been suggested that there was some acrimony between you at times. But this was not the case with regard to the way in which you, unlike, perhaps, some others, received the news in September 1981, that you were to be replaced. This is confirmed by the Prime Minister. She comments that in meeting those who were to be asked to give up office,

> I began with Ian Gilmour and told him my decision. He was – I can find no other word for it – huffy ... Christopher Soames was equally angry – but in a grander way. I got the distinct impression that he felt the natural order of things was being violated and that he was, in effect, being dismissed by his housemaid. Mark Carlisle ... also left the Cabinet – but he did so with courtesy and good humour.
>
> (Thatcher, 1993, p. 151)

Is that how you remember it?

MC   As you say, she says I went with good humour – I certainly tried to. Of course, I was obviously disappointed. It would be silly to pretend I wasn't. But I repeat – I could understand her reason for doing it – at the end of the day the Prime Minister must choose their ministers – I said to her, and this is public knowledge, 'Prime Minister, if you are asking me to give up my office, I will go back right away to the Department and I will write you the appropriate letter. I assure you that I realize you have the right to choose who your ministers are. It has been a great honour to be in the Cabinet for two and a half years. I realize you want to make changes, and I have always realized that.' I tried not to be bitter about the fact that I was dropped, and I don't think I was bitter. What I did say, and repeat again, is that I do not know what it was within the Department (if it was) that had happened that had caused any displeasure – my guess is that it wasn't really anything to do with this.

PR   Was anything hinted?

MC   Well, the press had been hinting I might go. I departed office in September, and the press through July and August had been running increasing numbers of items on the issue of 'Who's going to be in the reshuffle?' As it became more obvious there was going to be a reshuffle, the speculation started on, 'Who were the failures and who would be dropped?' And so in the week or two before the thing actually happened you would find yourself being written up as one of the failures who were going. Given this, I felt entitled to ask, 'In what respect do you think the Department has failed you? It seems to be a criticism not only of me, but of others as well?' She was gracious enough to say that she accepted this.

PR   Was there was an element of the kind of inspired leak from No. 10 to the press which became such a feature of future reshuffles?

MC   Oh yes, and this is what I objected to. But whether this was from her or from her press secretaries isn't for me to say. I always said, I did not object to going – I resented, if you like, the build-up over the two weeks before; the implication that somehow one had failed and had made no worthwhile contribution. I don't believe that to be true, for the reasons we have discussed. I think I made a consider-able contribution. As I go around schools today I still find legacies of my days in office.

PR   I suppose one possible explanation for your move is that one of the Prime Minister's most important thinkers and supporters, Sir Keith Joseph, very much wanted to be Secretary of State for Education?

MC   Keith, if you are able to interview him, would, I think, be kind enough to say that I had made a contribution. He wrote to me telling me that he had no idea until he went into the Department how much we had achieved in those two and a half years. I am sure he meant this and that he was being perfectly genuine. I had written to him to congratulate him, and he wrote that he had no idea how much had been done earlier. We did achieve a good deal.

PR   Were there things which you had not done, or would have tried to do if you had been given the time to do so?

MC   Yes there were. What we didn't do, and I accept this, is we didn't produce a great National Curriculum or anything like that, partly because we tried to work through the local education authorities. I think you will find that towards the end of my time I made a speech to the National Association of Headteachers in which I said to them:

'For heaven's sake stop carping and look at what we've achieved over the last two and a half years. Look at how successful your financing has been – much more than you might have expected.'

PR   Did you have any regrets on leaving office? In particular, any feeling of business uncompleted? If you had stayed a bit longer, what would you have tried to do?

MC   I would have liked to have stayed a bit longer, obviously. But I am not sure that I can really identify anything uncompleted. We made it clear we were going to support A levels; we gave quite a boost to polytechnics; we had a fairly successful series of Industry and Education Meetings which were held in different parts of the country (I seem to remember one in Birmingham). No I don't think there was any one particular thing. The work is ongoing, isn't it? We weren't out to denationalize the Inspectorate or something – sorry, privatize is the word now isn't it?

PR   Sir Keith took over after you. He is often described as possibly the most important thinker in terms of education which the Tory party has had in recent times.

MC   Although I am not quite sure what he actually did.

PR   That seems a fair question. John Patten told us that in his early days Sir Keith was reputed to have wandered around the Department asking plaintively, 'Where are the levers? Where are the levers?' This was a question he was to continue asking for some time. Even Margaret Thatcher is reported to have said in a television interview in, I think, the run up to the 1987 election something like, 'It has taken us far too long to get to grips with education.'

MC   Perhaps the main criticism made of me, let us be clear about this, and I am prepared to accept that there was some truth in it, was that I was not disposed to be as radical as some wanted. I will accept that as a fair criticism: but on the other hand I must say, equally, that I got fed up with constantly hearing people talking about falling standards in education. The plain truth is that at the time standards were not falling. What people should have made clear is that standards were not as high as they wished them to be. But the claim that education standards were falling and teachers were failing was rubbish: they were not. We were not, perhaps, doing as well as we hoped, but that is a quite different point. The fact that I started with that general philosophy means that I was not out to make the radical changes that others wished to do.

PR   When I talked to Kenneth Baker the two words which he picked out to describe the thrust of his policies were 'standards' and 'choice'. Whereas I found that John Patten's key words seemed to be 'choice' and 'diversity'. What words would you use to describe your agenda for change?

MC   Like Kenneth Baker, I would stress 'standards' and 'choice'. But unlike him I do not accept that standards were as bad or as low as some were claiming. Some people would probably claim I was complacent in 1979, and that is why I did not do anything worth-while. I don't accept that view. I think history will show that we did quite a lot in those two and a half years. Because of the view I took, I did try to defend the image of the teachers. Given this, one of the things I would have liked to have done was to have achieved the setting up of a General Teaching Council.

PR   You did try. Why did it not happen?

MC   I did try – I would like to have achieved it, but the unions were not keen. I saved up announcing our wish to set up a General Teaching Council until I could do so at a National Conference of the NUT. Fred Jarvis had begged me to do this. But when I stepped forward they immediately started booing. However, I went on and made the announcement. Afterwards I said to him, 'Well Fred, there was no point in keeping that to announce here was there?' Remembering back, I seem to recall that they did not actually boo during the announcement, but they didn't show it any appreciation either. For my own part, coming from my background as a lawyer, from the Bar, I believed that teaching should be looked upon as a profession. As such it should act professionally, and that means setting their own standards validated by an appropriate professional council. It is as simple as that.

PR   To have the power and responsibility for determining who can enter the profession and on what criteria, as is the case in Scotland?

MC   I think so. There should be a General Teaching Council anyway.

PR   The possibility of setting up such a Council is currently being aired by people like John Tomlinson and John Sayer, although there is not too much evidence that the government is as keen on it as you were.

MC   I got a paper about it the other day, but I must confess I haven't read it yet. I do remember John Tomlinson. He was Chief Education Officer in Cheshire at the time. He would probably tell you what a disaster I made of things. On second thoughts, perhaps he would not.

PR   Can we return to an earlier point in our discussion? What do you think Sir Keith Joseph achieved during his four and a half years in office?

MC   You should really ask others what he achieved during that period. I think for me it would be difficult, to be honest, to remember in enough detail to say much that would be useful in answering your question. What I would say is that he would obviously bring to any job that he did a high intellectual capacity, a very questioning mind, and very clear aims. I could also say that I suspect that his inability to put those aims into immediate operation was a result of the fact

that, at the time, he had to work through the local education authorities. I suspect this was a much greater source of frustration for him
than it had been for me.

PR   Because, by the time he came to the DES, he had begun to develop
       a radical agenda for educational change?

MC   I am sure he wanted to draw upon a much more radical agenda
       than I did. I also think that it is very difficult to do so in education.
       When I was appointed I thought there was a need for a period of
       stability, and during my period of office I tried to achieve this.

PR   Keith Joseph's defenders argue that inevitably it takes time to think
       through a radical reform agenda. This seems, for example, to be
       John Patten's view. But that by the time Sir Keith had left office this
       had largely been accomplished and it was this which enabled his
       successor, Kenneth Baker, to move as fast as he did.

MC   I agree with much of that. Certainly I am sure that a great deal had
       been achieved during Keith's time in thinking things through. But
       earlier you asked a very fair question, 'What had been achieved
       during his period?', which I would like to return to. I suspect a great
       deal of thought had been given to things which at that time he was
       unable to put into operation. In retrospect, I have some reservations
       about some of the ideas which were developed at the time. For
       example, I had some initial concerns about the idea of grant-main-
       tained schools. In part, I was worried about what this might mean
       for those pupils who might get left out. In fact, on this, maybe, I
       would have been even more radical than the radicals. If we are
       going to have grant-maintained schools, I would go all the way and
       have every school funded by the central government rather than
       have some LEA schools and some grant-maintained schools.

PR   Brian Sherratt is on record as having advocated just this – he
       believes that the Conservative government in furthering its policy in
       favour of grant-maintained schools should have done what the
       Labour government eventually did in pursuing its policy for
       comprehensive schools – legislate this into existence.

MC   That may be, but when I came to office I believed that schools had
       been through an awful lot of upset during the last few years. There
       had been a great debate going on, for and against comprehensive
       education, for and against the 11-plus, for and against grammar
       schools – schools had been thrown into turmoil. It seemed to me
       that what was badly wanted was a period of stability. A period of
       stability in which we should try and get control of spiralling govern-
       ment expenditure, but do this in a sensible way. In a way in which
       it would be possible for schools to be properly provided for. To
       create conditions in which we could enable and encourage parents
       to play a bigger part in the management of their schools and the
       education of their children. I felt that we should start trying to look

at what was really going on in schools before making decisions about what should happen in the future. I thought a period of stability was necessary.

PR   The years since your resignation have been, for a variety of reasons, characterized by turbulence rather than stability in education. Thus during Sir Keith Joseph's time there was a good deal of industrial action, and since then educational reforms have come thick and fast. In all of this the 1988 Education Reform Act has been central. What was it intended to achieve, and how successful has it been?

MC   Before tackling your last question, I would like to stress that the early 1980s was a period of relative stability for schools. On the 1988 Act, I would repeat my concern that if you push for grant-maintained schools you have got to think of what you do with the children that are left over.

PR   In 1992, the DfE published a White Paper entitled *Choice and Diversity: A New Framework for Schools* which summarized the main features of the government's educational reform agenda. In doing so, it claimed that this agenda had an underlying coherence. A coherence which could be expressed in the 'five great themes [which] run through the story of educational change in England and Wales since 1979: quality, diversity, increased parental choice, greater autonomy for schools and greater accountability' (1992, p. 2). Do you regard this as a fair description of the government's educational reform agenda since 1979 and how successfully do you think it has been implemented?

MC   Sorry, before we discuss this, can I go back to one point that you were making earlier? You asked whether there was any particular theme which informed the 1980 Act, and I said that there was no great theme; but there was a theme, and that theme was parental choice. We emphasized the parents' right and ability to choose a school of their choice. Now, the criticism made at the time, with hindsight, I now see, amounted to the claim that I was not radical enough. Taken out of context, such criticism may have some justification, but at that time we were opening the door for the first time in a way designed to enable parents to have more say – as against the local education authority say – as to where their child was educated. Maybe we should have gone faster, as some of our critics armed with the benefits of hindsight have argued, but for a first attempt, we did make quite a push in that direction.

Let me turn to the 1988 Act. I'm all for as much parental choice as possible, but, you know, I did sometimes worry, if all its benefits were to be realized, whether this would meet the needs of all children and not just those in the top 70 per cent?

PR   Its defenders – people like Kenneth Baker and John Patten – argue that it is the bottom 30 per cent to 40 per cent who have, for years and years, been most poorly served by what had existed in the past. John Patten, for example, argues that we have for too long been too much concerned with input, and too little concerned with output.

MC   The danger with the comprehensive school, it always seemed to me, is that to provide an adequate sixth form you had to have a school that was too big at the base. This tended to make for impersonality, and for people to get lost. This view made me a bit of a heretic. I was not opposed to sixth form colleges in certain areas, because it seemed to me that you could combine smaller comprehensive schools with sixth form colleges very successfully in a county like Hampshire. At the time the ideal was thought to require each school to have its own sixth form. I wanted to make sure this was not achieved at a cost of making schools too big.

PR   The 1988 Act tried to set up the local management of schools, a National Curriculum and assessment, open enrolment, grant-maintained schools ...

MC   Oh yes, there was a heck of a lot in it.

PR   How compatible were these things? It is sometimes argued, for example, that there is a fundamental ambiguity at the heart of its proposals in so far as the National Curriculum entails a greater centralization of power whereas LMS is based upon more decentralization.

MC   Well I am not sure about that, but I am certain that the original National Curriculum was far too centralized and far too prescriptive. But then I also think that this is being put right, or largely put right as a result of the Dearing Report.

PR   Do you regard yourself as a fan of the 1988 Act? I get the impression that you have quite a lot of reservations about it.

MC   Well, to be absolutely honest, by then I had left the House of Commons and was working full time at the Bar. My involvement in things was slight. I have to stress that. I had gone into the Lords, but this did not mean that I was able to spend a lot of time on the passage of the Education Bill. In 1988 I was heavily involved in doing a review of the parole system for the Home Office, as well as doing quite a lot of work in court, and so I did not take any part in any of the debates.

PR   You must have had views on it?

MC   I did, and, in fact, I made my maiden speech on it in the Lords. I had reservations about it. These were concerned mainly with my uncertainty about how successful the changes proposed would be in improving provision for the less able.

PR   Many of my colleagues in local government say that the Conservative party on the whole has been pretty hostile to local authorities over the last decade. Is that a fair criticism and did you and do you share that hostility?

MC   I don't, but I think that the local authorities have not, in general, been very popular in recent years. In terms of the views of my party, I suppose the issue comes back to a point I made earlier. If you have a radical agenda of reform which you want to implement, it is very difficult to do so if you can only exercise indirect control over the system. But there are problems with direct control. I know that for fifteen years we have had Conservative government, but within our kind of two-party system you should keep in mind what the other party might do when it's in power, as well as what you might like to do. If you abolish the powers of the local education authorities, then you may choose to impose one form of centralized control over education, but this means that somebody with a very different political view may choose to impose another once they win power. I'm putting this very badly, but I didn't want really to upset the equilibrium that existed and the balance of powers upon which it was built.

PR   So you would have wished for less radical reform, believing that it would have been possible for the Conservative party to achieve many of its most important aims by revising incrementally rather than reforming fundamentally the system?

MC   But I did add that I suppose if one was going down the line of grant-maintained schools, on reflection now, perhaps we ought to have gone the whole 100 per cent hog.

PR   It looks like there is now a fairly broad consensus on the need for a National Curriculum and for LMS, although some of this breaks down when people start to talk about the details. In the light of what you have said above, what do you think the Labour party will accept, and what will they try to change?

MC   I don't know what they'll do. They have said they are going to abolish the Assisted Places Scheme overnight. They seem to have changed their views on that. At the last election, I seem to remember that they said they would continue to support those pupils who were already being assisted. I have no doubt the idea of the National Curriculum will remain, and also no doubt the idea of assessment at different ages will be retained: they will scrap, presumably, published league tables.

PR   What of the inspection system which Kenneth Clarke set up?

MC   The OFSTED scheme? Do you think they would get rid of that?

PR   I don't know. I wondered what you thought?

MC   I don't know. On publishing results there is a dilemma: clearly parents are entitled to see or have the power to see such results, and in doing so to see what the schools are doing. But equally, you have got to be careful that you don't publish things which are so distorted that you give a totally unfair picture of people's endeavours and efforts.

PR   If you were to attempt a balance of advantage and disadvantage, how would you judge Conservative policy on education since your time as Secretary of State?

MC   I'm not sure whether or not standards are, in fact, significantly higher than they were. What I do know is there has been a lot of disruption over the last few years.

PR   You make two points about standards, don't you? Firstly, you doubt whether they were as low as is sometimes claimed, and were diminishing. Secondly, you are not sure that the evidence exists to demonstrate that they are higher than they were and that they are continuing to improve?

MC   What I attacked is the suggestion that they were dropping, because almost all the statistics which you might consider – such as the number staying on in higher education, the number passing O levels, the number passing A levels – showed an upward trend. To claim that they were diminishing in real terms seemed to me to fly in the face of the available evidence. Furthermore, to still be making such claims in the late 1980s was to invite the question, 'Well, you have been in power for the last ten years. Why have you failed to do anything about it?' So it didn't seem to me politically very sensible to make such claims, nor did I believe that they were true. If, however, you say standards had not risen as fast as you had hoped, that is a quite different matter.

PR   There have been other justifications for the reforms of the late 1980s – for example, that education has been too producer-led, too controlled by the educational establishment, and that it is right for parents and others to have greater choice.

MC   I'm all for parents having a greater choice. I'm all for parents having a great say. I am all for parents having greater involvement. I do see that headmasters should have a good deal of flexibility. I do think the National Curriculum was a bit too restrictive and prescriptive in the form it was first produced. But we do appear to have had an awful lot of shake-ups over the last few years, and I am not sure what effect this has had on standards. I am not sure that there has been any noticeable change upwards in standards.

PR   What happened after you ceased to be Secretary of State?

MC   I stayed in Parliament until 1987. I got very involved with the Commonwealth Parliamentary Association. I took over in 1982 as Treasurer International of the CPA and continued to do that until 1985, and then became Chairman of the UK Branch between 1985 and 1987. I went back to chairing the Home Affairs Committee. I also started building up a bit of my law practice again. When I left Parliament in 1987 I went back full time to the Bar. I was then asked by Douglas Hurd to Chair the review into the parole system, which I did. This took about twelve months on a part-time basis; and then in April 1989 I was asked to become chairman of the Criminal

Injuries Compensation Board, which I continue to do on a part-time basis. All this has made me very rusty on educational matters, as you have been able to see.

PR   It seems to have been coming back to you as we have talked. In any case, it must be difficult to remember things which took place thirteen or fourteen years ago?

MC   You are right. Things have been coming back to me as we've been going along. I suppose my strongest memory of my time as Secretary of State is that it was very hard work.

PR   Do you see those years as the high point of your political career?

MC   Oh yes, clearly. Yes, of course they were. Two years in the Cabinet is a unique opportunity, obviously. Don't get me wrong. All I am saying, if I have to be honest, is that they weren't easy years. People would say: 'This or that is not up to scratch. Well, that's Mark Carlisle's fault. He isn't up to it.' And I say, yes, I enjoyed them. It was a great honour to be in the Cabinet, but it was not an easy time to be in charge of a major spending department. We had a lot to do; we did a lot, and we achieved a good deal. I think we achieved a period of reasonable stability. In the years that followed, it is that stability which I think has been lost.

PR   You seem to feel there has been too much change. There have been something like eighteen Education Acts over the last fourteen years.

MC   There has certainly been a lot of change, a lot of change. But don't go away with the impression that when I say it was hard work I didn't enjoy it – that's absolutely wrong: what I am saying is that it was not an easy period in which to be in charge of a spending department, for the reason I gave earlier on. I did it to the best of my ability, and I don't feel that I made too bad a hand of it at the time.

PR   You were at the DES for just over two years, weren't you? Tony Crosland, who many would describe as one of the ablest people to have been Secretary of State in the post-war era, once reckoned it took at least two years to become really conversant with all aspects of what the Department does. Yet, the life expectancy of Secretaries of State for Education in the post-war era has been about two years.

MC   That is true. The life expectancy of Secretaries of State for Education up until the mid-1980s was very short – about two years. I did just more than the average. Go some time and look at the photographs of those who have held the office in the Secretary of State's waiting-room outside his office at the Department. You will be amazed at how many there are.

PR   Do you think there is going to be another one soon?

MC   Quite possibly.

CHAPTER 3

Keith Joseph

WITH CLYDE CHITTY

Keith Joseph was born in 1918 and educated at Harrow and Magdalen, Oxford, where he studied jurisprudence. He was Fellow of All Souls, Oxford, from 1946 to 1960 and after 1972. He served as a captain in the Royal Artillery, worked as a barrister and was a director and then chairman of the family firm Bovis. After contesting Barons Court in 1955, he was member for Leeds North East between 1956 and 1987. He held various junior ministerial positions before serving as Secretary of State for Social Services from 1970 to 1974. This was followed by a period as Secretary for State for Industry before his appointment as Secretary for State for Education and Science, which he held between 1981 and 1986. He was raised to the peerage as Baron Joseph of Portsoken in 1987. He died in December 1994.

CC   What influences have shaped your views on education and on educational policy?

KJ   I was happy at school, though I felt under no great pressure to excel on the academic side. Cricket was my main passion and remained so when I went up to Magdalen College, Oxford. I was not active in politics at Oxford, and I took no part in the activities of the Union. I don't think I was an outstanding scholar, although I did end up with a first in jurisprudence. I think that was largely because I caught up with all my reading during the vacations. Since then, of course, like many other Conservatives, I've been concerned about standards and excellence and quality in education. And I have been very concerned that our system lets down the very children who are most in need. As long ago as December 1975 I said in an address to the Oxford Union (reprinted in *Stranded on the Middle Ground? Reflections on Circumstances and Policies*, Centre for Policy Studies, 1976, pp. 19, 32): 'We spend more than ever before on education and health, but with results which can please only the most blink-ered. We spend more on welfare, without achieving well-being, while creating dangerous levels of dependency ...'

And even then I was questioning the need for a comprehensive system of secondary schools:

> Are large, unstreamed comprehensive schools really ideal structures for education, for those who most need to benefit from school – the children from housing estates and older urban areas? The Labour Party, which 20 years ago seemed to be the guardian angel of education, has now been systematically subordinating it to political doctrinal objectives and thereby destroying it. The common ground, common ground with the people, in education is that education is about teaching *all* the young as well as possi-ble to read, write and number, to be sufficiently well-informed and self-disciplined to think for themselves and use their minds well, and to be motivated and enabled to earn their living by making the best use of their talents in existing opportunities for productive work. Any discussion of schools that does not start from this purpose and direct everything towards it is not about education as it is understood by most men and women in England.

And these are the issues I really care about. And more and more over the years I've come to care about those children for whom education isn't working. And we ask where did we go wrong and what can we do about it. Because it's the bottom 40 – the bottom 50 – per cent that are getting a raw deal from education.

CC Why did you choose politics as a career?

KJ Well, I didn't want to run Bovis, the family firm, and I had no wish to teach law at Oxford. And politics seemed to me to be the ideal way of getting things done. I started off in local politics in London, and then I became MP for Leeds North East at the beginning of 1956.

CC How did you become a cabinet minister?

KJ I held the portfolios for Labour and Social Services within the Heath Shadow Cabinet in the 1960s, and then when we got back into power in June 1970, I was given Social Services. After only a few weeks, our Chancellor of the Exchequer, Iain Macleod, died and people were apparently talking about me as a likely successor. But I never wanted the job. As I've said before:

> I never wanted to be Chancellor. I'm not an economist. I don't have any self-confidence in that field. And, energetic though I am, I dreaded the drudgery. I've always thought of the Chancellor as a 'poor chap'. And in the event, Edward Heath picked Anthony Barber.

(quoted in Halcrow, 1989, p. 45)

As far as Education is concerned, it's a job I wanted very much. After two years at Industry, I wanted to move to Education in 1981. When I knew that Mark Carlisle would be going, I went to Mrs Thatcher to ask if I could have the job. And after her experiences at the DES in the early 1970s, I think she was surprised that anyone should want to go there. There were meant to be calmer waters at the DES – though this didn't prove to be the case.

CC   What were your main objectives when you first became Secretary of State for Education?

KJ   When I started the job in September 1981, I was anxious to free up the system – to free it from unnecessary bureaucratic controls. I'd already questioned the whole nature of the relationship between the state and education provision. And I wanted to see if there was a way, a practical way, of delivering more parental choice of schools – particularly at the secondary stage. I've always been attracted to the idea of the education voucher and I've always worried about the state's involvement in education. You see, that had also been one of my chief concerns as Secretary of State for Industry. I thought there was a strong ideological case for abolishing the Department of Industry altogether, since really the state has no business getting involved in industry. We do not know how to go about it. And it's the same with education. We have a bloody state system; I wish we hadn't got one. I wish we'd taken a different route in 1870. We got the ruddy state involved. I don't want it. I don't think we know how to do it. I certainly don't think Secretaries of State know anything about it. But we are landed with it. If we could move back to 1870, I would take a different route. We've got compulsory education, which is a responsibility of hideous importance, and we tyrannize children to do that which they don't want, and we don't produce results ... I know that other countries do make a success of it, at least in part. Take France, for example: whether Napoleon was responsible, whether they've been at it a long time, whether there's a parental culture, whether the homes are more supportive, whether they cheat a lot ... I do not know. But all I do know is that when I went to the Department and showed them these lessons from Europe, they were merely polite. They weren't going to do anything about it, so I arranged for missions to go and see what the Germans did.

CC   Did you see the DES and the MSC as being in competition with each other during your period in office? Was it ever a problem to you, as Secretary of State, that the MSC seemed to be operating in a kind of parallel sphere?

KJ   A problem? A delight ... to find somebody like David Young that would agree with me. You don't understand what an inert, sluggish, perverse mass there is in education. The teacher unions were ... perverse, perverse; except for one or two of them, they didn't concern themselves with quality, or didn't appear to. I had union leaders make half-hour speeches without mentioning children. It was a producer lobby, not a consumer lobby. I was there for the consumers, so the MSC, which was in favour of consumers, was an ally, a joyful ally ... I'm not interested in kudos, not in the least. You see Rab Butler had designed a triple-based education ... and the third leg had gone: the technical schools. So I was delighted to give a push to David Young's Technical and Vocational Education Initiative.

You see, I believe that the secondary modern and the comprehensive systems ... have geared themselves to a diluted grammar-school curriculum. And that's been an error that successive governments, and the educational world, have applauded.

It doesn't mean to say that the children should not have good English and good mathematics and good science. God bless them, they certainly should, and as much history as can be conveyed, and all the other values, certainly. But it's got to be presented – and I don't know the way, I'm not an expert – in a way that interests them instead of what's happened. Now ... other countries seem to do better, it appears. My friends tend to say that I'm romantic, that really the French and the Germans do no better, or so they say. But I still believe that they do better, and I think that this reflects something that we can't measure or affect, namely parental attitudes, culture.

CC   Would it not be fair to level criticism at the Conservative party, historically, for their preoccupation with an academic, liberal-humanist curriculum?

KJ   Look, I'm not here to defend my party in every aspect. Of course not, of course not. We wanted to preserve excellence, as we knew it. And indeed grammar schools have on the whole, on the whole, done well. I would like to see, and the Conservative party nowadays would like to see, the non-grammar schools doing equally well for their constituency.

That is why I felt so strongly about the MSC's TVEI – we have tried to impose a grammar-school curriculum on everybody and it hasn't worked. We need differentiation and variety – a whole lot of new approaches. As I argued in a BBC television programme ('Good enough for your child?', *Panorama*, broadcast on 28 February 1983):

> TVEI will benefit the very large proportion of children who are not getting a benefit from school. They're certainly not getting a parity of esteem. They're either dropping out, or they're emerging from school without what they themselves, their parents or their future potential employers would expect them to have got at school. These are the children who will benefit from the government's new plans.

Actually the problem really goes much deeper than all this ... You know, I think you will know, that I'm an enormous admirer and friend of Mrs Thatcher, but sometimes I wish she hadn't raised the school leaving age (to 16), because it makes it harder to reduce it now. But I don't think we use the time well. Now, of course, in a period of high unemployment, it's not exactly easy to advocate lowering the school leaving age, and I know that our wretched neighbours, who are so much more prosperous and successful than we are, have got school leaving ages above ours. Nevertheless, for the benefit of the children, if you're going to compel them to stay at school, you must be effective, and if you can't be effective, then don't keep them compulsorily at school ... it's tyranny.

The first time that I met my civil servants at the DES, I said to them: 'Do you realize that the education system of this country is failing 50 per cent of the population; 50 per cent of the children go through the schools and it does them no good at all?' So the civil servants all looked at each other, and one said very smoothly: 'Oh Secretary of State, please don't say 50 per cent; it sounds an awful lot. Let's say 40 per cent.' So that became the new slogan of the DES: 'Do something for the bottom 40 per cent.'

CC   Why did you come to the view that it would not be possible to introduce a system of education vouchers?

KJ   Well, as I said earlier, I've always been attracted to the idea of the education voucher and I made this clear in my speech to the 1981 Conservative Party Conference. But at the time I also pointed out that

> there are very great difficulties in making a voucher deliver – in a way that would commend itself to us – more choice than the 1980 Education Act will, in fact, deliver. It is now up to the advocates of such a possibility to study the difficulties – and there are real difficulties – and see whether they can develop proposals which will really cope with them ...

I wanted vouchers simply because you transfer, in one go, from the producers to the consumers. But nobody is going to claim – and I do not claim – that all consumers are wise. Of course not – but some would be able to exercise choice which they can't exercise now, however limited. I also believed that if vouchers were combined with open enrolment, some of the least good state schools would disappear, and increased competition would galvanize the less good state schools to achieve better results. These were the prospects that attracted me to a combination of the voucher idea and open enrolment. In the event, I was a frustrated enthusiast because I was forced to accept that, largely for political reasons, it wouldn't be practicable.

CC   Political rather than financial?

KJ   Oh certainly not financial ... certainly not. Finances didn't enter into it. Finances didn't enter into it, no, it was political. In the sense that you would have very controversial legislation, which would take two or three years to carry through, with my party split, and the other parties unanimously hostile, on wrong grounds. And all the producer forces hostile. And then one would have decided either to go by way of imposition – from an appointed date there shall be vouchers everywhere – or one would have to go forward with a pilot scheme. And a pilot scheme would probably have been wrecked by producer hostility and could have produced only a mouse. And I didn't think that I had the moral courage to impose it. Of course it wouldn't be like imposing comprehensivization: it's imposing freedom – that's the main difference between the two.

Anyway, with great regret, I was forced to tell the 1983 Conference that 'the voucher, at least in the foreseeable future, is dead'. Of course I realize that I had upset many of my close friends and colleagues; but I just couldn't see a way of making the whole thing work. It may come back, if there is the political will. And opting out will help to free up the system – with open enrolment forcing schools to be more responsive to the wishes of parents. Not as good as the voucher, perhaps – but better than nothing. An important item on the national agenda.

CC   How far are you satisfied with what you achieved as Secretary of State?

KJ   I think what I can claim to have achieved is to have shifted the emphasis from quantity to quality, and that, I think, is now accepted across the House, across the floor of the House. When I arrived at the Department of Education, I found honourable and diligent civil servants who had scarcely had time to think about quality, because they had been so preoccupied with roofs over heads, with the growth of the child population of the 1950s, '60s and '70s, and I suppose I had to understand that. But I found them almost indifferent – no, that's unfair – almost unaware of the urgency of doing something about quality. And to the extent that I shifted that thinking, and to the extent that my arguments in the House with my opposite numbers achieved a certain amount of agreement, I was pleased that quality was the top of the agenda. And I remember reading with some pleasure – I don't take the magazine, but there was an article shown me from something called *Marxism Today*, in which the writer said: 'Why have we allowed the Tories to steal quality?' I take no joy from the fact that quality should be a partisan issue. No joy at all. But in fact that's what I achieved. What to do about it is quite a different matter. I'm very distressed by this country's complacency about state education. I'm even more distressed that a large percentage of parents are said to be satisfied. I'm even further distressed by the apparent complacency of the Inspectors, who are meant to be the guardians of standards. So I accept the responsibility for changing some attitudes in education.

That's an achievement, but God knows it was overdue. But for the particular components of policy, I'm not particularly proud. Some of the things I did are all right.

CC   I'm surprised by your negative view of your own period in office.

KJ   Well, I'm entitled to feel that I failed. Not that it would have been possible to transform the quality and effectiveness of education in a mere five years – not conceivable, not conceivable. All I would have liked to have done better was to lay some of the foundation stones. And I feel it's so very difficult in our state system, without the cultural background that other countries have.

People at the DES, they're imprisoned by the state system they have to operate. A system that tends to discount motivation. You compel children to go to school, you've got them as prisoners – and if some of them truant, too bad. Now that system is the one the DES has to operate. They are unlikely to say: 'Let's jettison the whole system.' They are unlikely to say that, and politicians who do reach that position are unlikely to come along and say: 'Let's go back to 1870.' And short of going back to 1870, one is very limited in what one can do. Very limited. I tried to escape from that constraint by way of examination reform. That's how I tried to change the system.

I wanted to stretch the academic and to stretch the non-academic in appropriate ways. Stretching was my favourite word. I judged that if you emphasized that, much else would follow. But I find now – and that's what people said at the time – that was simply what my officials *encouraged* me to imagine I was achieving. I invented the GCSE; I invented the differentiation. I said I'd only agree to unify the two examinations (O level and CSE) provided we established differentiation. And now I find that, unconsciously, I have allowed teacher assessment – to a greater extent than I assumed. My fault, my fault. It's the job of ministers to see deeply, and now it's all flabby. And if you have a flabby examination system and also compulsory attendance, you can't guarantee benefits and results. So I failed again.

CC   What would you see as your main intellectual and political contribution to redirecting Conservative thought, if one can put it that way?

KJ   Well, it was far easier, you see, to do this in the economy, where things like abolishing wage controls and price controls and foreign exchange controls and dividend controls were obviously justified. Trade union law and council house sales – all straightforward, done by a simple decision, and it just happened. Not so in education: a lot of sensational policy, much more complicated, much more difficult. So I can claim some credit for being part of a team that made changes in the economic framework, and that was doable; and, once done, very hard to change back. Far harder in areas of social policy.

And you have to understand that when I was at the DES, there was that awful pay dispute going on all the time. And that soured relationships. I was in conflict in one way or another with all the teachers' unions over pay and conditions. And I was criticized for not finding enough money for Education. They said that I didn't 'play the Whitehall game' and fight hard enough for Education. I accepted the Treasury case for 'financial stringency', and therefore perhaps Education lost out. But I couldn't go in for 'double standards' and argue for something I didn't believe in.

CC   How do you view developments which have taken place in educational policy-making since you left office? Would it not be fair to say that you have serious reservations about the framework for the National Curriculum?

KJ   Look, the most important word in my GCSE initiative was the word 'differentiated' – which isn't widely understood. Namely, that you test people according to their potential, not by a common academic standard. And for that reason, there are meant to be *differentiated* papers and *differentiated* questions, as you know. Now I'm not convinced about the 'national' – the word 'national' – in the phrase National Curriculum. Because I want more breathing space, more air, more variety. But you don't find me defending either myself or the Conservative party. Or criticizing people. Because I reckon that we've all made a right old mess of it. We've all got it wrong. And it's mostly hurt all those who are most vulnerable.

But I am unhappy about the new National Curriculum. As I said in a debate in the House of Lords (18 April 1988), the government's plans will put the secondary school curriculum into 'too tight a straitjacket'. I like a lot of the new Education Reform Act. I like the opting-out scheme, and so on. But I am worried about the National Curriculum. It will be too academic and squeeze out vocational subjects. We face a catastrophe in this country through low expectations of less academic children and poor standards. We need to *stretch* the less academic by giving them things to do they *want* to do. We simply must not squeeze out non-academic, vocationally based subjects. That's what TVEI was all about – stretching the less able. Children enter primary school all keen and eager to learn, but they're bored and demotivated by the time they leave secondary school. So we're failing them all the time. We must not go on failing them.

I mean, there's only one thing that matters in education – and that's motivation. And that can't be commanded or achieved by the state. That's the main problem. There are whole areas that the educational world ignores and that never reach the press. I was a core curriculum man, I think; but I also wanted variety and diversity. I don't want a large testing industry to be imposed on our schools. I do not want everybody to have a watered-down grammar-school curriculum, because that means too many of our children have to fail in academic terms.

   I think the so-called education establishment should have been much more vocal, much more attentive to quality. And by quality, I don't mean excellence; I mean potential. I don't just mean everybody else. I'm a disaster too; I'm one of the club. I mustn't pour out the vials of wrath; but I do think the children have suffered very badly in this country.

CC   Finally, can we talk of what its like facing the prospect of a reshuffle or of leaving office and government? We mentioned earlier that in one reshuffle there were rumours that you might become Chancellor? You made it clear that this was not something you wanted, because you did not see yourself as an economist and because you dreaded the drudgery. A number of your senior colleagues, including Kenneth Baker, Nigel Lawson and, most importantly, Margaret Thatcher, suggest that when you were appointed to Education, this was what you most wanted. They also indicate that when you left the Department and government, this was at your own initiative?

KJ   Reshuffles can be difficult. When I first came to Education I wrote a note to Carlisle in appreciation of what he had done. I did want to go to Education but after four years there felt that I had had enough. There were some achievements, I think that I am entitled to to claim to have contributed to a shift in emphasis from quantity to quality, but as I said earlier I also believe I am entitled to feel I failed. Even so, I was glad later to read Margaret Thatcher's comments on the reshuffle of the 21 May 1986. 'Keith Joseph had decided that he now wished to leave the Cabinet. The departure of my oldest political friend and ally, indeed mentor, saddened me. He was irreplaceable; somehow, politics would never be the same again.' As Kenneth Baker has reported, I left him a list of thirty issues which he would find in his in-tray. Many were detailed points. Also I tried to give him some advice, suggesting that he did not make the same mistake that I did of seeming to attack the teachers. I also told him 'I have no bitterness. I have been wanting to go since before Christmas'.

CC: Finally, and once again, what do you hope to be remembered for in Education?

KJ: That I have put in place the building bricks from which a change in effectiveness may emerge. What would I like to be remembered for? Drawing attention to the 40 per cent who get little benefit from education, perhaps? I don't know?

CHAPTER 4

Kenneth Baker

WITH PETER RIBBINS

Kenneth Baker was born in 1934. He was educated at St Paul's School and Magdalen College, Oxford, where he read history. He did his National Service as a lieutenant in the Gunners during 1953–55 and thereafter worked in business (Shell, Aquascutum, Minster Trust) for a number of years. After contesting Poplar in 1964 and Acton in 1966, he was elected Member for Acton in 1968, St Marylebone in 1970 and Mole Valley in 1983. After serving in various junior ministerial positions, he was in 1985 appointed Secretary of State for the Environment. Between 1986 and 1989 he was Secretary of State for Education and Science, where he was responsible for the Education Reform Act of 1988. Since leaving Education, he has been Home Secretary (1990–92) and Chairman of the Conservative Party (1989–90).

11 May 1994

PR   Could we begin by talking about your views and attitudes on education and how they were developed and shaped by your background, your career and your personal experience of education? How did these views and attitudes influence what you tried to do when you became Secretary of State?

KB   Politicians usually have decided views on education. In this they are much like those who work in education. All politicians have gone through the educational process. They have had first-hand experience of it. They will also have been involved in it in various ways as Members of Parliament. One's own education, I think, is very important.

    I went to Holy Trinity, a state Church of England primary school which was in Southport. It was located in an old Victorian building with a yard. We had playing fields but they were some way out of town. I can only recall visiting them two or three times in all the years that I was there. It was a conventional education of a rather old-fashioned sort which was really rather effective. Many years later, in 1986 I think it was, when, as Member for Mole Valley, I was holding a surgery, a small and elderly lady came in and asked me, 'Were you the Kenneth Baker I taught at Holy Trinity?' I remembered her as a young teacher – Miss Makin. Shortly afterwards, as Education Secretary, I had the pleasure of taking her with me on a nostalgic visit to our old school. I remember those days very vividly. The essence of that type of education was to embed in you the very basic, simple skills of reading and writing and arithmetic. I remember chanting mathematics tables by heart, learning poetry by heart, doing a lot of writing, spelling, punctuation, and things of that sort. It was a good education, I have no doubt about that at all.

Then, because we were evacuated, I took two 11-plus exams, one for Lancashire and one for Middlesex. I suddenly discovered that there could be very different kinds of exams – one of them was a modern-type exam which I did not really know very much about ...

PR   If I remember, there were very different pass rates in the 11-plus in these areas – Lancashire had one of the lowest, and Middlesex one of the highest.

KB   Really? I can believe that. I took the Lancashire exam in Lancashire and the Middlesex exam in Middlesex. In my judgement the Middlesex exam was much easier and the Lancashire exam was much tougher. This may account for why the pass rates were so different – I don't know. On the strength of my results, I went to King George V Grammar School, which was in Southport. It was a good, traditional grammar school. While I was there I started to learn Latin and French for the first time – that is something I remember clearly. After a year, the evacuation ended and we returned to Twickenham where we lived. I went to Hampton Grammar School. Hampton was also an excellent grammar school. I remember reading Shakespeare for the first time. But after I had been there for two years my father suddenly said to me, 'Do you want to go to St Paul's?' I think I had mentioned that another boy from Hampton had gone there. My father did this because he felt he could, by then, just about afford it. Even so, as a middle-ranking civil servant, I think it was a very big sacrifice for him. We lived modestly but both my parents felt that the really important thing was to give my sister and myself the best opportunities in life that they could.

I was interviewed by A. B. Cook, a legendary Pauline teacher of the time, and asked to do some maths problems and write an essay. I must have done well enough, because I was offered a place. So, for the next five years, I went to St Paul's. It was a very good school, a very academic school. It was founded in 1509, very much as a school where the ablest sons of the rising middle classes, especially of London merchants, were sent over the centuries. They tended to be very competitive, to want to do exceptionally well. It was also a very cosmopolitan place. Not least because Colet had decided, in his wisdom, back in 1509, there should be 153 scholarships (the number of fishes in the miraculous draft) for children of all creeds and nations. That was an exceptional idea for 1509. It meant that over the years St Paul's has always attracted a dissenting element. There were a large number of Jewish boys in the school, as well as some Indian, Chinese and African boys, and even some from America. All this made it much more cosmopolitan than the normal English public school. It was a very good school.

PR   Your experience of schooling seems to have been uniformly very positive?

KB   Yes, it was, of a piece, very positive. I was lucky to be taught by gifted people at all the schools. I remember the maths teacher and the English teacher at Hampton Grammar. I remember my Latin teacher at King George V. At St Paul's, I was very lucky, we had an outstanding history master, P. D. Whiting, and also an outstanding English master, C. P. Longland, who is still alive. I remember them as being very dedicated to their subjects, with a gift for stimulating the same kind of enthusiasm in their pupils. St Paul's was very demanding; there was lots of homework; you had to work hard. They were long days, and there was Saturday morning school.

PR   With a strong emphasis on order and achievement?

KB   There certainly was. Every school has to work within a disciplined environment; without this you cannot have a worthwhile process of education. I remember one man, an absolutely hopeless teacher, total disorder reigned in his class and nothing happened. In fact during my school years I experienced two teachers like this – one at Hampton and one at St Paul's. It might have seemed a bit of a laugh at the time to us, but it was actually very bad indeed because we were getting nothing out of their lessons.

With the support of P. D. Whiting, I was accepted to study history at Magdalen College, Oxford. Before taking up my place, like many of my contemporaries, I decided to do my National Service first. I ended up as a second lieutenant in the Royal Artillery and spent some time in the Suez Canal Zone. I enjoyed my National Service and learnt a good deal from it which was to be of great value to me in my life in industry and politics.

In 1955 I took up my place at Oxford. I was the first member of my family to go to university. Even so the background of my family had been very educational – I think I stress this in my book *The Turbulent Years* (1993). My grandmother, whom I never met, was an Irish girl who came over in the 1880s and trained at Wandsworth Teachers' Training College. I still have some of her books, including her annotated copy of *Hamlet* from her student days. She ingrained in my father and my uncle the importance of education. Her sister-in-law (my grandfather's sister, my great-aunt Ida) ran education in South Wales for the Catholic Church before the turn of the century. So there has been a tradition in my family, from the days of my great-aunt Ida and followed by my other aunts, of there being lots of teachers around. My wife, Mary, had also been a teacher. Once she had graduated, she trained as a teacher and taught for six or seven years. When I first met her, Mary was teaching in a remedial class in one of the first comprehensive schools in London. She continued teaching until the birth of our second child. All this has meant that I have always had a very high regard for the teaching profession, and have been fully aware of its importance.

PR   Were you ever attracted by the idea of becoming a teacher?

KB   Was I attracted to it? I rather enjoyed, and I still enjoy taking a class occasionally when I can get to a school. I don't get to schools as often as I did. But when I get the chance, I like to take a class either on poetry or in history.

PR   But being a teacher wasn't ever really a serious option for you?

KB   Not really, I wanted to go into business and politics principally, and that is what I decided to do.

PR   Why politics?

KB   Well, it gets into your blood. It is a kind of addiction. In that sense, I suspect every politician has an understanding of the kind of temptations which drug addicts face. It gets into your blood it's hard to escape. A life in politics has a certain attraction. Especially if you want to change things. I wanted to change things for the better. I still do. Politics is a way to do this. It is certainly not the only way to do so, but it is an important way.

PR   You have had a long and interesting political career and have held several of the most senior posts in government, including Environment Secretary, Education Secretary, Home Secretary and Chairman of the Party. I was struck by some of the less than flattering comparisons which you make in your book between the Department of Education and other Departments and between your experiences as Education Secretary and the other senior governmental roles you have held. In your book you suggest that 'Moving from the Department of the Environment to the Department of Education and Science at that time was like moving from the manager's job at Arsenal to Charlton. You crossed the River Thames and dropped down two divisions' (Baker, 1993, p. 166). You also comment that there were times as Education Secretary when you needed more police protection than you did when you were Home Secretary.

KB   Well two things – first, I don't believe that at the time Education had a high place in the batting order of government departments. Certainly, my previous department, Environment, had a much greater influence within the government as a whole than the Department of Education and Science; particularly during the 1970s and 1980s. This was so because the Department of Environment had been created as a monster department by Ted Heath. Thus, for example, at one stage, it even carried responsibility for Transport. It was a huge and important department and had a vast range of responsibilities, ranging from the environment right through to local government and planning. It was also a department in which very important decisions were being made and was at the centre of a constant turmoil of legislation all through the 1970s and 1980s. It was involved in setting up new finance systems and new planning systems, and, of course, the issue of the environment in general had become very important. It is not surprising that it had a certain esteem about it.

Education didn't have quite that degree of esteem, and it seemed to get into a lot of trouble in one way and another: it had gone through the tremendous turmoil of the reorganization of secondary education on comprehensive lines in the 1960s and 1970s. And there was a growing disquiet that things were not all right in the State of Denmark, or in this case the State of Britain. This concern was powerfully expressed, initially, by a Labour prime minister, Jim Callaghan, in that famous speech he made at Ruskin in 1976. What he said was bitterly resented by the education establishment and by Shirley Williams, his own Education Secretary. It was felt that education was a specialist matter – as such, it should be left to the specialists. You shouldn't have clumsy politicians tramping around within the secret garden of the curriculum. But there was a growing disquiet about what was happening in education. First, because many people who had gone to grammar schools were very saddened to see their old schools under attack. Second, many people were very saddened that the great hope which had been invested in the idea of the secondary modern school had not been fulfilled. Third, many business people were saying, 'Well at 16 we're getting applicants who are barely literate and not numerate. What is happening to our education system?' And so this was a matter which was being forced upon our attention and which had to be addressed by all politicians – not just Conservative politicians. There was disquiet within the Labour party as well.

There were attempts in the late 1970s to begin to address these problems, and particularly what many saw as one of the fundamental problems, and that was the curriculum. Various bodies were set up – for example, the Curriculum Development Council. Such developments had not, I must say, got very far or achieved very much. Earlier you asked me about my attitudes to education, how these had been shaped and how they had influenced my views on educational policy. As I have said, I was very lucky – very lucky indeed – to experience English education at its best. When I became a politician I found that most parents didn't have any real choice about the education of their children. Many constituents would come in to see me and would say, 'I want my child to go to such and such school, but I have been told that he can't be allocated to that school. That he will have to go to another school instead. But it's further away; it's not as good; what can I do?' Those sort of questions came up frequently. What could such parents do if they were not rich enough to send their children to private education, or if, as was true of many of them, they did not want to do so?

At the same time there was a doctrinal desire to destroy which drove on some part of the movement towards comprehensive reorganization. To my mind, this was dreadful. The desire to destroy the grammar schools for spurious advantages of a social nature was, I think, quite wrong. I was also sad to see technical schools have disappeared. Of course, there had never been many of them. They were depicted by their opponents as being narrowly vocational – a kind of throwback to the mechanics institutes of the nineteenth century. It was argued that you shouldn't let people do such things. It was thought of as frightfully *infra dig*.

The whole thing was a tremendous mistake. It meant that many excellent grammar schools had gone on the basis of the claim that 'We will make all schools like grammar schools.' It was a false bill of goods from the very beginning. There was growing disquiet and concern that the reasons some schools were being closed had very little to do with the quality of the education they were providing. I had personal experience of one particular episode – the way St Marylebone Grammar School was destroyed in the early 1970s. It was the best school within my constituency by a long chalk: certainly better than the two neighbouring comprehensives. It was one of the best schools in the whole of Central London. There was a deliberate political vendetta conducted against it by the ILEA, which I think was outrageous. I was deeply shocked and appalled by it, and I did all that I could, and I could just see that I was not going to win. With Labour in power and Shirley Williams as Education Secretary, ILEA, led by Ashley Bramall, who was also Chairman of Governors of Marylebone Grammar School, decided to strike the school down. They fixed the Board of Governors – it was really appalling. No consideration was given to parents or to the children. I got very angry about the whole thing. It was an act of educational vandalism based on bigotry. I vowed that I would do everything I could to bring an end to an education authority where dogma took precedence over good education.

When I became Technology Minister in the early 1980s, I wanted to do something about technological education. I did not see this as a question of making pupils just motor mechanics or lathe workers, because the new technologies and the new jobs were going to be based on the microchip. And so within three months of taking office in 1981, I persuaded Margaret Thatcher to launch a scheme to get a microcomputer into every secondary school. At the time, over half our schools did not have any kind of computer. We mounted this initiative from the Department of Trade and Industry, and we were prepared to pay half the costs from the funds we had. The initiative started with Keith Joseph, then he went over to Education, but his new Department was very lukewarm. I soon discovered that they loathed me doing this, and objected very strongly, resenting another department interfering in 'their schools'. I came up against all kinds of difficulties. Questions were asked about why should I be coming in and doing all this? They argued that there would not be enough software, and that if the initiative was to work it would be necessary to train large numbers of teachers. I said, well, we will provide some of the software and pay for some of the training. It was very successful – within a few months over a thousand schools had applied. As soon as the demand from secondary schools was satisfied we opened the offer up to the primary schools as well. I think I can probably say now, even now, that we are more sophisticated in using computers in schools than probably any other developed country, including America. We use them in very sophisticated and integrative ways, and across all the different disciplines. We do not relegate them just to the computer room. This is very important. This has made it possible for all our children to become computer literate.

That was my first significant brush as a minister with the Education Department and the education system. I found that I had some supporters, and I also found some who thought what I was trying to do and the way I was trying to do it was a total anathema. My next step was to try to extend some of these ideas into colleges of further education. I started to visit colleges of further education and quickly discovered how good many of them were. I also found out that they were thirsting to be free of local government. This was even more true of the polytechnics. We tried in 1980–81 (or rather

Mark Carlisle and William Waldegrave did) to move polytechnics out of local authority control, but it got nowhere – the whole proposal ran into the sand. But I learnt from this experience. When we did it in 1986 it went through easily – it was among the least controversial things which I did. Former Labour MPs working in the sector looked upon me almost as a hero.

PR   Price and Fowler?

KB   Price and Fowler wanted it because they wanted independence and more academic freedom to run their institutions. They wanted greater business and managerial freedom even more than academic freedom. The academic freedom of the polytechnics had not been seriously challenged, but certainly they felt hamstrung in other ways. They wanted to be able to get on and expand, and this was a time in which this was the big expanding area of higher education.

In summing up my views and attitudes towards education, I would stress that education was the way in which the Baker family had moved on in society or up the social scale. My grandfather had been a docker – a wonderful man – and education had been our ladder. I am not just well disposed towards education – I worship it.

PR   Can we try and put our discussion into a broader context? It is often claimed that educational policy was characterized by a high degree of consensus between the parties during the Boyle/Crosland era, but that this has increasingly ceased to be the case since 1979. What was the educational policy of the Conservative party between 1979 and 1986? Can I preface this by suggesting that there were those within the higher echelons of the Conservative party who at the end of this period were frankly disappointed with the lack of progress which had been made in implementing the Thatcherite revolution. Sir Keith Joseph is on record as admitting as much. In an interview reported in the *Independent* he is quoted as saying: 'What we haven't done, but still need to do, are in the obvious areas of education and health ... In my view, there is a lot still to be done to give people more choice in education ...' (13 November 1987). This view was expressed with even greater bluntness by Margaret Thatcher in response to a caller who asked her in an *Election Call* broadcast what she regretted she had not actually done during the previous eight years. She responded: 'I wish we had begun to tackle education earlier. We have been content to continue the policies of our predecessors. But now we have much worse left-wing Labour authorities than we have ever had before – so something simply has to be done' (Reported in the *Guardian*, 11 June 1987). On this account, did the real break with the canons of the educational policy of the post-war era come after 1987 and not before? In this context, it might be argued that this transformation might best be dated to your years in office as Education Minister?

KB   I think a lot of that is true. If you look at our manifesto in 1979 I think you will find about two or three inches on education – there's hardly anything. In 1983, I think there is about half a page [this was set out in a six-point programme for the new administration, some of which was already being implemented]. In 1987, which is the one I was directly responsible for, there are several pages of highly specific proposals. We did not address the problems of education widely enough during our early years in office. There were some initiatives under Mark Carlisle, and then Keith Joseph came along. Keith, as I say in my book, was, I think, intellectually seduced by a very clever department who wanted to do its own thing. They have long been one of the feudal armies in the great battle structure that passes for British government. They wanted to do things their way, and tended to count ministers in and count ministers out.

PR   Margaret Thatcher does not seem to have remembered her years at the DES with much affection. You comment that when offering you the post of Education Secretary she warned you 'about the Department. She had clearly had a searing time dealing with the officials there when she herself had been the Education Secretary from 1970 to 1974 and she believed that these officials had thwarted Keith too. I remember her saying to Keith at a meeting in 1983 that "You have an awful department"' (Baker, 1993, p. 161). How would you describe the attitudes and influence of the senior civil servants within the Department during these years?

KB   I discuss this in my book. When I took over I found morale within the department poor. The morale of ministers was low,

> due in no small part to an inability to push distinctively Conservative policies past powerful civil servant's opposition. Of all Whitehall Departments, the DES was among those with the strongest in-house ideology. There was a clear 1960s ethos and a very clear agenda which permeated virtually all the civil servants. It was rooted in progressive orthodoxies, in egalitarianism and in the comprehensive school system. It was devoutly anti-excellence, anti-selection, and anti-market. The DES represented perfectly the theory of producer capture, whereby the interests of the producer prevail over the interests of the consumer. Not only was the Department in league with the teacher unions, University Departments of Education, teacher-training theories and local authorities, it also acted as their protector against any threats which ministers might pose. If the civil servants were guardians of this culture, then Her Majesty's Inspectorate of Education were its priesthood.
>
> (1993, p. 168)

PR   Even so, your account of your relationships with senior department officials is a good deal more positive than Margaret Thatcher's. You could count on the support of the Permanent Secretary, Sir David Hancock, to deliver what ministers wanted, but you seem to imply his 'writ' was limited essentially to higher education, and you describe him as 'the nominal Head of the Department' (1993, p. 166). He had come from the Treasury, whereas

> schools policy remained the fiefdom of those officials brought up and bred in the DES tradition. They had seen to it that key policy battles with Ministers had been won by civil servants. Keith's idea of education vouchers had been scuppered by them first delaying, and then proposing a super voucher scheme which was so radical it frightened the Cabinet and was rejected as unacceptable.

In your time, the most powerful of these officials was Walter Ulrich, Deputy Secretary for Schools Branch. You remember him as 'a prodigious worker and a talented draftsman', but 'no particular fan of Government policies'. *The Turbulent Years* contains revealing accounts of how he operated. How did he operate with his subordinates, the Permanent Secretary, ministers, and Secretaries of State?

KB   As Secretary of State my working method in every Department was to hold round-table meetings. I would sit on one side of the table, flanked by the appropriate minister and my PPS, and my minute-taking Private Secretary. On the side facing me would be the civil servants. When the Permanent Secretary attended he would sit immediately opposite me, even if he was not the policy expert on the subject under discussion. This seating arrangement deferred to his status as Head of Department, and he would be flanked by officials in descending order of seniority. But at the DES, it was always Walter Ulrich who sat himself in the seat opposite me, so that he would be my main interlocutor when we discussed schools policy. Nor did he allow his subordinates too many contributions. David Hancock [the Permanent Secretary] would be relegated to sitting at the end of the table, and on one occasion the unofficial relationships became crystal clear. Walter was holding forth on some policy or other when I put forward an alternative view about which David had sent me a minute. 'Who came up with that?' demanded Walter contemptuously, not knowing it was his senior. 'I did', said David plaintively, and everyone burst into laughter at this vivid illustration of their relationship.

Even Secretaries of State were not immune from Walter's formidable intellectual bullying. It was one of Bob Dunn's [a member of the ministerial team] complaints that when ministers in Keith's time eventually reached a political decision about a policy matter, Walter, if he didn't like it, would unpick it by sending a dissenting minute and then re-argue the issue face to face with Keith. Bob felt that too often both Keith and Chris Patten [another member of the ministerial team] would end up admiring Walter's fine Wykehamist mind and concede the intellectual point rather than persist with the political argument.

PR   Early on, he tried these tactics with you, but you 'made it clear that you had an agenda which [you] expected officials to deliver':

> There was only room for one boss in my department. Walter and his colleagues came to understand that, and once we had established what our relationship was to be I found Walter and the DES civil servants as capable of producing good-quality policy papers as any of their colleagues in other departments.
>
> (1993, p. 167)

Even so, they sound a formidable lot? Were they?

KB   They were formidable people, there is no question about that. There was to some extent, certainly with Margaret, a sense of guilt that she had signed more orders abolishing grammar schools than any other Secretary of State for Education and Science. She felt she had been taken in by the Department of Education and Science; as you say, she had no great affection for them.

PR   In fact, you said this to her in one meeting?

KB   Oh yes. She scowled and looked down. But she knew that it was true, really. You asked me about education policy before 1979. Let us begin with Labour policy from 1974 to 1979. For the most part this was really just tidying up the Crosland agenda; the further implementation of comprehensive education, the expansion of the polytechnics. In addition there was a contraction of the university sector during their time of office which can be explained by the fact that they got into such an enormous economic mess. It was definitely *not* a great period. They lacked objectives, they lacked targets, they didn't really know what to do. They were far to close to the teacher unions, and particularly to the NUT. The teacher unions were not at the time a progressive element in education, nor have they been since – there's no question about that. I always drew the distinction between the teacher unions and the teachers – I was never against teachers. I made a big point of never attacking the profession of teaching.

PR   I recall that Sir Keith advised you not to 'make the mistake I did of attacking the teachers'.

KB   He caught a cold on this very early on. But more generally, after 1979, Keith's role in shaping our policies on education and beyond is very important. He was certainly the most intellectually distinguished of all of Margaret's ministers. He had very clear ideas and views of startling simplicity, and he knew perfectly well that quality was what it was all about in education. Where Keith was not successful was that he found it very difficult, I think, to deal with the actual administrative consequences of that understanding. And then he got into the great teachers' strike and that, quite frankly, bogged down the whole reform agenda for education for almost two years.

By making quality the centre of the education debate, he made possible the other later changes we were able to introduce.

One of the most important things I had to do when I became Education Secretary was to resolve this as quickly as possible. I had to grasp that nettle and cut through it. I had attended various meetings at the DES related to this issue, as the Secretary of State for the Environment is one of the major players in this game. I had been struck at just how ineffectual Keith and Chris Patten were in dealing with this – I don't believe either of them grasped the issues in a way which would have enabled them to bring it to a head. They seemed to be drifting on and on. I have explained in my book how I went about trying to resolve the strike, and I am not sure any useful purpose is served by going through it all again now (1993, pp. 171–6). Suffice to say, I had to do some very tough things which didn't make me loved by the teaching unions. We took away their negotiating rights but set up a system which ensured that teachers got better rewards than they had ever been awarded in the history of the profession. The Interim Advisory Committee is an excellent arrangement. We put people on it who I knew would, within certain reasonable constraints, improve the lot of teachers very significantly. That is exactly what they have done.

PR   You seemed very good at getting money – better than Sir Keith perhaps?

KB   I had to argue very strongly, and there were bitter, bitter debates, and it wasn't easy. I had to fight every inch of the way, but undertaking big reforms like we did meant that there was an implicit obligation to provide the money, and I demanded that the bills be met. I said, 'You can't do it otherwise.'

PR   Otherwise you couldn't have settled the teachers' dispute as swiftly as you did?

KB   We had to – it cost a fortune, an absolute fortune.

PR   I seem to recall the figure £600 million, but presumably it was a good deal more than that?

KB   That was just the extra right at the end. It cost billions. It would have cost much less if only the Treasury had been sensible enough to have done a deal a year earlier. When the documents come out, all this will be written up. It was a classic case, in my view, of the Treasury messing up the Department – messing up the whole negotiating process. But I wasn't going to have that, since I was put in, as it were, as a white knight to do something. When a minister is put in a department in that way, you have a period when you can do quite a lot. During my first nine months I was able to establish educational policy for the following nine years, if you like; or even for the rest of the century and beyond. The fact that I was able to settle an industrial dispute that had gone on for so long greatly enhanced my reputation among my colleagues. I was seen as someone who could resolve things in education and who therefore had to be listened to. I then set about fashioning the other policies, all the other policies, including the curriculum policy.

PR   And you did it without further major strikes, despite all the threats?

KB   I was lucky to some extent in that there had recently been a major strike. I think the teacher unions hadn't realized how unpopular they'd become by forcing the strike. When children are being sent home from school, and when teachers walk out, the general public start to become very uneasy about all this – they don't like it, although they do tend to like teachers. They tend to think it's wrong for people who are in authority to strike – just as they tend to think that people in uniforms on the whole should not strike. The teaching profession was doing itself no good at all. We were able to appeal to the parents over the heads of the teacher unions – they had not experienced that from any minister before.

You might say the same thing for the Department. In making policy I was a very hands-on Minister. I got very involved in the minutiae of education, and they didn't expect it. In fact I found it fascinating. This meant, for example, that I had to try to understand all the different types of testing, and that's quite testing in itself. Of course I learnt a lot in all of this – my own views changed as they went along, to some extent as a result of what I learnt.

PR   Did you come to the DES with a detailed agenda of change beyond that set out in the manifesto, or did you develop one very quickly once you got there?

KB   I had some ideas from the word go. I knew that we had to do something about the curriculum because I had attended various meetings where Keith Joseph and Chris Patten and others had talked about it. Much of that discussion seemed to me to be incredibly woolly and vague. As I say in my book, the contribution of colleagues to this debate around the table was not one of the most glorious moments of collective discussion I've ever attended. It was largely derived from personal reminiscences of their own education (I started rather like that myself). It was very hard going, and so hard going that I decided to explain less and less to them, and I think I was justified in doing so.

PR   In your book you describe what happened when Sir Keith Joseph tried to generate a worthwhile debate on the nature of the school curriculum. At the time he was particularly concerned with what he came to call the 'clutter of the curriculum', by which he meant the various extraneous subjects which schools had begun teaching over time. As you say:

> When he took proposals to colleagues, and to the Cabinet Committee of which I was a member, the discussions were rambling and inconclusive. Most

> Ministers around the table could not distinguish between the curriculum, covering the full range of knowledge that a child has to absorb, and the syllabus, covering the detailed programme of study leading to an exam. Their views were drawn mainly from their own experience of education or occasionally based on that of their children.
>
> (1993, p. 189)

This experience was to have an important influence upon how you went about developing policy in this area. You were 'convinced that the key to raising educational standards across the country was a National Curriculum' and told the Prime Minister this shortly after your appointment. A few months later you discussed your preliminary ideas about what would be involved and received an encouraging reply. The Department, you stress, was 'glad to be given the green light to develop proposals for a National Curriculum, a policy for which they had considerable sympathy' (p. 191). As yet 'the public had ... no idea that this was on the educational agenda' and so you decided to tell them. This was reasonable enough, but your decision to make such a major policy announcement 'without first referring back to colleagues' was not what might normally be expected. You justify this decision by stressing that you 'did not want [your] curriculum proposals sunk in a mire of other people's individual memory and prejudice'. To prevent this happening, you 'decided to reveal the curriculum proposals' on the Sunday television programme *Weekend World,* which had scheduled an interview with you. It was, you acknowledge 'a gamble', but you were supported by the Prime Minister, who said to you 'never underestimate the effectiveness of simply just announcing something'. Do you still accept this account of policy-making on the National Curriculum? If so, how was it developed?

KB   On the first question, yes. On the second I should say that, within the Department itself, a consensus had begun to develop which acknowledged a need for a greater level of prescription – the records will show that. Subsequently, much of the basic work was done in the Curriculum Development Council – by people like Professor Blin-Stoyle. There were, of course, a variety of different views on what the National Curriculum should look like. I had very strong support from the Department in favour of a wide and broad curriculum rather than a narrow curriculum. I also believed that very, very strongly. I was not going to settle for a three-subject curriculum. As such, I feel that the curriculum as it has developed in recent times is in some danger of being too watered down.

PR   History may be on your side. As early as 1864 the Clarendon Commissioners made a case for a common curriculum which valued breadth and balance. They argued that

> If a youth, after four or five years at school ... quits ... almost ignorant of

geography and of the history of his own country, unacquainted with any modern language but his own, and hardly competent to write English correctly, to do a simple sum, or to stumble through an easy proposition of Euclid, a total stranger to the laws which govern the physical world ... with an eye and hand unpracticed in drawing and without knowing a note of music ... his intellectual education must be accounted a failure.

The common curriculum advocated by Clarendon, and by Robert Morant forty years later, is in many respects strikingly similar to the National Curriculum which was sketched out in the 1988 Education Act.

KB   I felt that very strongly.

PR   Since those times, classics is out and technology is in.

KB   Basically that. There was to be more practical work, much more practical work than in the old system, which was important. I was very proud of what emerged from the National Curriculum discussions; but it proved very difficult to produce in practice. Some of my successors have messed around with it rather too much. For my part, my biggest regret was that I was not able to open up the number of teaching hours issue. I knew that the curriculum we were developing was going to be demanding, but we never expected it to take up 80 per cent of the school week. I should have pushed harder for one extra teaching period a day. If there had been an extra teaching period a day – and I began to get round to pushing for this in 1989 – it would have been possible to accommodate many of the more difficult issues which focus on aspects of the argument about fitting a 'quart into a pint pot' as far as our curriculum proposals were concerned. It is wrong that within the English education system the hours taught by teachers in front of a class are lower than any country in Europe, and significantly lower than in America and Japan.

PR   The number of hours seems to vary from school to school in this country. The second report on *Taught Time* (OFSTED, 1994 London: HMSO) concluded that 'the taught week varied from 20.0 to 25.4 hours in primary schools surveyed and from a little under 22.5 to just over 26.7 hours in secondary' and that 'the total time spent in school by pupils varied by 4.1 hours a week in the primary school and by 8 hours in the secondary schools'.

KB   I had not picked that up. Not lengthening the school day and the school week was my biggest regret. We weren't able to do it because the strike had just been resolved, partly on the issue of the number of hours in a year that teachers have to teach. But an extra forty-minute period a day, or even an additional thirty-minute period a day, would have been very helpful.

PR   Before we consider the 1988 Education Reform Act, can we spend a little time on the development of policy on the City Technology Colleges? I would like, in particular, to explore two points with you

Firstly, in your book you stress that your 'first policy initiative was the creation of the City Technology Colleges (CTCs)'. You regard it as an important initiative designed, *inter alia*, to increase choice, diversity and standards in education. Furthermore, it offered a way of shifting 'power towards the parents and children who were the consumers of education and away from the education administrators and vested interests who were the producers of education' (Baker, 1993, p. 177). Three main aims are identified, and it is the second of these which I would like to focus upon. In this you argue that it was your intention to use

> the CTCs as beacons of excellence and exemplar models for what could be done in other state schools. I wanted a new ethos which entailed giving more powers to head teachers to set the tone of their school, to spend their budget as they wished and to hire the staff they wanted. We wanted CTCs to be test-beds for new teaching methods and new school management methods which could be used in other schools.

(p. 178)

Later on you point out that 'thinking and discussions about CTCs broke crucial ground for some of the main changes eventually included in the Education Reform Act which we developed some months later for the 1987 Election Manifesto' (p. 181). It would be hard to deny this last claim, but there is one area at least in which you seem to have had a significant change of heart.

In the comments quoted earlier, you talk of creating a new ethos of management which would entail giving much greater powers to headteachers, but in the 1988 Education Reform Act almost all the new powers allocated to enable site-based school management were given to the governors and very few were allocated to headteachers. In describing the role of the governing body and the headteacher, Circular 7/88 calls for both parties to exercise their statutory duties in a collaborative partnership. But the language of the Circular does not seem to be predicated on the notion that the partnership is an equal one. It is not easy to share the confidence of the authors of the Circular that 'local management will give head teachers powers to match their existing responsibilities'. Rather, it seems that, taken as a whole, the mandatory powers apportioned to headteachers as compared with those allocated to governing bodies seem relatively slight. Of course, governing bodies can delegate many of their powers to the headteachers, but it is for them to choose the extent to which they are willing to do so. As such, it is not surprising to find that accounts of the powers of the headteacher to be found in the 1988 legislation and beyond are for the most part couched in the language of enablement rather than of entitlement. What is rather more surprising is that this outcome does not square with what you seem to have initially envisaged. Did you change your mind?

Secondly, can we consider what we can learn from the setting up of the CTCs about your views on effective policy-making more generally? You saw the creation of the CTCs both as preparing the ground for the major changes set out in the Reform Act of 1988 and as 'an interesting case study in the development of new policy' (p. 186). You make two points on the latter claim. First, that 'when one wishes to innovate, there is usually a choice between using existing institutions with their established practices and reforming them from within, or starting completely anew' (p. 186). Second, that

> The CTCs were key in the process of reform because they were the first element to be announced, and incorporated many of the changes that I wanted to introduce into the whole system – parental choice, per capita funding, local managerial control, and independence from the LEA. If I had started out by focusing just on per capita funding and tried to get the support of my ministerial colleagues and their Departments, then the whole process would have become bogged down in the Whitehall system. That is what happened to Keith Joseph's ideas ... No, the only way was to get something up and running which incorporated the essence of much-needed reforms. That way everybody could see the reforms in operation, understand their significance and realise that we meant business.
>
> (p. 188)

I have quoted this at some length because it seems to me to say something important about your views on effective (and ineffective) approaches to policy-making. You are sceptical about the merits of general statements on major reform as a means of initiating change. Rather, you prefer to push through something specific and practical which illustrates the benefit of a general approach and only then to attempt more radical reform.

KB   That's exactly my approach. If one had taken all the range of educational problems that I was faced with at the time, like the polytechnics not being funded at a level they felt appropriate, the university sector in a sulk, the whole structure of further education in need of change, the reforms in the curriculum and running of schools which were necessary, etc., etc., etc., etc., and had tried to advance, as it were, on a broad front, I would have got nowhere. In order to crystallize change, in order to create the circumstances that make change possible, I believe very strongly that you have to set up something as quickly as you can to demonstrate how it can be done. That gives you a spearhead you can then use to achieve the other things you want to do. I chose the City Technology Colleges because they crystallized nearly all the other issues. What was to be taught in these colleges; who was to own them; how they were going to be funded; and we had very interesting discussions because it raised all the major issues which subsequently found their way into the Reform Bill. We had big round-table discussions about the rim and the wheel; who should be at the rim? Should it be the individual colleges or the LEAs? Once the Department saw that I was determined to do all this, and to do it in this way, they helped me. I would never say that the Department of Education and Science tried to thwart me. And I don't say that in my book either.

PR   I seem to remember you describe them as becoming a first-division department?

KB   I tried to get them up to that, and I think they achieved it. They helped me, because they realized that I was set on this course and I was determined to do it – and I kept on saying, 'You know, the Prime Minister will support me.' It was a great thing to say that. In fact, I didn't discuss it with her very much at that stage. But it's always a good argument. And I had a bit of the wind with me, and when you're a minister with a bit of the wind with you, you can do so much more. What's more, the Department likes a minister who wants to do things. When they saw what I was interested in, they were good at identifying the options. For example, if I wanted options on what to do on the powers and responsibilities of LEAs, governing bodies, headteachers, etc., they would say, 'If you want to achieve this or that, then the structure of the governing body should be such and such; the powers of the head should be such and such; if you want to remove them completely, then you're going to have to do this or that.' They did the same on open enrolment and the National Curriculum and the other aspects of the reform legislation. They were helpful. There's no question about that. But they were not equally helpful on everything. For example, they were not all that helpful over grant-maintained schools, but we're coming to that later. But they were generally helpful, and on that basis we began to fashion the whole set of ideas which finally found their way into the Act. But for my part, I had to do something to announce it, to make it happen. I used the setting up of the CTCs to do so. In any case, I am very proud of the CTCs. There are fifteen now; I would have preferred to have seen more. We were attacked for their cost. But when you build a new school it costs £7–8m, and we found it very difficult to get LEAs to let us have schools surplus to their requirements at an educational rate. They wanted to sell them off and get a lot of money; and so that was the real cost. But I'm very proud of those and they're very successful schools. They have already become beacons in their area, and others will follow and expand and develop. They were very much a tin-opener to the whole operation.

PR   As 'incoming Education Secretary' you had

> two watchwords: standards and choice. Those twin themes, exemplified by the introduction of a national curriculum with testing, and city technology

schools and grant-maintained schools, were the ways I intended to achieve my overriding aim. This was to improve the quality of education for all our children in whatever part of the country they lived.

(Baker, 1993, p. 165)

In determining what needed to be done, to what extent did you begin with these principles and then attempt to identify the reforms which would be necessary to put them into practice?

KB　Yes, broadly, I did. I asked, 'What can we do to improve standards?' That question led us into the whole issue of the curriculum. I immersed myself in such questions and attempted to understand them from the point of view of the educationalists. In turn, this got us involved in issues to do with testing. I was clear that there should be some sort of testing system. Again, I had to go as deeply as I could into the different types of testing system. We had great doctrinal debates within the Department and elsewhere about the relative merits of paper-and-pencil tests and of the costs of failure and that sort of thing. In my view, a lot of very sloppy sentiment had come into education in the 1960s; a desire to try to find excuses for failure in socio-economic terms. There was a reluctance to acknowledge that such failure could often be better explained by the fact that the teaching had not been good enough, that the discipline was not good enough, that the rigour was not good enough. I do not suggest that such thinking was endemic in the system as a whole, but it did exist within quite a lot of schools.

I certainly wanted greater choice. I had made this clear even before I became Education Secretary. The analogy is with the housing sector, where there is no choice if people were just council tenants. We opened up a whole opportunity of choice through the sale of council houses, the creation of housing associations, the creation of housing societies and all the rest of it. Suddenly, council tenants who had had no choice at all found they did have choices. I wanted to create similar choice in education, so that parents would have greater choice on which schools and which types of school they could send their children to. You might think of it in the following way. There was this huge continent which was state education, catering for over 93 per cent of all children. Then there was private education, a relatively small island with 7 per cent. And there were no links between them at all; no other types of islands or semi-continents. What we have done is to create a lot of semi-continents in the CTCs and in the grant-maintained schools. I was also very interested in the administration of the whole system. I had been a business manager and was therefore interested in the mechanics of management. In thinking about what change was necessary, we could draw upon the experience of some local education authorities which had pioneered new approaches. For example, Cambridge in particular, Surrey to some extent and Solihull had all experimented with delegated budgets. There had been some good work done on this dating back to about 1983–84.

PR   I think Solihull began in 1981.

KB   Really? It was clear, looking at what happened in these places, that the schemes they had put in place were showing positive advantages. Budget responsibility was handed down first for relatively little things like books and small items of expenditure such as window repairs. Later there was a move to delegate more significant items down. It soon became clear that schools given this responsibility were getting better value for money as a result. I believe that if you give people control over their own budgets they are much more likely to be conscious in making spending decisions that it is their money that they are using. They are much more likely to ask, What is the best use we can make of the resources that are available to us? I wanted to promote that attitude, and in order to do so we devised our ideas on the local management of schools. That has been a major success. It has been a very important development and has shown what can be done. Furthermore, it had in itself the seeds of further important change. Both those who are in favour and those who are not recognize this. Once you start down that kind of road you are bound to encounter some opposition from some of the local education authorities.

PR   Developments like LMS are hard to reverse. Once schools have experienced being able to manage to their financial affairs in such a way, they are likely to be reluctant to give it up.

KB   As you say, this is an innovation which will be hard to reverse. In any case, I feel that it was inevitable anyway. Some local education authorities introduced it with reluctance and went about delegating financial responsibility as slowly as they could. They wanted to stay as much in control as they could for as long as they could. I think it would probably be fair to say that this would be true for most of them. A few were supportive but they were relatively rare. They were the enlightened ones. It is often assumed that I am – and I am often described as – the doctrinal destroyer of local education authorities. Not at all. But I was quite conscious of the fact that by doing what we were doing we were bound to weaken their central control. I did not mind weakening that central control, because I did not think that some of the things that some of them were doing were effective.

       We wanted to enable schools to have a greater say in the management of their own affairs: that is why we strengthened the governing bodies; that is why we wanted to get wider representation on the governing bodies; that is why we gave them greater powers. Governing bodies prior to my Act – and I served briefly on one in the East End of London – were mainly concerned with things like the state of the washers on taps in the lavatories and the order of events for speech day, if there was a speech day; and very little else. As a governor, you were lucky if you were even given vague reports about progress and success, or if you were told about one particularly brilliant pupil. More often than not, that was it. I wondered what such governing bodies ever did. Why were they there? What were they doing? We wanted to give them much greater powers. I was told that if I did this then people would not be willing to take on such responsibilities. That they just would not come forward in sufficient numbers. We have discovered that people are willing to come forward. This proved that if you make a job worthwhile, worthwhile people will come forward to do it.

You raised the issue of the relative powers given to the head and the governing body in the legislation. I suppose we might have given – in fact we probably did give – rather too much to the governing body and not enough to the headteacher.

PR   Other countries which have gone down the site-based management route have not usually given to governing or similar bodies anything like the powers they currently enjoy in this country. Rather, they have tended to devolve these powers to headteachers.

KB   I think that is true. I am trying to recall the various debates and discussions we engaged in at the time. I think we took the action we did because we were advised that the governing body was a legal entity, and as such could be given duties and powers much more easily than a headteacher. I'd have to check the records.

PR   Did you see yourself in the 1988 Education Reform Act as passing a very radical piece of legislation – something to compare with the 1944 Act?

KB   Yes, I think I did. I think it probably is. You need to see it in context. At the time we had been trying to deal with a whole series of matters. In higher education alone there were things like polytechnic reform, like academic tenure, like the statutes of universities. Each of these taken separately would have been quite major matters in their own right, but they and much else could all be swept up into a single big Act. This meant we were able to move forward at a pace. I suppose I was lucky, there is no question about that, because with so much to do, I had managed to persuade colleagues before the 1987 election to put all our key proposals into our manifesto. This justified what we did, and it also committed us to trying to do it. Our proposals had been made public and our plans were well thought out and well planned. So we set about implementing them. There were tremendous disputes, of course, about the implementation, in particular, of the National Curriculum.

We also created a new type of school, the grant-maintained school. Let me explain how that came about. Partially, of course, through our work on the CTCs. But equally important was my experiencing first-hand, when I went to the Department, the desire to close small schools. My ministers and I were faced with dealing with closure proposals. I started to read through the files of these closures and I found that some very good schools were being closed; that some very popular schools were being closed. I also found the Treasury was telling us that we must close schools. We set up a committee, whose findings were not accepted, under Mr Fraser, to examine the system by which decisions were made. He was, I think, a former Permanent Secretary of the Scottish Office, and he later became the government's efficiency guru. We had to appoint him because at the time the Treasury was saying, 'You've got to close more schools. You've got this enormous number of secondary places surplus, and primary places'; so they insisted that we set up a small committee under Fraser to examine ways of speeding up the process so that we could close more schools more quickly. What was proposed would have involved reducing the degree of representation by Members of Parliament and school governing bodies. It was based on a 'Don't see the delegation' sort of approach. I could not accept that. I started seeing delegations of those objecting to particular closure proposals, and in doing so I became very impressed with the commitment and the ability of governors all over the country. In Labour areas as well as Conservative; it wasn't just a matter of middle-class schools in Surrey or little village primary schools within the Tory shires. The governors of Labour city schools which were under threat also came to see me. Once I started looking into this, I found some of the schools which LEAs planned to close were very good schools indeed. And then I began to look at the rest of the schools in the area and I saw that some very poor schools were going to survive. I mean schools which were poor by almost any standard you care to name. I acknowledge that I'm using subjective measures, but there were also objective measures you could use as well. I came to the conclusion that this was not at all satisfactory and that other voices than that of the LEA should be heard more loudly. In particular, the voice of local parents; and not just, as it were, the voices of the local education managers.

I became more and more personally convinced of the need to enable parents and others to play a fuller role than had been possible in the past. From that idea, in part, came the development of the CTCs, and they, in turn, were the genesis of the grant-maintained schools movement. I don't recall anybody putting papers to me on this from the government. The Adam Smith Institute, I think, at some stage tried to claim credit for this. I have to tell you that I saw no paper from them on this at all. The No Turning Back Group said, at some stage, that they had one. But I can recall no paper I had from them.

PR It was your idea?

KB Well, I would not put it quite like that. I think it was developed by the ministers at the Department. A lot of the policies we developed were produced through a process of discussion, debate and examination round the table. I am a great believer in that way of doing things. But certainly the idea of grant-maintained schools owed more to me than I think to anybody else. I remember seeing Margaret in the division lobby just before the Christmas of 1986 – we were discussing education in a general way – and I said, 'I want to try out an idea on you which would mean giving parents a bigger say on closures of schools, and on the possibility of schools operating outside the local education authority as a result of a choice by parents.' And she said, 'What a very interesting idea. Please pursue it. I am broadly in sympathy with it.' I think that response can be traced back to her time at the Department. I think that left Margaret with a sense of guilt as far as the grammar schools were concerned. She never forgot that, and she never really forgave the Department. And so we developed the idea of the grant-maintained school. It was very controversial, very much objected to. I say quite a bit on it in the book, and you will know from others the battles that went on and the ways that various authorities tried to stop it happening.

I wanted to release the energy in the system. An energy which was being constrained by all sorts of historic devices, of traditional ways of doing things. I genuinely wanted to energize people; to allow them to do the things they had always wanted to but could not within the existing system. I wanted to energize governors who wanted to get more involved in the management of the school. I wanted to enable business people who wished to do so to get involved. We were not going to achieve this by going through the local education authorities, I was quite clear about that. When you come to reform, something you have to decide is whether you basically try to do it from within or whether you do it from without. If you do it from within, you've got to make quite sure that you're not seduced, as Keith was, by the system. The powers of seduction are enormous. The powers of inertia are enormous.

PR And the powers of opposition?

KB And the powers of opposition. There are lots of very clever people in the education system of our country, all of whom are protecting their particular interests. Some are doing so for selfish reasons; some for idealistic reasons; and some because they genuinely believe their way of doing things is better. I always respect my opponents. I never underestimate them, apart from the management of the main teacher unions, which on the whole I did not respect.

PR   You make that pretty clear in your book.

KB   So we got the changes going. I would stress again how much they had to do with energizing people. I really am a big believer in letting people do their own thing. If you get good people in positions of responsibility, don't overbear them, don't try to boss them around, don't tell them what to do – let them get on with it. That was the liberating, the freeing-up side of what I was trying to achieve. The other side of the reform was to be achieved within the guidelines of a newly developed National Curriculum.

PR   Did you make any compromises in the 1988 Act which you came to regret?

KB   Well, as I said earlier, the big thing that I regret is not pressing harder for more teaching hours. The lack of hours was the source of many of the problems we had with regard to the National Curriculum. It meant that we had to make unnecessarily difficult decisions. Should all pupils have history and geography or history or geography? What can be included in technology? What should be included in English? It would have been so much better.

PR   What about some of the ways in which your reforms have been interpreted subsequently? For example, the setting up of a complicated system of assessment.

KB   That was a regret. We had several meetings when the experts explained to me the need for what they described as a fair assessment system. I knew it was becoming too complicated. All my instincts told me it was getting too complicated. It was something I would have redressed if I had stayed on in the Department, for I could see disaster staring us in the face. We did have some experience of assessment issues. We had, for example, to implement the GCSE proposals. This was a very worthwhile development, and the main credit for it should go to Keith Joseph. Its introduction changed the examination system in fundamental ways. It was a big thing. I had to implement it and having done so became very much more aware of what examinations could and could not do, and also of the ways in which they could go off the rails. I knew that the assessment system which was being set up on the advice of the Black Report was beginning to go off the rails. It was much too elaborate and much too complicated, for the best of possible reasons.

   The whole thing got too tied up with the issue of the school league tables and the publishing of school results. At the time, many within the educational establishment argued that the whole idea was outrageous and they tried to do all they could to prevent it happening. It is now very popular with parents and the public. This is one clock that will not be turned back. Much of the clock will not be turned back.

PR   Are you satisfied with developments since then? There are some people who say the 1993 Act takes a significant new direction from the 1988 Act. Do you see educational policy and legislation since 1988 as having developed essentially in line with what you were trying to achieve in the Great Educational Reform Act of that year? Are you satisfied with what you did at the time and are you satisfied with the results which this had?

KB   In retrospect, I would have liked to have stayed a bit longer than I did. I would have liked to have embedded the reforms of 1988 in a bit further. It is not possible to get such a major piece of legislation perfect the first time. It was clear at the time that things were going to have to develop. What we did could not be set in aspic for ever. No changes are. In particular, I would have liked to have been able to take the development of the curriculum a bit further and to have sorted out the problems that have developed over testing at an earlier stage. Things have got really ragged on this over the last couple of years and the failure to grasp the mistakes in the English test have led to the abandonment of lots of other things which should not have been lost. In my view the difficulties we now face are, quite frankly, mainly due to carelessness. They could and should have been avoided. Had I been there for a couple more years, I would have certainly developed more CTCs, possibly of a different nature, but this is now back on the rails again.

    Finally, I had begun to address the question of teacher training, which I think is very important. During my time as Education Secretary I visited a number of teacher training colleges and university departments of education. What I saw varied in quality. Several were very theoretical, and almost all gave too little attention to classroom-based practical training. For this and other reasons, I wanted to develop new ideas for teacher training which took place on the job and which was much more school and classroom based. We therefore put in hand a number of innovations such as the Licensed Teacher Scheme, the Articled Teacher Scheme and the requirement that teachers in training should spend more time in schools and classrooms. My successors have taken these ideas forward, and as a result the nature of teacher training has been much improved.

PR   Can I ask you a bit more on policy development on GM schools? You made clear earlier in our discussion the importance which you give to this aspect of your reforms. In a sense they were at the core of what you were trying to do. Do you think this is an initiative which has stalled over the last year or so? This is being explained in various ways, but some at least are claiming that what has happened is a direct consequence of your decision to leave the choice on whether a school goes GM to parents. There has even been some talk that a commitment to legislate for all schools to become grant maintained might be included in your party's manifesto for the next general election.

KB   I was trying to take people along with me and change things as well as I could – I acknowledge I was a very controversial figure – and one of the instruments we had for this was to rely on parental choice. The great majority of grant-maintained schools are very good indeed. They have unleashed the talent I always believed exists in schools but which was frustrated by the existing system. They have energized those talents. Of course, as a result, other schools have also begun to improve. If you're trying to sum up the consequences of the 1988 Act, you have to do so on the basis of an assessment of the general level of improvement of the education system of our country as a whole which it has brought about.

PR   And you feel that there has been such an improvement as a whole? What do you see as the evidence for this?

KB   Well, I was very encouraged, reading the papers this morning, to learn that our staying on rate at 16 is now 72 per cent. Cynics say, 'They would because of unemployment.' I think this is just a cheap comment. There has been an important change of attitude. As a result of cumulative change which stems from the 1988 Education Act, there has been a growing determination to persuade young people to go on with their education – that it is good for them to go on. This may be the most important educational change which has taken place over the last ten years. I'm rather proud of this because, I think, I had a hand in making it happen.

PR   There are those who claim that your legislation on LMS would have achieved what you wanted from GMS.

KB   I've heard that argument. I think that it would have taken a very long time. It's a bit like the CTCs. You had to do something to galvanize the change. I remember it being put to me in 1987 by some sophisticated chief education officer saying, 'Well, LMS will do it all: why do you want to go to the further stage of letting them become truly independent?' And I said, 'Well, the last mile is often the best mile'. If you take that further step of actually owning the assets, and become responsible for the whole operation, there is a greater sense of responsibility. Few local education authorities liked the idea of GMS, but then they never want to lose anything. They are the great monopolists. I thought it was an important and necessary step in making real change possible within the system as a whole.

PR   The latest legislation will require a governors' vote on GM every year. Will this not just demonstrate that large numbers of governing bodies reject the idea of GM and that they will do so every year?

KB   You'll have to ask John Patten about that.

PR   What was it like working with a prime minister who had herself served a substantial term as Education Secretary?

KB   In a way it was – this is a bit of a paradox – both easier and more difficult than it might otherwise have been. It was easier, because there was that sense of guilt on her part which I have referred to earlier, and this meant that she felt something had to be done. It was more difficult, because she brought a bundle of her own ideas and prejudices on what needed to be done which could be quite difficult to cope with at times. For example, she really did believe strongly in a simple and restricted National Curriculum and simple tests. But, strangely enough, she also had an almost romantic view about some of this. Yes, she would say, you have got to have music, it's important; and history is important. And the history of music is also quite important. But I don't think she rated foreign languages very high on her list of things. We did not always agree. She used to be set up by others, like Brian Griffiths, to hound me down. I faced a lot of pressure, when the Bill was being formed, to produce proposals which others wanted. After the 1987 election I was open to a lot of pressure from pressure groups. I had to fight my corner, and I won most of my battles. I wore them down. When I produced the curriculum documents, I knew many of those who were trying to get me to change things had, when they came to see me, never read them closely. They were several inches thick, but I read them. I am not saying I knew them in detail, but I knew them well enough. It was worth doing so. It helped me wear down the opposition.

PR   My reading of your book suggests that Margaret Thatcher was not always an enthusiastic supporter of everything you were trying to do. For example, you make it clear that she wanted a more restrictive National Curriculum than you did, and a much simpler form of testing than you did, that she would not have been averse to an element of parental contribution to the funding of GM schools and even of the CTCs. She also seems to have envisaged that the policy of the government should be to encourage all schools to become grant maintained, and that this should be achieved as soon as was practicable. Did you share this goal?

KB   I did not believe it was possible to achieve this quickly. You had to get some up and going, and it was pointless to start with small primary schools. You had to get some big schools out of the system and running properly. I did not want to lose the argument and the whole initiative by having some marginal primary school becoming GM and messing it all up. That would have been awful.

PR   Would it have been administratively difficult to manage a more rapid transition?

KB   It would have been very difficult.

PR   That was an argument which Anthony Crosland used against instant and universal legislation on the reform of secondary schools on comprehensive lines. In explaining to Maurice Kogan why Circular 10/65 was not backed with statutory power, he remarked:

> You must remember that at that time most local authorities were Labour-controlled and sympathetic to what we were doing – as indeed were some Tory authorities. So plans were coming in as fast as we could cope with them. For the whole time I was at Curzon Street the thing was going as fast as it could possibly go. The limitation was one of human and physical resources and not of statutory powers. But of course the situation changed later when the disastrous local election results of 1968 and 1969 put the Tories back into power almost everywhere.
>
> (Kogan, 1971, p. 191)

KB   Precisely. It is exactly the same thing. You have to manage most change at a measured pace. Like so many things with Margaret, when she picked up an idea and became very enthusiastic, she always wanted to go further than anybody else. She did say to me, 'I want the majority to be grant-maintained schools' at a time when we hadn't actually got even *one*! One out of twenty or thirty thousand! It would have been impossible to do it all at once. Quite impossible. One has got to begin slowly initially, and then progressively build up upon a good start. This has been what has happened, and schools have been opting to be grant maintained ever since. I never set myself a particular target or expressed views on what proportion of the total we should try to achieve. Going back to my analogy of the islands, I believed that the islands would be different sizes, of different groupings of schools. I do not object to that. After all, it was choice and variety that I was after.

PR   Have you been satisfied with what's happened since?

KB   Broadly, yes.

PR   Are there things you regret?

KB   Well, I think too much has been made of the difficulties of the curriculum and of testing, quite frankly. I have been sent all the papers on the Dearing proposals, and I shall read them very carefully. I hope I shall not find that too much ground has been lost. I suspect that probably quite a lot has been. If it has been, that will be a great pity, because the curriculum which I set out to develop was a real attempt to try to introduce a standardized system across the country, but one with a sufficient degree of flexibility to meet most needs. I fear that the present changes may allow a return to too much flexibility. But I wouldn't particularly want to be quoted on that, because I want to read through the papers and see how they differ from the papers which I went through at that time. I will start this weekend.

PR   I wonder if you have read the comment on your National

Curriculum which suggested that its problem was that it had lots of builders but no architect?

KB [*chuckles*] I think that's a little unfair, because the overall structure (made up of three foundation subjects, the core subjects, and the other foundation subjects, if you like) constitute the architecture. They produce the pillars – I had to set up committees; I had to have builders; we had to have people who were going to devise a science curriculum, a maths curriculum, a geography curriculum, a history curriculum and the rest for the first time. I was given a pretty free hand in deciding who should do all this; and I went out of my way to make it as reasonable, fair and balanced as possible. But I knew what I wanted. And the building is still broadly what I set up. But I do think that some of the higher points have been lowered. I think it's become a bit shadowy. I think some of the windows I opened might have been closed a bit: a pity really.

PR In retrospect, do you feel that your years at the Department will be what you will be remembered for most? Was the 1988 Education Reform Act *the* most important of your achievements?

KB I've still got some years to go, I hope. But I suppose when the muse of history takes out her sieve, I think it will go back to that. I also think the education reform of 1988 was the biggest single measure of social reform which was undertaken in the Thatcher years.

PR You'd rate it that highly?

KB There was no other measure of social reform that was as comprehensive ...

PR In front of all the other kinds of privatization?

KB Yes, as a *social* reform; as opposed to an industrial reform. It was the biggest measure of social reform which we undertook; and it was the most comprehensive measure of its kind. I suppose the only comparable measure would be the health reforms. I don't know. Possibly also the sale of council houses. But it was a major social reform.

PR Have the health reforms been as successful as the educational reforms?

KB I can't comment on that. I am very proud of the educational reforms of my time as Education Secretary. Yes, I suppose I might be remembered most for those. You will really have to assess that.

PR I have always been impressed with the equanimity with which you seem to cope with what must have been some very difficult times. Did you enjoy being Education Secretary?

KB I did. You had to be very cool about it.

PR Did you ever get used to the eggs being thrown at you?

KB I enjoyed it, eggs and all. But I don't know that I am finally in the best position to make an overall judgement on the reforms. I was too close to them. What do your fellow colleagues within the education world make of them now? What assessment are they making of them?

PR   This is a personal view, but what I *am* hearing is that Sir Keith's image is being somewhat refurbished from what it was at the time when he was Education Secretary. I can still remember the days when he was regarded as a kind of ogre within the education world. If it can happen to Sir Keith ...

KB   It can happen to me. [*both laugh loudly*]

CHAPTER 5

John MacGregor

WITH PETER RIBBINS

John MacGregor was born in 1937. He was educated at Merchiston Castle School and at St Andrew's University and King's College London, where he studied economics and then law. He was then a journalist, a business executive and worked in a merchant bank. After being a Special Assistant to Alec Douglas-Home (1963–64), he became Head of the Private Office of Edward Heath (1965–68). In 1974 he was elected as Member for Norfolk South. After serving in various junior ministerial positions he was appointed as Chief Secretary of the Treasury (1985–87), and then Minister of Agriculture (1987–89), before becoming Secretary of State for Education and Science in 1989. After a relatively short stay, he moved as Leader of the House of Commons (1990–92) and then Secretary of State for Transport (1992–94).

8 September 1994

PR   What has shaped your views on education and educational policy? How far has your own education influenced your views?

JM   Inevitably one has to go back to one's own education. There are three aspects I would pick out.

First, although I was heavily involved academically, the school I was at put great stress upon a very wide range of sporting and extra-mural activities. The fact that the school offered so many alternatives to the academic life was one of the formative influences of my life. We were expected and encouraged to live every single day to the full. That expectation has been with me ever since: it has always been a part of my approach to education. Indeed, when I did all those inevitable prize-givings which are the lot of the Secretary of State, I always used to quote – not that I am a Kipling fan – those famous couplets from 'If'. The view they express was very much a part of my own educational experience:

> If you can fill the unforgiving minute
>   With sixty seconds' worth of distance run,
>   Yours is the Earth and everything that's in it,
>   And – which is more – you'll be a Man, my son!

Second, and on the purely educational side, I have always believed in everyone striving for excellence to the limit of his or her abilities. That was also inculcated in me at school, and it remains important today. Indeed, from the nation's point of view, it is perhaps even more important today because, in this fast-changing world of intense competition, youngsters face a much more difficult life after school, particularly in getting jobs, if they have not developed their skills and abilities, and a readiness to adapt to change. That is why I always emphasized the importance of high standards and of not putting up with second best (even down to poor spelling or grammar) when I was Secretary of State.

Thirdly, and in purely educational terms, perhaps the most important formative influence has been related to my studies at university. I had originally wanted to be a Scottish advocate. To do that it was necessary to get an MA. I went to St Andrew's, where you had to take five subjects in your first two years. I did not know what fifth subject to study. I decided to take 'Political Economy', and that decision changed my life. It meant, among other things, that I did not become a Scottish advocate. Ever since, I have felt that the English system encourages a narrow specialization too early. When I was Secretary of State I wished to see what I could do to change this.

PR   You were born in Glasgow. Were you educated there?

JM   I was born in Glasgow, but that was simply because that was where the nursing home was. In effect, I was born and brought up in a coal-mining village called Shotts, which is half-way between Glasgow and Edinburgh. The coal has now run out there, but in my early days there still were coal mines. My father was one of the local doctors. There was a famous A. J. Cronin novel called *The Citadel* ...

PR   I remember seeing the film.

JM   I haven't seen the film – but I read the book many years later on a beach when on holiday with my family. For those who have read the book or, in your case, seen the film, the bit that was relevant was the young doctor's early days in a South Wales coal-mining community. That reminded me greatly of my own childhood. I went to one of the two local primary schools there. Of course, at that time, during the war, what was on offer was very basic. It was 'education by rote'. Even so, it was a very, very thorough education. I have always acknowledged how important that was. First, there was the solid grounding it gave. Second, the vast majority of children attending the school came from mining families, very far from professional backgrounds. It gave me a feeling I can only describe, as Rabbie Burns does, that 'A man's a man for all that'. I have held absolutely to that important sentiment throughout my life.

After primary school I went to a prep school in Dumfriesshire, and was then sent to a public school in Edinburgh – Merchiston. Initially my father was very worried about whether he could afford this. I don't think he really wanted to send my brother and me away, but the nearest secondary school was a long way away and he and my mother came to the view that, rather than having to do all that endless travelling, it was better for me to go to a school in Edinburgh, which is what I did.

PR   Do you remember any of your teachers as having exercised a special influence on you, either at primary or secondary school, or at university?

JM   Some had an enormous influence. Let me start with a simple example. In fact I was talking about this just the other night with my wife. I have a great passion for music. The person who really brought it out was one of my masters at secondary school. In the evening, after prep, he used to play classical music to some of us. I began to love it then, and this has lived with me ever since. I once did a *Desert Island Discs* on Radio Norfolk, and I realized afterwards that quite a number of the discs I had chosen were the ones that I'd first heard during those evenings. I could give you many other examples of such teachers and of the ways they have influenced my life for the better. I think we would all be able to give such examples.

PR   What was it about him which has made you remember him over the years?

JM   I should stress that the influence of other teachers has been even greater and more important. I just happened to think of him first. The headmaster of my prep school was a second example. He believed in living a full life and was a strong Christian. He had a very strong moral influence on me. My history master at secondary school was a third – I have always loved history – who played a powerful part in fostering my love of history. In fact he wrote me one of the nicest letters I received when I gave up being a cabinet minister. Towards the end of his letter (he is fairly elderly now), he talked in a way that seemed beautifully to summarize the essence of Mr Chips. He wrote of how worthy a thing it is to have spent a life and a career as a schoolmaster, and to follow the different ways in which his pupils had developed afterwards, in ways he had influenced; and how sad it was that sometimes today the motives and achievements of such teachers are denigrated. Reading it reminded me of just how important an influence this wise and dedicated man had had on me.

On a different note, one of the things that I lacked in my own education which I have always regretted, and on which I was therefore pretty hot when I was Secretary of State, is that I did not do any science. At that time, if you were a scholar, which I was, you had the opportunity to move faster ahead and to specialize more in the arts. As a result I had no formal scientific education. There were also teachers at university, both in history and in political economy, as economics was described within the department ...

PR   Adam Smith's original term?

JM   Well, yes you are right. It was Professor Nisbet who, in some respects – only in some respects – most of all in thinking about social policy from an economic point of view – had a strong influence on me. He was not an econometrician, so I never went down that route in economics. But I also have to say that I've learnt a great deal more about economics since I left university in every practical way possible. Professor Norman Gash, the authority on Robert Peel, also influenced me. I found his lectures absolutely absorbing.

PR   His book on Peel is excellent.

JM   It is a marvellous book. When you become a member of the Cabinet you are asked to give a book to the library at No.10. I was surprised to discover Norman Gash's book wasn't there, so I was very pleased and proud indeed to present it and to let him know that I'd done so.

PR   A fine choice.

JM   So there you are, I have mentioned several teachers who influenced me, and I could have mentioned many others. I really do very strongly believe that good teachers can have a profound influence on people's developments.

PR   You certainly seem to remember your education with real affection.

JM   Yes, very much so.

PR   What do you remember of your days as an undergraduate? You told me earlier that you had initially wanted to be an advocate?

JM   Originally, I thought I wanted to be a Scottish advocate, which, as you know, is the equivalent of an English barrister. I suppose that there were a number of reasons for this. I was attracted to the law and I was involved in a great deal of debating at school. The two interests were not unrelated. But, in my second year at university, my views began to change. I was a scholar, so, after successfully completing the first two years, I moved on to the honours course. As I said earlier, I had been overwhelmed by my first encounter with economics, so I took economics honours.

That decision changed everything. I got involved in politics and, by a stroke of luck, was able to represent the university at the National Federation of Conservative University Associations.

Eventually I became chairman of the Federation, and that helped me to decide that I wanted to try and widen my horizons beyond Scotland.

PR   Had you decided by then that you would make a career in politics?

JM   No.

PR   Politics was your third career move, wasn't it? Had you not been a journalist and then a merchant banker before this?

JM   I had originally thought I would still want to do law. To make that possible I came to London, to King's College, and began an LLB. As you know, an honours degree in Scottish universities takes four years, so I was facing the prospect of three further years of study. In my second year at King's College I began to feel more and more strongly that I didn't want to be a full-time student any longer. So I became a university administrator and did the third year of my full-time law degree part-time in the evenings.

After graduating, I was attracted away from a career in law by an offer I received to become a journalist. This was on the editorial staff of *New Society*, which is no longer in existence but was then starting up as the sister paper to *New Scientist*. I was one of the first members of the editorial staff. After I had been there about a year I got a telephone call from Michael Fraser, later Lord Fraser, who was then the head of the Conservative Research Department, inviting me to lunch. He was looking for a second special assistant (now known as special advisers) to Sir Alec Douglas-Home, who was then Prime Minister – Nigel Lawson being the first special assistant. It was a most fascinating period, and it got me into politics.

PR   What is the attraction of politics? I have to admit that reading for a degree in politics cured me completely of any desire to become a politician.

JM   It has its attractions. It offers a very, very full life. Its one real penalty lies in what this means for family life. You don't get enough time. I say this in retrospect – you don't get enough time, particularly when the children are young, to be with them because you are so heavily involved in Parliament during the week and in your constituency at the weekends. I hope it hasn't done my children any real harm. But I do regret not having been with them as much as most other fathers could have been. That is one disadvantage. The other lies in the sheer work and hours that it entails, although I have never minded that as much as some.

If there are disadvantages, a life in politics also has its advantages. First, there is service to the community. Representing a constituency as its MP is a great honour. This is something I care about a great deal and on which I spend a great deal of time. Second, the opportunity to help people: I remain totally unpersuaded by the arguments advanced in favour of proportional representation, because I believe fervently that one of the great virtues of the British system is the direct link between the constituency and the Member of Parliament. This really does work. When you become a minister, you have to impress upon every Private Office that you have another job as well. You are not just a minister, you are a Member of Parliament, who might spend much of his time dealing with great affairs of state, but must also go back to the constituency and do a surgery for four hours on a Saturday morning. I have found that helping a constituent with a Social Security problem, or even with drains or whatever difficulty might arise, keeps my feet on the ground. This is one reason why I totally reject the accusation that MPs are out of touch – they are more in touch with what is going on over a wide variety of matters than those who are not involved can easily understand. I should also stress that direct contact with constitutents is also rewarding. Third, there are opportunities to do things at the national level. When I wrote my resignation letter to John Major, I stressed the things that I wanted to achieve when I came into politics. Many of them have happened. This is very rewarding. Fourth, and finally, there is the sheer mental stimulus of it all. Politics touches just about everything. It embraces many different subjects and walks of life, and employs many different skills. You have to run a large department; you have to think about policy; you have to deal with political and policy challenges; you have to communicate through the media; you have to be able to speak in the House of Commons and at endless functions all over the country; you have to be able to get on with people; you have to like people and enjoy discourse with them, and so on. It is all tremendously stimulating. When I sometimes reflect on the pressures of a political life, I also think about how fortunate I am to have enjoyed a series of jobs which have taken me into all sorts of different avenues rather than just one single job.

PR   The fun and the fascination of it all?

JM   The fun and fascination are there too. And, contrary, I think, to some popular belief, and certainly to what the media sometimes put over, you are working with a lot of very stimulating and intelligent people. One of the reasons why you don't get tired at night with the long hours is that the place is working. When I am on holiday, I can fall asleep in front of the television at 10 o'clock as well as anyone else. But, when you are here in the House of Commons at night, you have got several things you want to sort out resulting from what has happened during the day, and you can go and chat to a colleague while you might both be waiting for the vote, and get it sorted out. You are a busy person working with a lot of other busy people, and this makes it a most stimulating environment. I would add one other point which is also, I suppose, true of people who are doing responsible jobs in other walks of life. As a minister, you probably have only half an hour to meet a delegation and sort out some complicated problems. This means that delegation has got to think carefully about what it wants to put over to you. Dealing with people who really know what they are talking about means that you do not waste each other's time. You get to the root of things, and quickly, and I find that very stimulating and challenging.

PR   How did you come to be an MP? Talking to some of the other Education Secretaries, we have found a considerable variety. John Patten told us that the crucial point was when he won a local election by a tiny majority. He reckons that if he had lost this he probably would not have gone into a career in politics. Lord Carlisle said something similar. He had decided to have his name taken off the Conservative party list of candidates when in 1963 Runcorn unexpectedly came up. This was the one seat which he had always wished to represent, and so he changed his mind, and the rest is history. Was there a similar element of serendipity in your case, or did you carefully plan your way into Parliament?

JM   I don't think anyone can 'carefully plan' a career in politics. I suppose I had not thought of politics until I was asked to represent the Conservative Students Association when I was at St Andrew's. After that, I became very interested in politics, and certainly I was stimulated by the people with whom I began mixing in London when I got there. But I still hadn't thought seriously about a career in politics. Then, of course, as I explained, I was recruited to work at No. 10, where I became fascinated by the challenge and the variety of being at the centre. And so after Sir Alec Douglas-Home ceased to be Leader of the Party, I went to work in opposition for Ted Heath, as the head of his private office. That brought me into the centre of politics in a big way. Even so, I still was not sure I would necessarily make a long-term career in politics. There is an element of public affluence and private poverty which is one aspect of a political life. At the time, backroom politics paid very badly, and also I was not seeing much of my children. So in 1968 I decided to move to the City. I had come to realize during the previous three years that it was very important to understand thoroughly what makes an economy tick, particularly the international economy. When I went, I really thought I was going to make a long-term career in the City, but, by late 1973, I found myself, like others, pontificating at lunches and dinners about the economy and its management. It was at that point that I began, quite suddenly, to think that if I really did feel so strongly about these things then I ought to throw my hat into the ring. I was thinking this might take up to five years to achieve, but I was extremely fortunate to win a constituency almost on my first attempt. At the time we did not know South Norfolk at all. But my wife and I absolutely love it, and it was one of the best things that could have happened to us. So, in a sense, I got into Parliament much earlier than I expected or had meant to.

PR   I was interested in your account of the life of an MP. Were you really describing the life of a minister? There are an awful lot of MPs who are not ministers and never become one. In your case you have had five major cabinet jobs over the last nine years. Would your life have been much more disappointing and much less interesting if you too had spent it as a back-bencher or in opposition, as most MPs actually have to do?

JM   I have to be honest and say yes, it would have been much less interesting. I've been very fortunate to have been a minister for fifteen years and a member of the Cabinet for nine years, and that has added a very big extra dimension.

PR   How did you become a cabinet minister?

JM   I was asked!

PR   A fair answer. But it's more complicated than that, isn't it? In *The Downing Street Years*, Margaret Thatcher says of the September 1985 reshuffle that

> At Nigel's [Lawson] request, I replaced Peter Rees with John MacGregor. John had a good financial brain as he had shown as part of the Shadow Treasury Team. Although I considered him very much a Ted Heath man, I had been impressed by his acumen and diligence and felt he would do this demanding job [Chief Secretary to the Treasury] well – which he did.
>
> (1993, p. 420)

Could we talk about the role Nigel Lawson played in advancing you? You had, of course, known him for some time.

JM   Yes, I had, and then for a long time we had little contact with each other. But in opposition we worked very closely on finance Bills together. I've known Nigel for a long time, and very much admire him; I think he was a superb Chancellor. But to answer your main question, Margaret was wrong. If you go back and read the speeches and policies that Ted Heath was talking about when I was head of his private office from 1965 to 1968 you will find that he was advocating then very many of the so-called Thatcherite policies that we followed in the 1980s. On this you may remember Selsdon man?

PR   David Willets makes much the same point in his book on *Modern Conservatism* (1992 London: Penguin). Nigel Lawson may have coined the term 'Thatcherism' in the 1980s, but many of its key ideas predated the Thatcher years.

JM   That's right. I have kept most of the speeches which Ted Heath made in the 1960s, many of which I worked on. They contained ideas and approaches very similar to those we pursued in Margaret's premiership. So Margaret was wrong to imply – if that is what she meant – that I was not wholly behind all that we were doing in the early years before I was Chief Secretary.

PR You held five cabinet positions in nine years – is that rather a lot? You were Education Secretary for less than the 'normal' two years enjoyed by those who have held this post during the post-war era. Is that not rather a little?

JM Yes it is. It is the one major regret of my political life that I did not stay at Education longer. Margaret (and Nigel quotes this in his book) said at the first cabinet meeting following the July 1989 reshuffle, 'This is the Cabinet with which we will now go through to the Election.' I believed that that was going to be the case, and I am sure she did as well. And so I was planning on at least two years as Education Secretary, but of course what happened was that Geoffrey Howe resigned. This was not, of course, in her original plan, and she had to find a new Leader of the House. I was very pleased to be made Leader of the House, but I was very sad to leave Education.

With regard to your wider question, I think myself that there has been a tendency in the past to move ministers around too much. We are all much more aware of the needs of different departments than people outside realize when we move into a new post. Nevertheless you do, I think, ideally, need about three years to carry through the things which you want to achieve. In every cabinet job I've done, I would have liked at least one more year. But the requirements of the parliamentary process, the need to engage a lot of able and ambitious people seeking to expand their careers, the pressures of managing the House and the party, lead to constant demand for change. It is not always possible to have the ideal.

PR You wanted to continue to be Education Secretary, but did you want this post when it was first offered to you? In our conversations with other Education Secretaries we have found some interesting differences on this. Mr Clarke wanted another few months as Health Secretary. John Patten wanted to be Education Secretary so much that he didn't prepare for it because he thought he would never be given the one job above all others which he wanted to do. Mark Carlisle was pleased to be offered the post but would really rather have been at the Home Office. And Lord Joseph, we have been told, probably wanted Education more than any other post. What were your feelings?

JM If initially I had ever contemplated a ministerial career, I would have thought Chief Secretary was the job that most suited me. But if I'd ever asked myself the question, 'What is the ideal job that I'd want to do after that?' Education would certainly have been one of them. Education has had a very high priority in my life. I'm a Scot, and I have a Scottish attitude towards education.

PR   Mrs Thatcher confirms that. She says: 'I was ... happy to appoint John MacGregor, with his Scottish devotion to education, as the right person to deal with the nuts and bolts of making our education reforms work' (1993, p. 598). Nigel Lawson also remarks that you had 'a long standing interest in education and had thought a good deal about it' (1992, p. 606) and describes your appointment as Education Secretary as 'a particularly appropriate choice' (p. 610).

JM   Goodness me, you do read the books thoroughly. I have always had very strong views about the importance of education. My father believed that, like most doctors, he was unlikely to be able to leave us very much in the material sense but that, if he could leave us with a good education, that was the most important thing. That is exactly the attitude I have taken towards my own children. I feel the same very strongly for the nation as a whole, and I was bothered for quite a while in the 1960s and 1970s about our failure to achieve the standards and the technical breadth that other countries were doing. So when the opportunity came to do something about this, I was absolutely delighted.

PR   What were the attractions of being Education Secretary in general and at the time you were appointed in particular? On the face of it, you might not have been appointed Education Secretary at the best of possible times. After all, by the time you went to the DES, the Great Education Reform Act of 1988 was on the statute books, but much potentially unglamorous work remained to be done. As Kenneth Baker puts it:

> The whole movement of reform was rolling forward. However, it was going to take some years before all the changes in the Act could be fully incorporated into the education system. A period of consolidation was now required or, as one commentator put it, 'a really boring Minister, devoid of charisma, short on vision, is just what education needs'.
>
> (1993, p. 252)

Nigel Lawson is less flattering about the Baker legacy and suggests that 'things were still in a somewhat unsatisfactory and untidy condition when Kenneth left the DES ... and it was left to his successor, John MacGregor ... to start to make it work' (1992, p. 610). Margaret Thatcher also seems to have lost confidence in Baker as Education Secretary. She came to believe that

> there was no need for the national curriculum proposals and the testing which accompanied them to have developed as they did. Ken Baker paid far too much attention to the DES, the HMI and progressive educational theorists in his appointments and early decisions; and once the bureaucratic momentum had begun it was difficult to stop.
>
> (1993, p. 597)

She was particularly 'appalled' at the proposals the History Working Group produced in its interim report of July 1989, arguing that

> It put the emphasis on interpretation and enquiry as against content and knowledge. There was insufficient weight given to British history ... I told Ken that there must be major, not just minor changes ... The test would be the final report. By the time this arrived in March 1990 John MacGregor had gone to Education. I thought he would prove more effective than Ken Baker in keeping a grip on how our educational reform proposals were implemented, though I knew that he did not have Ken's special talent for putting our case to the public. On this occasion, however, John MacGregor was far more inclined to welcome the report than I had expected.
>
> (p. 596)

JM   I think she perhaps misunderstood what I was doing – I did try to explain to her from time to time. You have raised a series of issues, so let me try and consider each one.

The first focused on the attractions of being Education Secretary. These are very obvious. First, I have already said I am a profound believer in the importance of education. (My wife, incidentally, is also heavily involved in the educational field, both as a governor and in a variety of other ways. I think she had rather mixed feelings when I became Secretary of State for Education because until then she was the educational expert in our house.)

Second, as I think is widely recognized now, education is of absolutely fundamental importance, not only to the competitive performance of the British economy, and of all firms and everyone in it in a very competitive world, but also to tackling the challenges of technological change. If our young people are going to be able to cope with the world of the future, they need to have a very strong foundation in education. I kept pushing these ideas very hard in the speeches I made as Secretary of State. I was delighted to be able to do so.

Third, on the question of whether it was an interesting period to become Education Secretary. I came to the view very quickly that Kenneth Baker had carried through the major reforms, particularly in the school sector, which were necessary, and that my job was to make them work. That was a big challenge and one which, to my mind, had two phases to it. One, I had to gain the confidence of the very large numbers of good teachers who had become a bit disaffected and were a bit worried about the speed of change. Two, there were a lot of detailed aspects of the policy that were clearly over-complex and perhaps sometimes moving in the wrong direction. Furthermore, I wasn't always happy about some of the people who had been entrusted with achieving this. It was a big challenge to get this side of things right. So, if you like, my task was not to achieve one of those great creative drives forward in policy change, but rather to make a big change in policy actually work. A lot of people said that this is what I had been appointed to do, and that I was probably an appropriate person to do it. So much for schools. On the higher education side, and also on the challenges we were facing post-16, there was a great deal to do both in policy and implementation. I found this fascinating. I would say my time was a creative period for developments in this area: polytechnics became universities; necessary financial reforms were introduced in higher education; and a huge expansion was taking place in higher education.

PR   Your policy on student loans came to fruition.

JM   Loans were an important part of it. As you know, the cost of maintenance grants for students had inevitably been rising fast, with the expansion in numbers. Indeed, we were giving more financial support to students, when you take into account their tuition fees and all the other costs as well, than pretty well any other country in the world. Effectively, tax-payers on much more modest incomes than students would normally hope to have were contributing to the support costs of these students; that did not seem fair. And we did of course build into the scheme safeguards for those who subsequently either did not have careers or were earning less than the average wage. But the student loan scheme was only one part of the many changes that we were taking through. It was actually an exciting period, and that made me all the more sad to leave just at the moment when I was getting all these things moving – I had spent much of my first year doing the creative work on that side of things, and had hoped to build upon it subsequently.

PR   Can we return to some of these issues later? Before doing so, it would be helpful if you would say something about what you see as the thrust of Conservative educational policy since 1979. Could you also comment on the importance of education to Conservative policy-making during these years?

JM   I think education has been very important to us. You must remember that Lady Thatcher was a Secretary of State for Education herself.

PR   This does not seem to have been an experience she remembers with much satisfaction or pleasure.

JM   Well, she wanted to get things moving. To achieve rapid change for all the reasons we have all talked about so often – an emphasis on the development of appropriate people, skills and attitudes – in which training and education are one of the most crucial areas a government must tackle effectively if as a nation we are going to be able to sustain standards of living and quality of life in the years ahead. So it does come back to the Department for Education and to what can be achieved in schools and universities. That part of it,

I think, we have always given a high priority. The fact that in successive public expenditure rounds education has always done pretty well, I think, is an indication of the priority we have given it. Not that the quality of educational output should be judged purely by the amount of money that goes into it. I have never held that view. But money is important in this area. I am particularly proud of the fact that, as you know, when we were first elected in 1979 only one in eight of the relevant age groups went on to higher education. Now it is very nearly one in three: that's been very much part of my political drive from very early days.

You have asked what is distinctive about Conservative educational policies. One of the motivations for my political career has always been the belief in the importance of educational opportunity, and the commitment to the creation of such wider opportunity is very much part of our policies. The other two aspects which I would single out are the emphasis on quality and standards on the one hand, and on variety, choice and diversity on the other.

More generally, let me focus on two things. First, I have always been critical of the way educational thinking developed in the late 1950s and early 1960s under the influence of the teacher training institutions. High on my agenda, had I had longer as Secretary of State for Education, was to look closely at teacher training. I feel that some of the ideas about child-centred learning which were so influential during these years have a lot to answer for with regard to the lowering of standards which has taken place in too many of our primary and secondary schools. I take a fairly strong view of some of the ideas associated with progressivism. If you are not teaching children basic skills to a high standard, and correcting mistakes, they will not have the right foundation and a fair chance for jobs in life afterwards.

Another thing which we have been very keen to do is to tackle the problem of premature specialization. We have also been concerned with improving the opportunities of what is sometimes described as the bottom 40 per cent. Tackling this is, once again, an aspect of our commitment to the creation of genuine wider opportunities and expanding standards.

PR   It has been suggested that you were one of the more popular of contemporary Conservative Education Secretaries with teachers and other educationalists, and that one reason for this was that you were less obsessed than some of your colleagues with tackling the issue of what has been termed 'producer control' head on.

JM   I did not know about my relative popularity. Nobody told me about this at the time, only afterwards! It is one of the penalties of being a politician – nobody ever tells you things like that. But I don't think I was more producer-orientated. What I tried to do, and this is something I have done in every ministerial job which I have held, is to remember that if I was to improve educational standards, if our educational reforms were really to mean something, then it would be necessary to carry those with you upon whom you depend to achieve your results. The same is true in other walks of life. When I was Minister of Agriculture, I was taking farmers through massive reforms which were very necessary, but also painful for a number of them. I went out of my way all the time to go out and explain why they were necessary, and I tried to get them on my side. Now when I came to Education, I very quickly decided that the disaffection that had resulted, partly because of the speed of change, partly because of some of the pay issues, partly because of some of the things that teachers badly misunderstood about Keith Joseph, needed to be tackled. Such things had combined to create a lot of very disaffected teachers, even though, as I also knew, many of them agreed with our reforms and understood what we were trying to do. So I set out in my first year quite deliberately to go and meet them all over the place. I went to most of the teacher conferences (I didn't go to the NUT), and so on. I wanted to get them to appreciate what we were trying to do and to understand what their problems were, so that we could work together more effectively. Now, all this may have led to the perception that I was producer-orientated, and one or two newspapers certainly seemed to think so, but they misunderstood entirely what I was trying to do.

I have mentioned Keith Joseph, and I would like to say a bit more on this. I was getting from my own constituents a number of critical letters during Keith Joseph's period as Education Secretary, suggesting that he undervalued and even devalued the contributions of teachers. I found this constantly irritating because, as you may know, in the House and everywhere else, he frequently paid tribute to the excellent work that teachers did. But this was hardly ever reported by the media. I had something of the same problem. I noticed that every time I paid a tribute to the teachers in a recorded interview, it never appeared. So I thought the only way to make sure they knew I valued what they were doing was to get round among the teacher profession myself.

PR   Kenneth Baker describes Sir Keith as

> a kind, generous and courtly person. Not a worldly man. Keith was never involved in intrigues or secret meetings. He found much of the small change of politics tedious and uncongenial. His intellect made him one of the mainsprings of Thatcherism and her leading guru, although opponents less charitably dubbed him 'the mad monk'.
>
> (1993, p. 162)

He also says, 'Keith gave me some good advice, "Don't make the same mistake I did of attacking the teachers"' (p. 161).

JM I think of this as the other way round – always try to praise the dedication and contribution of the good teachers. Even so, I never hesitated to criticize those teachers who diminished the concept of high standards, and whose ranting and raving on television did a great deal of harm to the teaching profession.

PR In preparation for this meeting I reread our interviews with Kenneth Clarke and John Patten. I was struck by their belief that a key characteristic of Conservative educational policy reform in recent times is to be found in a shift in emphasis from a stress on input to output measures in determining improvements in quality.

JM I think I said that myself earlier, when I was talking about the increased amount of money spent on education – I would not want that to lead to the belief that I subscribe to the feeling that only higher funding produces better results.

PR If Nigel Lawson is to be believed, this may not be the view entirely taken by your predecessor. Having described Kenneth Baker as 'a most civilised man with an agreeably sunny disposition', he goes on to claim that 'not even his greatest friends would describe him as either a profound political thinker or a man with a mastery of detail. His instinctive answer to any problem is to throw glossy PR and large quantities of money at it' (1992, p. 606).

JM I don't know about that. But funding is obviously important in determining, for example, take-up, particularly in higher education. It seemed to me that if we were going to get the expansion in higher education that we all sought, it would be necessary for us to be realistic and also to look at what was the case in most other countries. We found they didn't have the student/staff ratios we have here; nor did students have the ability routinely to go to residential universities anywhere and have their living expenses (as well as their tuition fees) almost totally funded by the state. We had to change that culture because there just wasn't sufficient funding available to achieve the expansion. I do actually think, too, that one of the reforms we introduced has been much underestimated – that was to do with putting more of funding of universities on to a tuition-fee basis rather than on to a *per capita* tuition-fee basis, so that funds followed the ability to attract students to particular courses.

PR I asked you about the prominence that the Conservative party gave education and education issues since 1979. One performance indicator for this might be the amount of space allocated to educational issues in the various election manifestos of the party. I think there were only about six lines on education in 1979 and less than a page in 1983. In 1987, seven or eight pages were devoted to education, and only then would it be appropriate, as Baker argues, to hail the party's 'education plans' as the 'flagship of the Manifesto' (1993, p. 184). It seems that Mrs Thatcher may also share such a view, since she is on record as saying that one of her great regrets was that it took the party so long to get round to really trying to do something about education. From all this, might it be argued that the Conservatives did not allocate education a high priority until the mid 1980s?

JM   I would have to check back. I am struck by your manifesto points.

PR   You were in overall charge of putting together the 1987, manifesto were you not?

JM   Yes, I was. More precisely, I was the member of the Cabinet who masterminded the whole thing. But of course one has to acknowledge that the emphasis it gave to education stemmed partly from Margaret Thatcher herself and partly from her Education Secretary, because they provided a lot of the input. However, it illustrates the prominence I gave personally to educational issues. In fact, we had all held that view for some time.

PR   It is often said that during its first two administrations the government concerned itself centrally with getting the economy right ...

JM   That is true.

PR   And only once that was done, did Health, Education and other social issues come to the top of your agenda.

JM   I think that may be true. We came in faced with the need to work our way out of a recession. We had a variety of economic reforms to which, quite rightly, we gave priority, and there were also the trade union reforms – all this occupied a large part of that first Parliament. At the time, I was myself in an economic job as Minister for Small Businesses in the Department of Industry. I really threw myself into that, because I felt we weren't going to achieve anything significant or lasting unless we achieved a turnaround in the economy and recreated the entrepreneur ethic. So economic policies and, at one crucial point, the Falklands War, did dominate that very early period. And, of course, there is one other factor. As a former Leader of the House, I know that in any one parliamentary session there is a limit to what new legislation, particularly major Bills, you can take through. You therefore have to prioritize. Trade union legislation was certainly a priority in those early years.

PR   I think there have been nineteen Education Acts since 1979. That is utterly unprecedented, isn't it? Even so, there is little dispute as to which is the most important. Who should get the principal credit for the 1988 Act?

JM   In the end one has to say Kenneth Baker. A lot of other people made it possible, but Kenneth was the driving force.

PR   Some argue its key underlying ideas were largely thrashed out by others. Kenneth Baker acknowledges that 'Keith Joseph had planted many of the seeds for what would become elements of the Education Reform Bill'. Nevertheless, Baker does not underestimate his own significance, commenting that

> I realised that the scale of the problem could only be tackled by a coherent national programme, and time was not on our side. I knew what I wanted in the package, and knew I would have to drive it through my Department, persuade the Prime Minister and colleagues that it should be adopted in the form I wanted, and then steer a major piece of legislation through Parliament and around all the obstacles which the vested educational interests would throw in its way ... To be successful, a politician has to have both a clear vision and the determination to pursue it.
>
> (1993, pp. 164–5)

Conversely, Mrs Thatcher does not seem disposed to overestimate the role of her new Education Secretary. In describing how the proposal for reform set out in the 1987 Election Manifesto were achieved, she comments that

> Largely as a result of work done by Brian Griffiths, it was already clear what these should be. There must be a core curriculum to ensure that the basic subjects were taught to all children. There must be graded tests or benchmarks against which children's knowledge should be judged. All schools should have greater financial autonomy. There must be a new *per capita* funding system which along with 'open enrolment', would mean that successful schools were financially rewarded and enabled to expand. There must be more power for headteachers. Finally, and most controversially, schools must be given the power to apply for what at this stage we were describing as 'direct grant status' ... outside the control of the Local Education Authorities.
>
> (1993, pp. 570–1)

Nigel Lawson also offers a revealing account of how these policy ideas began to be translated into policy practice. He notes that

> The Cabinet Sub-Committee on Education Reform proceeded in a way unlike any other on which I have served. The process would start by Margaret putting forward various ideas ... she had the Number 10 Policy Group heavily involved in the subject, and its then head, Brian Griffiths, was engaged in little else at this time – and there would be a general discussion ... At the end of it, Margaret would sum up and give Kenneth his marching orders. He would then return to the next meeting with a worked out proposal which bore little resemblance to what everyone else recalled as having been agreed at the previous meeting, and owed rather more to his officials at the DES. After receiving a metaphorical handbagging for his pains, he would then come back with something that corresponded more closely to her ideas, but as often as not without any attempt by his Department to work them out properly, a gap which I tried to fill as best I could by having John Anson do the work, which I would then present at the next meeting. This procedure was repeated on most of the aspects of the reform. Kenneth remained in unruffled good humour throughout the process, and the outcome was the raft of proposals that appeared in the 1987 Conservative manifesto ...
>
> (1992, pp. 609–10)

JM   I wasn't involved in any of these discussions. This is an aspect of the way in which the Cabinet works that is often misunderstood. A lot of people underestimate the extent to which there are usually lengthy discussions of future policy well before the media cottons on to what's happening. Even so, the reason I hesitated when you asked me who was the major influence over the 1988 Education Reform Act was precisely because of the kinds of points you have just made. There were so many people involved in one way or another.

PR   In reading about all this, I found one thing particularly strange. Nigel Lawson, in effect, seems to admit going behind Kenneth Baker's back to the Prime Minister to put his ideas for educational reform to her. She then agreed he might do this and, in describing what happens next, he writes

> Back at the Treasury, I called a meeting with John MacGregor ... [and others]. I warned that they were not to breathe a word to anyone in the Department of Education: not only would they be unhelpful, but I had little doubt that Kenneth would be more inclined to embrace an initiative which he believed had emerged from Margaret than he would one that emanated from me.
>
> (1992, pp. 607–8)

Is this normal practice? Did it not amount to encouraging the Prime Minister to take advice from a third party without the knowledge of the person who should have been her principal policy adviser? And how does this square with Lawson's explanation for his own resignation? As far as I can understand it, Mr Lawson resigned because he objected, in principle, to the Prime Minister taking confidential advice from a third party which might be at variance with his own. Furthermore, in this instance, unlike, perhaps, in the Baker case, Mr Lawson, at least, knew that Sir Alan Walters was offering such advice.

JM   It is not a parallel situation. Nigel was a cabinet minister, and a very senior one. In any case, I wouldn't really wish to comment, partly because I can't remember the context, and of course, what one does not know is how much Nigel talked to Kenneth, or, for that matter, how far he expressed his views in other fora within Cabinet.

PR   In looking at the 1988 Act, how important do you regard it?

JM   I think it has to be regarded as one of the most important reforms of recent times. I say this, not least because it introduced the National Curriculum, which I think is a fundamental and necessary change. I have been interested to listen to some of the comments on the GCSE results over the last month or so, and I've been struck by some of the examiners who are saying that the improvements in pupil performance we are now seeing is, in considerable part, attributable directly to the influence of the National Curriculum now beginning to come through. There are also other vital improvements as a result of the reforms, such as the publication of school results; the emphasis now on comparisons; on parents wanting to make use of such information. Parents have, of course, always been very interested in their children's performance, but there is perhaps rather a more public focus on it now, and we have given them the information, the access and the opportunities to make use of it. I also believe that LMS, which started in my own county of Norfolk, will bring big benefits; and then there are the choice-related reforms like grant-maintained schools, which I believe are all going to have a very beneficial impact.

PR   It's sometimes argued that there is a fundamental ambiguity in the idea of greater autonomy through LMS and GMS, and greater central control through the National Curriculum. Do you feel that there is a genuine ambiguity here?

JM   On the National Curriculum, I inherited several policy groups as well as the NCC and SEAC, and I was very concerned about the prescriptive nature of some of the proposals with which I was being presented. This was particularly marked at 14-plus, but, nevertheless, I was worried about it at earlier Key Stages too. So I devoted a good deal of my time talking to teachers and others in the educational field to see what changes we needed to make in order to prevent things from becoming too prescriptive. But I think that is a separate concern from LMS. LMS was much more about financial control and the way in which decisions were taken on the deployment of funds within schools. On this, it has always struck me as ludicrous that highly experienced and responsible headteachers were having to waste an enormous amount of time making requests to County Hall for quite trivial sums of money, with months sometimes passing before anything was done. Rather than this we should try to create the kinds of systems which enable heads to manage, as happens in most other walks of life. There are great benefits from LMS from that point of view, but that is entirely different from the issue of the National Curriculum.

PR   True, but that raises another issue that I would like to discuss with you. You have talked about the need to free headteachers to manage, but very few of the powers redistributed in the 1988 Act are directly given to the heads – nearly all are given to the governing body.

JM   When I talked about heads, I may have been guilty of using a kind of shorthand in which I am speaking of the need for a more localized form of management. As it happens, it was during my period in office that for the first time governing bodies were given real powers, and initially it was clear that some were finding it difficult to adjust, and some began to complain about the burden of responsibility which they carried. I was never very sympathetic. It seemed to me that the problems were not insurmountable, and that people of quality would learn to be able to deal with their new responsibilities quite quickly. I think what it revealed was that we didn't have enough governors who were able to do that. We learnt of the need to have chairmen of governors who could give an appropriate lead. But I would not wish to exaggerate the problem. There are a lot of schools who have very good governors. I also think the evidence is beginning to demonstrate that in the vast number of cases the right kind of relationship has been developed between the chairman of governors and the headteacher. A mark of the good head is that he or she knows exactly how to make use of a good board of governors. A case in point often exists in the case of the decision to seek grant-maintained status. In very many cases this comes initially from the head, and then the head and the chairman of governors, having been persuaded, work together. I would guess that in the great majority of cases, whether of LMS or GMS, in practice it is the head who exercises the greater influence in the exercise of the autonomy now available to schools. Of course, it continues to be necessary for a head to make sure that he or she carries the board of governors with them. I also found that a lot of heads have been active in encouraging their governing bodies to recruit new governors with the skills that they knew were necessary. That was a big challenge, and I spent a lot of my time with industry trying to persuade them to encourage their people to go on governing bodies. There has been a good deal of success on this.

PR You seem to put the National Curriculum as first in importance of all the reforms which have followed the 1988 Act. Have you been satisfied with the way in which it has been developed and implemented? And what about assessment?

JM Assessment has, I think, been a source of some of the most difficult problems which we have faced. It was always going to be the case that carrying through a major reform like the introduction of a national curriculum and system of assessment was going to have teething troubles and was going to take time before it settled down. I am also very conscious that there is a belief that the system has had to cope with too much change and that this has left teachers feeling over-burdened. I must say I did tend towards the view, as I said earlier, that it was the National Curriculum which was in danger of being developed over-prescriptively. I was not an expert in some areas in which subject policy groups reported and we then had to implement. I did worry about the extent to which – and perhaps I am being rather unkind in putting it in this way – some educational experts saw the National Curriculum as the opportunity to put into practice their own pet views and pet theories. During my time as Education Secretary, I had to grapple with these pressures, and to put a break on the over-prescriptive zeal of the educational establishment.

That applies to the work of the curriculum working groups, and the way in which individual subjects were being developed, but also to the curriculum as a whole and the difficulties of finding space in the school week for all of the ten subjects. So I spent much of my time easing that burden, particularly as it applied to secondary schools.

On the other hand, I did not share the view of a lot of primary school teachers that they were vastly over-burdened with work. I also felt there was undoubtedly a need to widen the range of subjects and improve the standards. I found that good primary school heads and teachers who had complained to me when I first became Secretary of State about the burdens they faced, after a few months were beginning to tell me, 'Well, now we have really got into it we find that we're already doing a lot of what is proposed anyway. We understand it, and it is not as difficult as we had thought.' There is always a balance to be struck. There were two areas that did greatly concern me, I am not sure we've got these right yet. The first was Key Stage 3, where the attempt to cram a quart into a pint pot was at its most apparent. We clearly had to try to ease the pressures here. The second was post-16. I was very impressed by some of the suggestions that were coming from elsewhere, and not least those reflecting my Scottish background, from Eric Anderson, who advocated a mix of the kind of specialization to be found within the English system with that of the broader Scottish Highers approach. That was another reason I regretted leaving when I did, because I was very anxious to see if I could find workable solutions to these problems.

PR   What did you make of the DES? How would you rate it in comparison with some of the other Departments in which you have worked?

JM   There were good people there. Most of them were very hard working. A few were not so good, but that is inevitable in a large department. You have to learn whom to listen to. I did also think that, as a department, it was rather more insular from the rest of Whitehall than the other departments I'd been in. This may be partly because an awful lot of people in Education and in the department feel that this is a closed world. That 'You lot outside do not understand what we do.' That 'It would be better to just leave us to get on with things with the minimum of interference.' I thought it was important to break down that feeling. I tried to do this in various ways. One of these ways was to do all I could to foster the development of industry/education links.

I did also feel that, in the enthusiasm to carry through the reforms, particularly those to do with the National Curriculum and its assessment, the officials badly underestimated the effect which all this had on the teaching profession. Since, frankly, ministers travel about much more than civil servants, I think it is the job of ministers to achieve a balance in terms of the pace and scope of reforms and the pressures which this entails for teachers. Let me give you an example of what I mean, drawn from my early days as the Minister. If you recall, teachers were saying: 'We are absolutely inundated with bumf.' Some of this, of course, was coming from outside the Department. It was coming from a whole range of educational bodies in the private sector who were taking advantage, perfectly understandably, of the opportunity to promote their own products. But a lot was coming from and through the Department. While this was happening, some of my officials were saying: 'We are not over-burdening people.' There is a tendency among officials as a whole to write the vast reams that seem to justify their existence, and for them not to realize the effect that they are having. So I simply had the technique of putting each publication going out to schools from the Department on my window-sill in order to see how that pile was growing and growing, and growing. It let me see just how much we were putting out. There is also the bureaucratic tendency to do things that are unnecessary. There was one occasion – do you remember? – when we had two sets of forms which every teacher had to fill in at the end of the week for each subject. I asked the civil servants to justify why we were asking for these forms which took a great deal of time to fill up. One of the answers that came back was: 'Well, if we're asked a question in Parliament, Minister, as to how much time is being spent on history, geography and so on in schools – unless we ask these teachers to complete these forms, we won't know.' I thought, blow that, that's not a very important question, given the workload we put on the teaching profession. So I got the teachers' unions to come in and have a debate with my officials about the forms. I was convinced that the unions had got it right, so we just scrapped one of them. But having said this, I do think there are a lot of very dedicated people at the Department, and that most are dedicated by a desire to make the reforms work.

PR   What we have heard from some of your colleagues echoes what you've said. That the DES is a department isolated from the rest of Whitehall which has unusually close relationships with the profession it serves.

JM   I found a lot of signs of that. But it is also important that the profession goes on establishing better links with the world outside education, and I tried to encourage that, both in the Department of Industry and at Education.

PR   Some of your colleagues consider that it has tended to see itself as part of the educational establishment. Some have also expressed reservations about the quality of support that they have had from the Department when compared with that which they received in the Home Office, the Treasury, the Department for the Environment, or whatever. I suppose that's not really surprising …

JM I wouldn't put it as strongly as that. I rest on what I said earlier, that in every large department there are some very good people, and there are some who are simply not good enough. As part of our reforms of the civil service, we are beginning to sort that out, so that, as in every other walk of life, the not so good don't move ahead to further promotion. You must make sure that you get the right people into the key jobs. In thinking about the Department, I prefer to put it that way, but certainly the insularity did strike me. And also – and you will know very much more about this than I do – the world of education is full of people who wish to propagate their own views. It means that you constantly move into a maelstrom of argument, and that was particularly true of the debates on the reports of the History Working Group and its proposals for the history curriculum.

PR How would you judge yourself as a Secretary of State? What kind of Secretary of State were you?

JM I left certainly no more than half way through the job, and probably less even than that. I felt I had completed the first phase of doing something about making the National Curriculum workable. I had also completed the first phase of getting through the reforms on LMS, on the grant-maintained schools and the CTCs. I had done a great deal on the higher education side. I hope that I had begun to gain the support of the good teachers in the profession. But there was more to be done; the next stage was going to be the one that was really going to matter, and I wasn't able to complete it.

PR What was it like working for the one Prime Minister who had been Education Secretary? From all accounts, she was no great fan of the DES. In his book Kenneth Baker reports that she warned him about the Department, and he concludes that

> She clearly had a searing time dealing with the officials there when she had herself been the Education Secretary from 1970 to 1974 and she believed that these officials had thwarted Keith too. I remember her saying to Keith at a meeting in 1983, 'You have an awful Department'.
>
> (1993, p. 161)

JM I can understand why a lot of these criticisms were made. I am not the sort of person who in public statements likes to just criticize people for the sake of it, but I was fairly constantly frustrated at the slowness with which things happened in the Department on the one hand, and the over-burdensomeness and lack of worldly realism which existed on the other. This in part explains why I spent so much time trying to find out what was actually going on in the schools, and to see what I could do to get the kind of balance I talked about earlier right. So I understand quite a number of the criticisms. I think it would have been a very good thing for the Department if a lot more of its people had spent some time outside the civil service. That could be also helpful for schools. In this context I was very much in favour of the reforms which encouraged late entrants to enter the teaching profession. They could bring a lot of experience with them which would be useful to schools. I would also wish that more members of the Department had spent more time in other departments like the Department of Industry. One or two of the best people who were in the fairly senior ranks of the DES had been in the Treasury, and that is a Department which is full of very good people – of real high-flyers.

Interestingly enough, the Prime Minister and I didn't have any of the debates of the sort described in the books on the creation of the Education Reform Act which you quoted to me earlier. I had no fiery debates with Margaret on education. I did when I was in one or two other Departments, but not in Education. I think she was very supportive of what I was trying to do in higher education – such as the creation of the student loans scheme. She was happy for me to get on with it. I occasionally tried to explain to her why I was trying to regain the confidence of the good teachers. I fear she sometimes misunderstood that, and didn't realize that I was driving ahead with the reforms.

PR   Margaret Thatcher makes a number of points about your period in office as Education Secretary in her book. She was unhappy about the development of the National Curriculum under Kenneth Baker, and suggests

> John MacGregor, under constant pressure from me, did what he could. He made changes to the History curriculum. He insisted that the Sciences could be taught separately. He stipulated that at least 30% of GCSE English should be tested by written examination, yet the whole system is very different from that which I originally envisaged.
>
> (1993, p. 597)

JM   I would make two points on this. The first point is that the constant pressure from her was on history, and not on anything else.

PR   I think she commented on this that 'John MacGregor was far more inclined to welcome the report than I had expected'.

JM   There was a problem on history, and, frankly, I started to get pretty sick of it towards the end because it assumed an importance out of all proportion. Brian Griffiths is a great friend of mine, and we get on very well together, but he felt very strongly about history, and I spent a good deal of time trying to take him along with how we were trying to find a solution to the history issue. You will never satisfy the different sides of the history debate; it was typically academic. This did create quite a bit of toing and froing – quite a bit of friction.

But only in this area. I think on everything else I was going ahead as *I* wanted to do, and as she wanted to do.

The second point I would make is this, I do agree with the point she makes about progressive theorists and so on. That was a problem I grappled with, particularly in some of the appointments which had been made by my predecessor to SEAC and elsewhere, and to the National Curriculum Council. That is what was at the back of my mind when I was describing to you that I thought that things had become over-prescriptive and over-burdensome. I did what I could to pull that back. But the first membership had already been decided by the time I got there, and I wasn't able to make any significant changes in the composition of NCC and SEAC until the first round of tenures had expired. Then I looked for the kind of people I wanted to put on to these bodies, and, incidentally, sought in particular some people from outside the educational world. They were very definitely my own appointments. They were in line with what Margaret was saying was needed.

PR   Do you think she was satisfied with what you were doing? You mentioned that Geoffrey Howe's resignation forced an unexpected cabinet reshuffle, and since she needed a new Leader of the House you had to move from the DES. Do you think that was her only reason?

JM   You'll have to ask *her*. I would merely stress the point that we did not have many confrontations about education policies. The main one was on the History Working Group. Whether she felt that I was wrong to re-establish contact with some of the very good teaching unions or not, I don't know. But I feel very strongly myself that you don't achieve results unless you carry the people who must implement them with you. I knew out there we had potentially an awful lot of allies, and I was determined to make that very contact and that bridge with them.

PR   She says in her autobiography that

> I already knew my ideal solution: Norman Tebbit back in the Cabinet as Education Secretary ... He was tough, articulate and trustworthy. He would have made a superb Education Secretary who could sell his programme to the country and wrong-foot the Labour party.

And even though Tebbit refused this offer, she 'still wanted a new face at Education, where John MacGregor's limitations as a public spokesman were costing us dear in an area of great importance' (1993, p. 835). Do you remember that?

JM   Yes, I don't think they were costing us dear.

PR   There is a suspicion, widely shared within the education profession, that you were moved because you began to be seen as too willing to listen to them. You were perceived as being more friendly than the great majority of your colleagues, and that this ultimately cost you the job.

JM   Look, if Geoffrey Howe had not resigned there wouldn't have been a change anyway, and I would have been able to complete the second half of what I wanted and set out to do. But I *strongly* disagree with the notion this was, quote, 'costing us dear', unquote. There may have been one or two strident commentators and one or two newspapers who said this, but that was all. I firmly believe that if you are going to get results, you have got to talk to the people who bear the brunt of implementing a reform. The key is to know which people are the right people to talk to, and that takes a bit of time to learn when you first come into a new area. I firmly believe you have got to talk to, and learn from, the people who are sympathetic to what you are trying to do, and can help you through some of the problems that arise in the implementation of any complex reform. I don't regret that I did this for one minute: I think that was a strength. I also very firmly believe that our objectives and the broad principles of the framework we sought to implement were wholly right. Interestingly Margaret's comments were restricted almost entirely to some parts of the National Curriculum, and not to the many other important reforms we were also carrying through. For example, I spent quite a lot of my time on CTCs because it was proving, by that stage, a time-consuming process to get the last CTCs up and running, both from the point of view of getting the sponsors and finding premises. I came to the conclusion that we had almost run out of steam on the original CTC concept, and had to find a new way of carrying that particular reform forward. And that's just another example of an area that Margaret did not mention. But across the whole range of the reforms, including those in higher education, there was no disagreement between us. Furthermore, these reforms were happening and they were working.

PR   Can we turn to the grant-maintained schools? There seems to have been important differences among those involved at the highest level in determining policy on this. I get the impression from Kenneth Baker that he never saw this as universally applicable. Rather, he saw grant-maintained schools as being made up of a limited number of high-quality institutions which would act as catalysts, forcing the pace of improvement in the rest of the system. It seems fairly clear that this was not what Margaret Thatcher wished, especially for the secondary sector. From time to time she would make statements to the media in which she made her impatience clear and which seem designed to force the pace of reform or to shape it in ways she approved of. She admits to doing the same kind of thing on the National Curriculum over, for example, proposals for the history curriculum, of which she disapproved. As she says:

> I had become thoroughly exasperated with the way in which the national curriculum proposals were being diverted from their original purposes. I made my reservations known in an interview I gave to the *Sunday Telegraph* in early April (1989). In this I defended the principles of the national curriculum but criticised their detailed prescription in other than the core subjects which had now becomes its least reasonable feature. My comments were greeted with consternation by the DES.
>
> (1993, p. 596)

She seems to have enjoyed such public attempts to embarrass the DES. For some time, for example, she used to talk of "'independent state schools" – a phrase that the DES hated and kept trying to remove from my speeches in favour of the bureaucratically flavoured "Grant Maintained Schools"' (p. 571).

JM On grant-maintained schools, I certainly was much more enthusiastic than Kenneth Baker. I was very impressed by the enthusiasm and rejuvenation in morale that was being achieved by the early GM schools. I organized the first conference of grant-maintained schools at which we had present the chairmen and headteachers of the first 20 schools. It was in Leicester, and I remember it as a very rewarding experience. I wanted to give them this public support because I knew some were having real problems with their former LEA and were being forced into quarrels with their peers in other schools. They were put under pressure by some outrageous behaviour, and yet they were dedicated to the concept of GM status for the sake of the school. In one sense, of course, GMS is just moving a bit further on from LMS, which, when I arrived, was still at an early stage. I became convinced GMS reform was very important, and I put a great deal of emphasis on it. Even so, I knew it was bound to take time to build up the numbers, in part because of the complexity of the processes that had to be gone through, and in part because it was necessary for a number of GM schools to be seen to be working well if others were to take the same route. But I put a huge emphasis on GMS, and I have to say I have been delighted to see what's been happening since.

PR Even so, has some of the momentum now gone out of the GM movement?

JM In the early days was it was very easy for those hostile to the GM concept to mount an attack which was sometimes well-financed and scaremongering. There was also a lot of peer pressure from heads, other teachers and local education authority councillors and officials against those trying to get GM status. They were often very isolated, and I know they felt very much on their own. It needed, therefore, a determined chairman with good backing from the governing body, and a determined headteacher to persist. I still think that the idea of a parental ballot was right. I do not think that the momentum has gone out of the GM movement, with over a thousand schools now grant-maintained; incidentally, I was delighted that the thousandth school was in my own constituency! I always thought that some of the press comment, which tended to suggest that the concept would only be judged a success if well over half of all schools were GM, was quite wrong. By no means all schools would wish to take it up, but I am confident a lot more will. I believe that the sector will, by the next election, have reached a critical mass which will make it a difficult reform to reverse. There are so many who have seen the positive benefits and who are extremely enthusiatic about them.

PR   Kenneth Clarke seems to think that things have gone rather quiet on this issue for a bit, and that is what the DES wants to happen.

JM   Well during my time I pushed very hard for it. Even so, I do think it is true that there were people in the DES who didn't favour this reform, and who were always trying to squeeze it out. When I was critical earlier, that was one of the areas which I had in mind. I believe the answer in such cases is usually to put a good person in charge of the reform. This is what I did, and so we overcame that problem. But I was, and am, very strongly in favour of GMS.

PR   Looking back on the reforms, have they been successful?

JM   We always knew they would take five to ten years to implement, and a good deal longer still to achieve their full potential. That particularly applies to the National Curriculum although, as we are now seeing, it is already achieving a steady improvement in standards and results. Most of the other reforms have already had highly beneficial and noticeable results.

PR   Some argue that such improvements are more apparent than real. It is sometimes suggested that although more students are achieving higher grades, the standards which those grades represent are dropping. This is a view that has been expressed by some of your very senior colleagues.

JM   Yes, I know the concern about that. One has always got to be alert to the dangers that it might be happening, and I am sure it does happen in some cases, when you get such an expansion in numbers going on to the sixth form and then into universities. But I was always struck by those in the university world whose judgement I respected stressing to me that, by and large, there has not been a dilution, in standards, despite the expansion. I may add as a footnote that I do worry sometimes about the low grades of A-level results which some universities are prepared to accept for some courses.

PR   Is this not inevitable if the age cohort attending university rises from 8 per cent to 30 per cent?

JM   Yes, it probably is to a certain extent. I worry a bit about some of the softer courses that are sometimes now being offered. I remain a rather strong believer in rigour in standards. A way of tackling it is through the tuition-fee element, so that universities which really are attracting the most successful students and are shown to be doing a good job get more of the funds. But I think that overall this worry about standards is over-done. Most of us who have children who are going through, or who have recently gone through, the system are aware of the pressures they have had to face and how well they have responded. I think sometimes the criticisms are related to recollections of past days when only small numbers actually did A levels. Don't you?

PR   I do. I think such criticisms can be very dispiriting for the profession ...

JM   ... and for the children ...

PR   ... and for the children and for their parents.

JM   I had to deal with that when I was Secretary of State because, as Gillian Shepherd is finding out, exactly the same 'August stories' were appearing when I was Education Secretary, with the kind of dispiriting effect we have talked about. But to some extent this is a media issue. August is a period when there isn't that much news. Few journalists are keen to print good news, to the point that some struggle hard to find any kind of bad twist they can give to good news. This is something we all suffer from. I was in Scotland recently on a visit and was about to do a radio interview. I was asked what I was doing that day. I was going to go and visit a freight terminal for which the people in Scotland had been asking for a long time, and which links Scotland via the Channel Tunnel direct to continental markets. I said to the journalist, 'I hope you will ask me some questions about this, because it really is good news.' He looked at me and said: 'Show me a journalist who's interested in good news.' Of course he didn't ask me about it. There is an element of that in what gets said about education. If an educational guru is prepared to say standards have fallen, he will get much more attention than his colleagues who say standards are being maintained or improved. But you're right about the dispiriting effect. It is certainly something that one's always got to be very conscious of.

PR   What aspects of the reforms do you think are irreversible?

JM   I think that we are going to see the same as in many other aspects of policy, that the Labour party, having opposed so much of what we carried through in the 1980s, have now come around to the recognition that we were right, and will not attempt to reverse most of the reforms. Listening to Tony Blair's speeches recently, I have been struck by the extent to which he is claiming that the Labour party would pursue policies which, when I and other Secretaries of State were taking them though Parliament in the 1980s, were being bitterly opposed by Labour spokesmen. So I believe that the reforms in relation to higher education, the National Curriculum, local management of schools – I hope even grant-maintained schools, as they come to see their virtues – will all now be secure for a long time ahead. This is just another example of how the Conservatives won the battle of political ideas in the 1980s, and of how politics have now moved firmly on to our ground.

CHAPTER 6

Kenneth Clarke

WITH BRIAN SHERRATT

Kenneth Clarke was born in 1940 and educated at Nottingham High School and Gonville and Caius College Cambridge, where he studied law. He was called to the Bar in 1963 and practised from Birmingham before taking silk in 1980. He has served in a variety of junior ministerial positions and has worked as a Whip. Between 1974 and 1976 he was Opposition Spokesman on Social Services. After spells as Paymaster General and Chancellor of the Duchy of Lancaster he was appointed Secretary for State for Health in 1988 before moving as Secretary of State for Education and Science, where he served for eighteen months between 1990 and 1992. Since then he has been Home Secretary (1992–92), and is currently Chancellor of the Exchequer.

27 June 1994

KC   How nice to see you again. I'm trying to remember my last job but one, but I greatly regret that I didn't stay longer at Education, just as I greatly regret that I didn't stay longer as Home Secretary. I did a little over a year as Education Secretary, and I enjoyed it enormously. I expected to continue after the election, and I would have liked to have seen through a good solid stint of policy-making of the kind that I had had at Health.

BS   Well, could we begin, Chancellor, with how you developed your own ideas and attitudes towards education – could you tell me something about your own schooling – I have read something about it in your biography ...

KC   There is an excessive concentration, it always seems to me, in the debate on education policy, on everybody's own experience of schooling. There is a tendency on the part of many members of the public, who are not close to education, to form their own views about education entirely on the basis of their own memory of school. So whether people liked or hated their own school, there is a slight tendency to think that it was actually marvellous retrospectively and to compare everything that is happening now with then. I don't think I was ever guilty of that. My views on education policy were not determined by my own experience of education; but my own experience of education, for what it's worth, was state infant and junior school, followed by 11-plus sending me to an independent day school that took about a third of its pupils from the local authorities paid for by scholarship: from there I went to Cambridge, and from there I was called to the Bar by the Inns of Court.

BS   You were part of the Cambridge mafia.

KC   Yes, there were a whole lot of us who were contemporaries who were personal friends and all actively engaged in politics. And the Cambridge mafia is the nick-name given to the ones who became professional politicians – large numbers, actually, of Conservative MPs; six of them became, or have so far become, cabinet ministers.

BS   You were seen as their leader, I gather?

KC   Not necessarily. I don't think I was especially. If you'd asked the students at Cambridge to say who was potentially the outstanding man of that generation, if we'd had an American-type system, the man almost everyone would have rated as the one most likely to succeed in the class, or whatever it is at most of the American universities, would be Leon Brittan. But I was a light; I hope I was a leading light – I was chairman of the Conservative Association, I was president of the Union, I was chairman of the Federation of University Conservative and Union Associations, which was the national body and I went straight down to go on to the Conservative candidates list.

BS   You were particularly interested in politics when you went up to Cambridge. What was the attraction in politics?

KC   No idea – I just found it very interesting. Whenever I am asked that question I always say that I think it probably arose from my early reading of the newspapers when I was a small boy and the fact that I found the politics interesting.

BS   When you went up to Cambridge you hadn't determined at that stage exactly what your politics might be?

KC   Well no. Actually, I was nineteen by then, and I think that like most 19-year-olds I had not formed all my opinions in concrete for life: you go to university at a very formative stage of your own experience, so my views quite quickly became more clearly focused at Cambridge, and I was a pretty active Conservative by the end of my first year.

BS   What decided you?

KC   I was never attracted by socialism; I regarded it then, as I regard it now, as an old-fashioned political and economic system that is too controlled by interest groups as a political system and is extremely unsuccessful as a means of running an economy. I don't like a command economy, and I don't like the interest-group approach to politics, the block vote democracy representing outside interest, and the Labour movement: I was more attracted by people who wanted to modernize the country. We had a history of comparative economic failure since the war, and we were showing dangerous signs of being left behind by other modern liberal democracies. We were having difficulty in adjusting to our role in the world, which, when I was a student, was epitomized by the arguments over whether or not we should give independence to African states. This debate loomed enormously high on the political agenda of the day, while we were still considering whether or not to apply for membership of the European Union. The trade union and Labour movement was then bitterly opposed. I saw the leading Conservatives like McLeod, Butler and Maudling as enlightened men whose views were likely to produce a more attractive and modern nation-state, so I rapidly went in their direction.

BS You came to Education from Health, which you obviously enjoyed.

KC So far I have enjoyed all the jobs I've had, but I enjoyed Health more than any of the others, largely because I had a long stint at it and we had definitely delivered the changes I required by the time I finished.

BS Did you really want to be Secretary of State for Education?

KC Yes, although it is true I didn't immediately. It was the one reshuffle where I resisted the proposed move and tried to persuade Margaret not to move me before April of the following year, when the health reforms came into effect – I thought she was moving me at the wrong time and I wanted to see through to a conclusion the Health Reforms on which I had devoted such a large part of my political life by then. I very much wanted to be Secretary of State for Education, which is one of the jobs I had always found and thought attractive in government, but I didn't want to be Secretary of State for Education just yet. You know, if she'd asked me again in five months time, I wouldn't have argued.

BS Can we turn to education policy – how important and how radical do you regard the 1988 Education Reform Act?

KC I think it is extremely important. It was the first real attempt since the Butler Act to revisit the basis of education policy and to refocus what we try to achieve in the education of people. I regard the raising of standards for education and the orientating of education towards the needs of a modern society as the most important supply-side economic change we can make: I also think it is essential that we should remain a civilized state, as we are, and I think a strong educational system is essential for a prosperous society that enjoys a high quality of life.

BS   How radical do you regard it?

KC   Well, I think you have to be as radical as is necessary. 'Radical' is one of those words that is given an amazingly wide range of meanings. The most extraordinary people describe themselves as 'radicals', all across the political spectrum. I think we have to make sufficient change to achieve our purpose, which in this case is a better education system delivering higher standards.

BS   What are your views on Conservative education policy before 1986? The Conservative party manifestos are rather short on anything to do with education – a matter of a few lines.

KC   I think you're right. I think that's a fair criticism. It always rather surprised me that Margaret Thatcher, who had been an Education Secretary herself, did not give a higher priority to education in the earlier years than she did. I think she decided that the key issues that she was facing in the first two Parliaments when she was Prime Minister were the economic issues. The third Parliament was when she embarked on social reform. By that time she was laying heavy emphasis on inner-city policy, which you will remember was the most prominent aspect of our policy for the first year or so of the Parliament. We turned to education reform and then reform of the National Health Service; and that was the kind of third-term agenda that she set. Before that we had not made a high priority of it. It was not just the Conservative party, I don't think the Labour party had much of an education policy before that either. It seems to me that for as long as I've been in Parliament the whole thing had been reduced to a rather banal argument about the virtues and demerits of comprehensive education, and that was about the only subject that aroused any passion on either side of the political divide. By the late 1980s the change to comprehensive education was almost universal, and people were still using the rhetoric on both sides of a somewhat dead political battle: actually, occasionally they still do so, but far less than they used to, because the 1988 Education Reform Act has moved it all on.

BS   There seems to me to be a paradox in Conservative education policy which one could describe in terms of free economy/strong state – give schools the freedom to determine their own affairs, GMS, CTCs, LMS, create diversity, parental choice, reduce the power of LEAs, make schools autonomous – give them freedom: yet on the other hand legislate for a prescribed National Curriculum. Do you see that as a paradox?

KC   No I don't. I think the basic approach was similar to the ones we had adopted in other areas, and there was a consistency to it. Our view is that you should devolve the day-to-day delivery of great public services so far as possible: that the way in which the service is delivered should largely be determined by those who run them on the ground, be they vice chancellors, headteachers, GPs, heads of hospitals, or whatever. We don't see the need for a great bureaucracy of centralized planning and control, which is what the health service had, or in the case of the education service a kind of weak central overview with a powerful planning and control exercised by the local education authority. And so we believe in placing responsibility for the delivery of the service very much in the hands of those at the operational level. I agree with you that we seem to encourage diversity: we see no reason why people shouldn't try different methods of delivering the required standards and the required objectives. We rather believe in consumerism, so we want to see the interests of the patients, of the parents, reflected as far as possible, and the views of patients and parents responded to as far as possible. The thing about such a devolved system of responsibility is that there does have to be some accountability for what is delivered in the end. And the role of the centre as well is to set up the broad objectives – what it is that we are expecting to be delivered by those who are responsible for the day-to-day delivery on the ground. So the role of government is to set out a framework, describe the system, to say what it is we believe in the public interest should be delivered by that service, and then allow the people on the ground to go ahead, to seek to deliver it, and to be accountable for their success or otherwise in doing so. That is why we had a National Curriculum and set out the objectives. The idea was to define the subject matter of education in terms that made sense in the modern world, were consistent across the country and aimed at high standards and the depth, breadth of knowledge and understanding which children require nowadays if they are to be effective citizens in today's world. We then wanted to devolve the responsibility for delivering that. We also wanted to create more local, genuine accountability for delivery by openness, measurement of progress; they're things that we insisted on. I think that you could draw comparisons between that and the health service reforms. I actually think that is the way to manage a giant public service, which otherwise can be a confusion of responsibilities which, frankly, the education service was, I think, by the time we got to 1988.

BS   Those we've spoken to suggest that Keith Joseph was a great cerebral force behind the devising of Conservative policy on education. Do you think that's true?

KC   I think Keith Joseph, of all the people I have known, was probably more intensely interested in education policy than any other Conservative I have discussed these things with. Unfortunately, his period of office was bogged down in interminable financial arguments, and arguments about pay, largely because of the bizarre system of pay that we'd inherited from the Burnham Report. So I am sure Keith made less progress than he would have wished when he was in office. He also found that the Secretary of State's office, by the time he came to it, had precious little influence – there were few instruments which gave him influence over what happened on the ground. At it's worst, people regarded the role of the Secretary of State to be someone who did nothing whatever to influence the content of education or the way in which the schools were run, but was there to be blamed when anything went wrong by accusing him of depriving the system of money, which in the opinion of some was the only legitimate political subject for debate. So I don't think Keith had a terribly happy time at education. I think the industrial action had already started when he left office, and it all got dominated by that. He had a genuine interest in the subject, and he was genuinely concerned. Everybody knows that Keith was a man who was concerned and worried about policy, and he had a very deep social conscience and wanted to make an impact on education. But he wasn't able to take it through the process of reform. That was embarked upon under his successor.

BS   That's very interesting. When you took over from John MacGregor in November 1990, how did you find things – it wasn't altogether straightforward, I gather?

KC   Well, actually, I think things were going reasonably well: the Act had been passed; the outline of the reforms was in place; I was wholly satisfied with the outline of the approach we were taking. I mean, I had been involved in these things before; I was on the policy group on education before the 1987 election. I thought the outline was better than the detail, and I thought the reform programme was better than its implementation. There were an awful lot of details that still needed to be addressed, because the devil is in the detail of delivering any of these complicated, huge public services, and I thought there were weaknesses there. I also thought it was in slight danger of running out of steam, and that there wasn't the momentum of change under way that by that time we had got very satisfactorily running in the National Health Service. So when I took over I tried to bring to the job a new sense of urgency. I tried to get down to tackling some of the detail where it needed to be improved, and I was also somewhat dissatisfied by the way in which, well, the two bodies charged with the curriculum and the testing ...

BS   NCC and SEAC ...

KC   ... NCC and SEAC did not seem to me, either of them, to be going about the job of delivering on the ground what we wanted in the right way. There was a serious danger that they were going to deliver things that weren't actually what we had intended at all. And that was only one part of a system which was in danger of slightly missing the point in taking the reforms further and forward. So, as I say, I tried to tackle the weaknesses of detail; I tried to give an added sense of urgency, and I tried to sharpen up our objectives in certain reforms. I had a clear overall view of the reforms, so I didn't take long to pick it up because I had always followed the subject and knew it quite well. There are still aspects of the policy that need working on, to make sure that aspirations are matched by policy instruments that really deliver.

BS   The composition of those quangos, NCC and SEAC, was curious, wouldn't you say?

KC   Well, I've got to be careful. I mean I'm not sure I shall ever write my memoirs. We're a bit too near to events for me to comment in too much detail about this. I don't wish indirectly through your book to start offending too many people. [*BS and KC laugh loudly*] But on the other hand, yes, the composition of the bodies surprised me. I never got the sense out of them that they were wholly committed to the policy which they had agreed to deliver by accepting service on the bodies. Instead of having independent, well-qualified, powerful bodies delivering the policy – and I wholly defend their right to be independent, powerful, and to use their professional expertise – we'd created debating societies with a curious mixture of people who didn't seem altogether agreed on their purpose and certainly didn't seem altogether to be agreed on the purposes which I'd expected. So I had trouble with them from the start, yes.

BS   There are a number of very significant successes that you achieved as Secretary of State for Education.

KC   Well I think so, but I've no doubt that people still argue about that.

BS   John Patten, for example, regards the setting up of the independent inspectorate, OFSTED, as a very great achievement.

KC   That's very kind of him.

BS   Can you tell me something about your thinking behind the introduction of OFSTED?

KC   Well, this was in order to improve accountability for the standards we expect to deliver and to get some objective view of whether those standards were being delivered on the ground. I think the government was entitled to define a curriculum and to give an indication of the way in which it wants to see standards raised. You couldn't do that unless you had some powerful independent body which was respected, which could monitor standards being achieved on the ground, report on them openly to the general public and to parents in particular, and be of support to schools in the delivery of what we wanted. The old schools inspectorate was a perfectly reasonable body. A lot of the people in OFSTED are people who worked for the old schools inspectorate, but it had rather a different purpose. It didn't inspect a lot of the schools at all, except on a very, very infrequent basis. It regarded its most important role as developing ideas on policy of its own and advising ministers about those ideas; so they were keener on their input to ministerial policy than they were on changing anything in the schools themselves. And they didn't report very openly, except in broad-brush terms on matters of general policy all the time. They were very supportive of the schools, and in the main they were very good people. But the independent inspectorate reorientated the whole outfit and gave it a role that fitted the reforms. I think, actually, that until we created the independent inspectorate it was rather difficult to work out how the old schools inspectorate fitted into the outline I had in mind for how the education service should work.

BS   Is there a danger that HMI in, as it were, keeping an eye on inspecting the amateurs – the OFSTED inspectors – might have a vested interest in showing that OFSTED isn't perhaps as successful as they were?

KC   Well, they might. It's only human nature, I suppose. If any of them start producing those kinds of comments, I hope that future Secretaries of State will make allowance for human nature and try to look for some other objective assessments of whether OFSTED's doing the job properly.

BS   What actually was your assessment of HMI?

KC   Too soon after events for me to want to comment in too much detail. Also, it would be extremely unfair for me to make detailed comments about HMI, who would feel inhibited in answering back, as it were; I mean, they are public servants and they don't expect to be engaging in debate with their former Secretaries of State. And also, I don't want to give you the impression that I had anything against the HMI, really. There were some very good people in HMI, and some I worked with very closely. The Chief Inspector who retired during my time – he did in fact reach retirement age and was due to go – Eric Bolton; I worked very successfully with him. I liked him and I took his opinions seriously. I thought he was a good man and I thought we worked together very well. The only thing I would say about HMI is that it varied a lot. The ethos of those parts of HMI responsible for further education, for secondary education and for primary education was very different. There were three different cadres, really, of the inspectorate and they were really three separate animals. So they had a totally different approach to their job. And without being particular, for the reasons I've just given – it was too recent – I had a very different opinion, personally, of the respective quality of the different parts of it. As between those three, I have my own strong preferences about which I thought was doing the job most effectively.

BS   OFSTED was one of your major achievements, but there were of course several others which we should talk about.

KC   That's very kind of you. Well, firstly I gave a whole new impetus to the grant-maintained school system. I did that slightly by accident. In my first speech I talked about the need to accelerate the process of moving over to grant-maintained status.

BS   Yes, it was while you were Secretary of State that we became grant-maintained at Great Barr in 1991; in fact we corresponded subsequently.

KC   That's right. I remember. So quite early on I made various public statements and found that I'd changed the policy. My predecessors had been much more cautious, and there was an inclination to regard grant-maintained status as a cautious experiment which would be tried out in a few schools and then eventually, perhaps, moved on to others. I, personally, had no doubt that moving to grant-maintained status was desirable. I had no doubt that it was a natural corollary of the local management of schools, which I think was one of the unreserved and now almost uncontroversial successes of my predecessors. And I thought that people who opted for grant-maintained status would rapidly find that it was a tremendously satisfying thing to have done, and that it would arouse enthusiasm among staff and parents of schools that went grant-maintained. So I made a deliberate point of seeking to drive up the number of schools opting for grant-maintained status as rapidly as possible by exhortation and encouragement and insisting that we got on with the job of vetting the applications and responding to people who got through the ballot process and everything else. The numbers went up during my time, and I remember it going to the one hundredth grant-maintained school, I remember it going to the two hundredth grant-maintained school. I remember beginning to forecast that the majority of secondary schools would be grant-maintained, and that particular ball got rolling very rapidly.

The other thing that I had to achieve was to get in the final bits of the National Curriculum, which was rolling through this cumbersome process we had created. Again, I altered the policy almost by accident, because I knew that it came to the Secretary of State, and in theory the Secretary of State had the final power to make the final changes that he wished to the recommendations that came from the various subject groups and then made the Curriculum Orders. I don't think anybody advised me that none of our predecessors had made the slightest change to anything that came out of these committees. I responded quite strongly to draft recommendations on the subject of music and the subject of sport, I think. I changed the history and geography curriculum from the drafts put to me. I don't think I did so from any position of political bias. I thought parts of it were something of a horlicks, and seemed to have lost the point of delivering a key knowledge on the subject that was required. One of the things you will recall was that the word 'knowledge' had apparently become a word that wasn't included in any of the SATS that related to the curriculum, and so the corpus of the factual knowledge that people expect to have in their curriculum didn't seem very strong. I actually thought people who debated with me on the geography curriculum hadn't read the geography curriculum that they were arguing about. There was a whole school of geographers who carried on an agitated argument, telling me that things weren't there like environmental geography which I knew perfectly well were there; so that was very odd. History people only noticed that I tried to determine that contemporary events – current affairs – should not be part of the history curriculum. I had to sort a wild controversy about robbing people of their last thirty years. I thought I would have had a far wider debate about some of the other things I'd done earlier on.

I never did get round to doing what I really wanted to do with the curriculum, which I think has only been done since by John Patten and Ron Dearing. I also think, and I said it quite openly at the time, that this process of having subject committees, who had been subjected to far too much lobbying from outside interest groups wanting things put in it, had led to an overloading of the curriculum. The curriculum was massive. I never did think that it should absorb 100 per cent or more of every teacher's time teaching a prescribed National Curriculum. I thought the curriculum should spell out the essential corpus of subject matter, knowledge and understanding that needs to be covered, leaving some scope for the individual teacher to demonstrate his or her flair or interest in delivering the subject. So the general thinning out of it has gone on since – something that I would very much like to have done, and on which I certainly made speeches at the time.

What else did we do in my time? There were the CTCs – despite the fact that not everybody in the government was as keen on CTCs as I was, but we got all the CTCs, up to about fifteen, in place. Then the other thing that I began was to preside over the beginning of the testing system, and I tried to make some sense of those wretched SATs. I wasn't the greatest fan of the ten levels of attainment system, but it seemed to me that we had gone far, far too far down the track for me to try to change that. But the actual nature of the SATs and the way that they were conducted left a lot to be desired. There was, and there still is, a sort of fundamental political argument about whether or not we should have any testing at all. Well, I was a fervent believer in testing. Indeed, to the shock of my officials, I used the word testing when 'attainment tasks' had become a kind of politically correct form of language for them. I introduced the 7-year-old tests, if you remember, and presided over the first round of 7-year-old tests, which went better than everybody said, because a lot of the critics were the usual old NUT hands who were going to criticize anything. But they were not an unmixed blessing, there was no doubt. A lot of primary school teachers, good primary school teachers, had found them a bit of a nightmare in terms of controlling the class and also giving the necessary time to them to carry them all out. And whoever devised them, I was rapidly persuaded, had not had a very good understanding of what it was really like to conduct a class of 7-year-olds. I'm trying to remember the trouble with the particular test that all the primary school teachers got very worked up about. It was science. There was one that involved a most fantastic amount of splashing of water, which people found that a class of 7-year-olds would no doubt enjoy – the 'sinking and floating' test.

BS   They had to measure ...

KC   Yes, the test certainly didn't work as it was supposed to work – everyone got very wet. So I listened to an awful lot of complaints about these things. I pointed to the relevant part of SEAC. I changed some of the personnel, largely thanks to happy retirements from the previous holders which gave me vacancies. I am not saying that the people who retired were the people who were wrong, but I had some vacancies. I appointed at least two primary school teachers, including one head by whom I had been wildly impressed when she took me to her wholly excellent school in Surrey. After showing me her school, she sat me down and gave me a most ferocious lecture about these SATs, and why they had created chaos in her school, and what was wrong with them. She persuaded me that she was genuinely not opposed to the idea of tests and results being available to the parents – it was just these particular wretched tests that she objected to. So I appointed her to SEAC. The second round of 7-year-old tests went extremely well; they went smoothly; every school did them, I think. Far more did them than are doing them at the moment. We produced the results, and my recollection is that we produced the first league tables with the minimum of fuss, and we got those more or less into the primary school system. When I left we were still modifying the secondary tests, and I was embroiled in interminable arguments about what they were like. Parts of SEAC appeared to be determined just to grind on regardless with their particular approach, come what may. These tests were presented to me and my junior ministers, and as far as I can see with our comments going in one ear and out the other. They were hopelessly over-elaborate. They were obviously going to be impossible for teachers to do in any reasonable amount of time, and involved interminable heaps of paper and instructions which were driving every headteacher or every teacher in the country completely wild. And behind my public remarks about pencil-and-paper tests that could be done and examined in a reasonably objective fashion, lay a lot of arguing about the draft tests that were proposed that in my opinion were in danger of discrediting a perfectly good policy. That was the sort of detail that I said I was concerned with. That happened on the curriculum front as well. I mean, the two quangos were producing mountains of paper, Swedish forests were going to produce cross-curricular themes and advice on the contents of the curriculum. And then SEAC producing these amazing sort of SATs to test it all. I was involved in trying to simplify it for a little over a year. But I will confess that I'm not sure that people who were receiving the mail in individual schools noticed much difference.

   I personally was involved in interminable rows with this bureaucracy that we put in place that was producing all this stuff that was in danger of discrediting the policy.

BS   Until you appointed Brian Griffiths.

KC   Yes, we made changes. I appointed two people to head the two bodies who seemed to me to have a very clear idea of where we were going; people I knew I could work with. I had no personal quarrels with the previous two. They were perfectly OK. But I decided that I just had to have people heading these things up who clearly shared my sense of purpose and who I thought were strong enough to get control of a couple of bodies that had slightly lost their way.

BS   And then there were the universities and the polytechnics.

KC   Yes, I was very pleased to do that – I got awarded 'Radical of the Year' for doing that. Polytechnics have flourished already as a result of being taken out of local authority control. And they were very wounded by the status thing. I wasn't so receptive to polytechnics arguing that they had second-class status compared with the universities. Some of the principals did persuade me that it was really difficult to attract the best pupils, because children thought that universities were all better than polytechnics, and they also had some difficulties in their overseas relationships because people didn't understand what a British polytechnic was. But leaving that on one side, what seemed to me mad was to have two totally different systems of distributing money, and relationships with the Department, with bodies all of whom would have been called a university in other countries in the world. I thought the best polytechnics were achieving higher standards than the weaker universities – but that's essentially a faculty by faculty thing anyway – and I thought we could devise for the lot of them parity of esteem, parity of status, and a system which was a fairer way of distributing the money for teaching and research, and would encourage and bring the best out of all of them. And I was rather pleased to do that. Further education colleges ...

BS ... and sixth form colleges ...

KC ... and sixth form colleges, I took on the same path. Principals of polytechnics used to complain to me that until we had taken them out of local authority control – which I think we did in about 1988 – some local authorities had treated them as rather troublesome comprehensive schools whilst giving them far less attention than they tended to give to their comprehensive schools. Now the further education colleges and the sixth form colleges were full of good people who I think were also suffering from not being allowed to run their own institutions. My principle, as I've said, was you give responsibility to people; give them the chance to run their own organization, and make sure they are properly accountable for what they do, and make sure that in particular you are giving them incentives to deliver the right results through the means by which you distribute the money – finance institutions. I still have some contacts with sixth form colleges and with further education colleges from time to time, and I am not surprised to find that, regardless of their politics, all people running them are enjoying like mad the ability to expand and to develop and build closer links with the local community and local industry, and do their own thing.

BS And the same principle would apply to schools, presumably; so why is it that the government has been reticent to enable – or to put it bluntly – force, more schools to opt out?

KC [*KC chuckles*] I'll make one confession, indiscreetly, as it were, after the event. If I'd been Secretary of State in 1988 I would not have put in this balloting system. In my experience it produces quite extraordinary local political campaigning of intense bitterness. I mean, you don't need me to tell *you* that, Brian. You know directly from your own experience.

BS I remember it vividly.

KC I don't think it is an accurate representation of democracy in action. What happens every time anybody seeks to opt out is that parents who have an interest in their own child's education and in the standards of the school feel that they don't know enough about how it's run anyway: they listen to the most bewildering, wild arguments about the consequences for the school of changing the status quo. Some local authorities spent vast amounts of money on propaganda, and there was canvassing of parents, and legal action and all kinds of things surrounding it. I am afraid I was never able to persuade my colleagues that we could take the ballots out of the system once the government had put it in the Act, so the ballots remain, and they remain the biggest single obstacle in the way of moving to grant-maintained status, which in my opinion is demonstrably a success where it's in place. I think it's a pity that all this local campaigning gets in the way of parents understanding it elsewhere, and stops us going even faster.

BS   I agree entirely. The ballot has proved to be an impediment. And with greater devolution with LMS schemes, governors and heads mistakenly rationalize their situation to the effect that it's not worth generating all that political acrimony for the sake of full autonomy. And it means that parental choice is circumscribed, diversity restricted and the educational dependency culture kept alive.

KC   That's right, and I think we have quite enough experience of how grant-maintained schools work now, and how they should relate to the Department for Education or anybody else, and I hope that we move as rapidly as possible towards a full universal system. If I am allowed to make one comparison with Health, I resisted all this stuff in the Health Authority, although lots of local authorities tried to run local votes and ballots when we were consulting on trust status of the hospitals. The result is that in the health service we have nearly 100 per cent NHS trust status for hospitals, community hospitals and community services, and as far as I am aware my former opponents in the Labour party and the BMA are not advocating reversing this, although it was over their dead body that it was being proposed. I think that if we hadn't had the ballots on grant-maintained schools we'd have reached the same outcome.

BS   And there was teacher appraisal.

KC   Teacher appraisal – I had a little difficulty on that. Anything, anything that touched on pay, terms and conditions I had a lot of difficulty on, but we got it in place, which was pretty good. Everybody was quite responsible. And I don't know how it's working – I have lost touch with that – but at least we had teacher appraisal where we had none before ...

BS   Well, it can be rewarding to discuss one's professional performance with professional colleagues. It's a way of valuing teacher performance. Most teachers will find it helpful to reflect upon their achievements and to discuss with colleagues areas for professional development.

KC   Well, I don't get too many complaints about it. It works in nearly every other walk of life, and it can be helpful. I mean, people feared it meant that you could be sort of hired and fired on some sudden appraisal of your role – but, no, it can be helpful. The other thing we haven't mentioned is the review body. The trouble in all the public services is that you can get absolutely bogged down in pay, terms and conditions being the only things that everybody talks about. In the case of the BMA it remains the case. I had private meetings with them and I have no recollection of them ever raising any other subject with me apart from pay, terms and conditions. As far as the teachers' unions were concerned – it featured pretty big. I inherited a Bill which I regarded as a complete horlicks – which was about to change the teachers' pay system, and go back to something that will look worse than the Burnham Committee to me – the main problem being it seemed absolutely doomed to create the maximum amount of conflict because of confusing the role between the Secretary of State, the local authorities and the teachers in what was neither fish nor fowl in terms of bargaining process or imposition. Within three weeks of being appointed I had a new Prime Minister who was very keen on education, and he worked very closely with me throughout my time. He made lots of speeches on education. If you get the Prime Minister on your side and working with you, you get things through the Whitehall system rather quicker than you otherwise would. The Prime Minister agreed that this Bill was a mistake and that we should take the plunge of having a review body system. I think that is the right system for public servants like teachers, nurses, doctors, who do not wish to take industrial action against their pupils and patients. But these people are constantly fearful that they are going to be unfairly treated if they deprive themselves of the right to go on strike. So I introduced an objective review body process which is still going well.

BS Now, you touched on this earlier – why, in your view, is Conservative education policy superior to the alternatives? [*KC laughs*]

KC Well, I think because our interest is about standards; I think because of our belief that schools and colleges should be given their head when it comes to delivering what we are asking them to do; I believe that schools and colleges should be open and accountable for what they achieve to the local public and to parents, as well as to anybody with an interest in education. Conservatives wish to see a reduction of the bureaucracy. We wish to see the most effective distribution of the money deployed by the people on the ground. But essentially our aim is to raise standards to the higher levels required by the demands of the modern world. We haven't just discovered higher education. The 1990s mean that the general level of attainment of people in this country has just got to be that much higher than we could get away with fifty years ago. The alternatives are muddled; I don't think the opposition parties have any clear overview of policy. They hark back to their own political past, and they are far too much in hock to the organized interests of the professions and others in the trade unions. The whole argument about the way in which education is to be delivered and how you achieve higher standards is bedevilled by a lot of curious philosophical debates that have taken place over the last thirty years. The Labour and Liberal parties are too seduced by the fashionable remedies of the 1960s for their arguments to slip into my soap box or party platform oratory of the days when I was at Education.

BS   Teacher training?

KC   Oh yes, I embarked on the reforms of teacher training, moving to school-based training. The two things you have to do with people who are trained to teach is firstly to get them up to satisfactory levels of education attainment themselves. Secondly, to enable somebody who has got the academic level we require to acquire the skills of teaching real classes. I was probably influenced there by the fact that the system used by lawyers and by doctors is that you train to the required academic standard, but you acquire your professional skills alongside and under the supervision of senior practitioners on the ground in the trade. And I as a barrister, as a pupil, went into the courts with the pupil master. A junior doctor works his way up the medical profession by spending a lot of his time, if he's working properly, alongside a consultant whom he calls in when he's got a problem but from whom he acquires the actual application of the professional skills. I think more of the teaching profession should have been effectively trained in this way. Would-be teachers should be got up to the right academic level, but then should acquire the skills of the trade under a system much more closely supervised by schools themselves, and in which the schools themselves play a much bigger and active role.

BS   What's it like being Secretary of State for Education – what kind of a job is it? What I would really like to know is, what sort of Secretary of State were you, because they all have their different styles – some relish the cut and thrust of intellectual debate, and one hears of the different ways in which Secretaries of State manage the Department and so on.

KC   Well, I think it has probably changed. I think the job has changed a bit from before 1988. I've known Secretaries of State for twenty, thirty years. I made my maiden speech on education; I was Education whip under the Heath government; I used to see Margaret Thatcher once a week in action when I was a junior whip. But going back before then, and since then, and thinking of some of the Labour ministers more particularly, you could have a very quiet life as Secretary of State for Education. The influence over events the Secretary of State for Education had was not too great. Secretaries of State have always immersed themselves in the interminable arguments about the 11-plus and comprehensive education, which were almost the only subject that they debated at national level, otherwise it was a lot of school visits and generally presiding benignly over a system. And then if you go back years and years ago – the first Labour government after the war, because it followed the Butler Act – George Tomlinson was a very popular figure. I have read a biography on him once, but I had no impression that George Tomlinson *did* very much personally as Secretary of State for Education, apart from being a popular figurehead. There were others, still alive, to whom I could be equally unkind, who I think passed without trace through the Department of Education. So post-1988 it became much more like Health – you are heavily immersed in an area with lots of policy and with lots of controversy. The controversy is inevitable – a pity, but education has always been a controversial political issue in most of the country. You work under high pressure, and, well, it's very combative, and you try to avoid that and turn it all around back to some discussion about real educational things – contents, standards – and keep the show on the road.

What sort of Secretary of State was I? I suppose you're asking other people, so I shall in due course be horrified to discover what they think. I think I was a very activist Secretary of State, as I have been in most Departments I have been in. I had a very clear agenda which I rapidly put together because I felt familiar with the subject – things I wished to push on. So while I was there – and I hope everyone in the Department agrees with me – there was never a dull moment, and it was not a quiet life, and we were pushing ahead very strongly in the direction that I wanted. How did I find the Department? Curate's egg. Good in parts. The Department had a more powerful agenda of its own than any other Department of State in which I have ever worked. When I arrived, I think in some parts of the Department – this is unkind, most unfair to some of my colleagues – it took a certain time for people to accept that, yes, I was changing what they were doing, and insisting that the Department was delivering the government's policy. I had more trouble on that front in the Department of Education than any other Department I have ever been in. It wasn't universal, and, to be fair, this could have led to far more trouble in the Department than it did, but for two things, I think. Firstly, the Permanent Secretary, John Caines, was extremely good at sorting all this out. I got on very well with John Caines, and I think he helped me to avoid a lot of trouble I could have got into. Firstly he, as my Permanent Secretary, accepted that I was the Secretary of State and that the Department should deliver what I wanted, and in his very quiet, avuncular way, I think he oiled the wheels and made sure that the clashes did not arise between me and parts of the Department. Secondly, the other thing that I hope avoided us all getting into trouble was I never objected to people freely – and sometimes ferociously – expressing opinions with which I disagreed. It is the duty of the Department to advise the Secretary of State when they think he's wrong, and I do not wish to be told all the time things I wish to hear, nor do I remotely resent the fact that people enter into combative debate with me. That was not the problem. Some of the people who did argue the toss with me most ferociously were some of the people I most enjoyed working with. I had plenty of time for that. There was one individual – I won't name him, but I personally had the highest regard for his ability – who knew his subject backwards. I was dealing with a star performer on education policy but so long as, in the end, after I had heeded advice, I was allowed to determine the course we were to follow and the pace at which we went, I never resented the debate. That remained a slightly permanent struggle all the way through.

But I enjoyed working with the Department, and I hope that with one or two exceptions of the kind that you no doubt have in any large organization, most of them enjoyed working with me. They were stirring times, I think, and we never got into disaster. When I left, I didn't want to leave, although I didn't argue this time – the Home Secretary is a senior job, and you might never get offered it again. I was surprised when John Major asked me to move. I'd been working so closely with him on education policy before the election, I'd convinced myself that he would just ask me to carry on for another couple of years, and I expected to do so. I didn't argue, but had we carried on for another couple of years, I would have enjoyed it.

I think it was all trundling along in the right direction, coming along pretty well. And I remember, my last excitement, my last few days in office was trying to get that Bill through in time before the House was dissolved. And we had desperate trouble getting Royal Assent to the Bill before Parliament was dissolved. There were intense procedural arguments in the Commons and the Lords where I resisted all attempts to get me to ditch it, to ease things, and I was determined to get it to the Lords in time for the Lords to finish it and get the Royal Assent, which we did, I think, on the last day of Parliament – it certainly seemed like the nick of time.

BS   The pressures of the job must be enormous. Perhaps we could talk about how you cope with the pressures – some newspapers, for example, would have us believe that you like to spend time at Ronnie Scott's, that you enjoy the odd pint or two. I find it hard to believe that you have the time, frankly.

KC   Ronnie Scott's – well that's simply not true. It must be about six years since I've been there. You're absolutely right: I simply don't have the time.

BS   Do you cope with the pressures just by working, or do you have other outlets?

KC   Well, I suppose it's a matter of temperament really. I work very hard indeed – always have done. I like working hard. I am used to working hard, and for very, very long hours. And at the same time

I seem able to switch off and just have a nice time, enjoy myself. People have told me that I don't seem to be a worrier at all. I'm fortunate in that I have a retentive memory and can work very quickly. I can absorb information well. I've been at the forefront of politics for so long that I know a lot about a Department before I go into it. There's nothing much new to me within Whitehall, because I've been at it for so long really – by virtue of Cabinet and all these Cabinet committees. So I do work extremely hard, but also if I go to a party at a conference I'll stay up quite late – so does my wife – we both enjoy having a nice time.

BS   A mutual acquaintance, Sir Joseph Pope from Nottingham, once described you to me as fearless, quite fearless in politics – very courageous.

KC   Well, that's very nice of him. I've been in politics for some years now – I suppose I know how far I can go: it's not really for me to say, but yes, fearless, and I would like to think that I am courageous in political life, yes. I would like to think that the adjective 'determined' is a fitting one to describe my work as Secretary of State for Education.

BS   Is that why Mrs Thatcher gave you the job, do you think?

KC   Well certainly education had become a high-profile issue. All during that period, even though John McGregor was very popular there, it became very high profile. There were some very good journalists, which there aren't at the moment – very vocal and determined and very engaged journalists – who turned education into an increasing issue. And it coincided with the introduction of the GCSE, which was just beginning to come through, and parents were beginning to realize that GCSE was not nearly as rigorous an exam as O level. And it wasn't just the GCSE issue, it was general standards. Mrs Thatcher realized that something had to be done about it. The message from the Department was that educational standards were going up whereas everyone knew that they weren't, and GCSE was an example of that. The same with grant-maintained schools, which was another principle policy issue you were asking me about earlier in our discussion – it had been rather swept under the carpet, so much so that the Department would not even talk about the whole grant-maintained initiative. I opened this whole issue up. I promoted grant-maintained policy as the policy for the future. I said that educational standards were not high enough. I identified with the worry expressed by members of the public, and said that we had to do better than this. Education was slipping, we had to keep A levels – the gold standard; we've got to keep up the standard of GCSE. It really was a matter of back to basics. Grant-maintained status was one of our big issues, and so were CTCs, which nobody really would talk about either. There was a battle royal going on in the Department itself. It was happening before I arrived in the

Department, and it was certainly very apparent when I arrived there that they didn't want these issues discussed. They didn't like grant-maintained schools. They didn't like the CTCs. They were trying to minimize the policy. So I took it as an issue and ran with it. I talked about it; I made speeches about it, and I did the same thing with the CTCs; I did the same thing on standards; I did the same thing on the curriculum, and I took the officials head-on on the curriculum, and said it's not good enough – I took bits out myself. So, to answer your question, yes, I'd like to think that that was pretty courageous stuff, really.

BS   The newspapers sometimes like to portray you as a night-owl, a beer-swilling bruiser. But having sat with you for just over an hour now, my impression is quite the reverse.

KC   I work hard, but I am not a night-owl. If I go to a party or something, I enjoy it – but I don't go to very many parties.

BS   So essentially you are working all the time?

KC   Well, I do work very long hours. You know, I have a full day which ends, probably, at eight o'clock at night or something, and then I will have either a dinner or formal dinner, and then I'll have to work after that pretty late. I am a pretty active politician. I've always been put in to do specific things – to make big changes, really. There were the big health reforms; a lot of different work at the Department for Education, and also at the Home Office – you know the police reforms. I don't just sit here and enjoy the status quo. I have had some pretty radical, major things to do. But yes, I do enjoy life, and I like a pint every now and again, and I don't hide the fact. I like smoking, so sometimes I'm photographed smoking.

BS   And why not?

KC   Well, why not, exactly.

BS   When the muse of history takes out her sieve, what assessment will be made of Ken Clarke as Secretary of State for Education?

KC   Well, what assessment will be made of Ken Clarke? I would hope people might think that he began to put education back on the road towards higher standards; that he started sorting out the difficulties with the curriculum and the testing – getting them back on track. He started getting these bodies to work for him rather than for the Department – these various bodies, SEAC and NCC. And he was really instrumental in beginning to get education back towards the more traditional delivery approach, and towards delivery of higher standards.

BS   Presumably you anticipate a change at the DfE?

KC   Well, you know, I don't really know.

BS   You're obviously the bookie's favourite to succeed John Major at some time. But I don't suppose I can draw you on that topic, can I? What would your comment be on such an observation?

KC   Well, there's no vacancy.

BS   You felt passionately about education?

KC   Yes, I did feel very strongly, very strongly indeed, that education wasn't up to standard, and that children weren't getting the opportunity that I had had. I felt that children were being short-changed.

BS   And you wanted to redress the balance?

KC   I really wanted to redress the balance. If I'd been able to, I'd have reintroduced grammar schools. OK. Must break off now, I'm afraid, and finish correcting my speech. I'm sorry I can't give you longer just now, but I must return to what I was doing before. I hope that's helpful.

BS   Thank you very much, indeed.

KC   I shouldn't think that any former Secretary of State has given you that length of time, has he?

BS   Well, judging by the tape-length we've used up, you'll probably qualify for the bronze medal, Chancellor.

KC   By the way, I believe I was due to visit you at Great Barr just before I was moved to the Home Office.

BS   I'll invite you up when the book's published!

KC   Please do, and this time I shall do my best to come.

CHAPTER 7

John Patten

WITH BRIAN SHERRATT

John Patten was born in 1945 and educated at Wimbledon College and Sidney Sussex College, Cambridge, where he studied geography as an undergraduate and postgraduate. He taught at Oxford during the years 1969–79, being Fellow and Tutor at Hertford College from 1972–81 and Fellow between 1981 and 1994. He was member for Oxford between 1979 and 1983 and has held Oxford West and Abingdon since 1983. After holding a variety of junior ministerial posts at the Northern Ireland Office and the Ministry of Health, he served as Minister of State for Housing, Urban Affairs and Construction (1985–87) and from 1987 was for five years Minister of State at the Home Office. In April 1992 he was appointed Secretary of State for Education, where he served until 1994.

Part One: 18 May 1994

BS   Secretary of State, perhaps we could begin by looking at how you developed your own ideas and attitudes towards education? Could you tell me something about your own schooling, your experiences of school, and how perhaps they shaped your view of education over the years?

JP   I've never been one for introverted self-examination of the influences on my life. But my education was formal, old-fashioned to the extent of being soundly anchored in the 1950s, in two tough – both intellectually and in terms of discipline, behaviour and ethos – voluntary aided Roman Catholic schools. First, St Peter's School, Leatherhead, a primary school for boys and girls, where I went from 5 to 11. At the time the head and a couple of the other teachers were nuns. One, Mother Mary-Anna, the head then, is still alive, and now living in retirement, happily, I think, in her eighties in a convent in

Kent. We correspond at Christmas time and on those sort of occasions. She wrote to me after some years. And I did the 11-plus and I then moved on to Wimbledon College, which was then a Jesuit grammar school with a lot of Jesuits who lived in the college and taught, and a lot of young trainee Jesuits, scholastics – it's a long business becoming a Jesuit. These days it's a Roman Catholic boys' comprehensive school in the London Borough of Merton. It moved status at some stage or other – I don't know quite when – but I left there in 1964. It was a very formal education with the classes – let me see if I can remember what they were called: when you went in at 11 it was called Figures; the next class was called Rudiments; the next class was called Lower Grammar; the next class was called Grammar; the next class was called Syntax – that's when you did O level – and then you switched into the sixth form and that's where, by and large, it became less formal, more civilized. You didn't have to wear school uniform. You could wear sports jackets or suits, but always with a college tie.

BS   I believe the media tried to make out that you were something of a rebel for not wearing uniform in the sixth form?

JP   We didn't have to wear uniform in the sixth form. But in the last year it changed and the new headteacher said that we had to wear uniform. But by that stage I'd only got a term or so to go. So I think that's the media, you know, slightly elaborating. And the lower sixth was called Poetry and the upper sixth was called Rhetoric. Rather suitable names. And that's when it became much friendlier. I started off doing history, geography and English, but I was passionately interested in geography and after only a few weeks of doing English I decided that I would do geology instead because it matched up with geography. I was then very interested in physical geography, although I ended up being much more interested, right at the other extreme, in historical geography. And I did A-level geology by going to classes, with the encouragement of the school – they were very good about it. They didn't teach geology themselves, and I went to Kingston Technical College, as it then was – now Kingston University – and did A-Level geology from there. I then duly proceeded from there on an Open Exhibition to Sidney Sussex College, Cambridge, in 1964. And I got a 2:1 in 1967, but none the less was able to stay on and do research. And I did my doctorate and moved on to Oxford in 1969 when a vacancy in historical geography, which was my subject, fell vacant in Oxford. It's a highly specialized subject. And thereafter it's all in *Who's Who*.

BS   What influences, then, did your school have on your thinking on education *per se*?

JP   Well, both schools taught me the importance of working hard, competitiveness with oneself rather than particularly with other children. I've never, ever, felt particularly competitive towards anyone else. Tough, demanding, long hours, don't mess about, get on with it.

BS   And is that your ...

JP   Yes. That's very much my feeling. [*BS and JP laugh*] *Very* much my feeling.

BS   And does that come over, do you think, in your educational policies since 1992, or in your thinking on education prior to 1992?

JP   I didn't think a great deal about education politically before 1992. I was successively in the Northern Ireland Office, the Health Department and the Home Office for a very long stint. Obviously, the one job for which I might have thought myself suited was this one, and I never, therefore, thought that I would ever be appointed to this job, because it's axiomatic in government that you don't normally appoint 'specialists'. Even though I was by that stage rather a post-dated specialist. So I hadn't thought much about it. I was an enthusiast for the 1988 Education Reform Act; for grant-maintained schools; for local management of schools – all of those things. And I guess if anything, up to 1992 my mind was shaped by the work of early reformers like Keith Joseph; I thought he was a great thinker. And then to Baker, MacGregor and Clarke. And I've always thought that children flourish best if they compete with themselves. I think hard work is an economic, but also an ethical, issue. And that's about as far as I got when I suddenly found myself here, much to my surprise and delight. Keith Joseph was apparently, in the old DES, given to wandering around the corridors when he first came and saying, 'Please show me the levers; I can't find any levers.' And he did most of the ground-clearing thinking, I think, which underpinned much of Ken Baker's work, as Ken himself, I'm sure, acknowledges. It may have taken Keith Joseph several years to begin to find the levers, but he began to switch the whole ethos of government educational policy from inputs towards outputs. That was always on his far horizon, I think. And he wanted to find the levers to make this happen. And that's really what we've been doing over the last six years. That's not to suggest that earlier generations were indifferent to results. Not at all. But we're now focusing on what produces results – outputs – in an increasingly competitive age. Parents whose children failed the 11-plus under-standably questioned the selective system of education, but the 'comprehensive schools for all' solution failed to address the problem; it failed because it put form before content; it put organization before results. In the 1960s and 1970s there was increasing unease about the manner, the pace of comprehensive reorganization, not to mention some of the wilder educational theories of the time. It's hardly surprising that increasingly education became polarized – both at local and national levels. There was a general lack of confidence in standards of performance, results, outputs; and it wasn't just the concern of the radical right. So these were the tensions my predecessors had to grapple with; tensions which were already apparent in the early 1960s – with Edward Boyle, Anthony Crosland; and even more so by the time Edward Short and Margaret Thatcher were in this seat. And then of course we had the oil shocks, the economic difficulties of the mid-1970s; and Jim Callaghan's speech at Ruskin College captures very well, I think, that sense of unease aggravated by economic difficulties.

BS   So the Callaghan speech was triggered by the economic fears associated with the oil crisis, but really there was a deeper unease?

JP   Yes, that's right. There are two important features. First, the whole education system was producer-driven; some saw it as indifferent to the needs and wishes, of parents, of employers and the wider general public. It was never quite clear who was responsible for what, and it became clear that central government took no responsibility for the school curriculum; that central government had few, if any, levers on standards of performance in schools. Second, schools were failing pupils of average and below average ability; there wasn't the right quality, breadth and balance for these pupils. And these issues, taken together, called for fundamental change. The Department, up until the mid-1980s, concentrated on the supply and organization of schools – there was a certain complacency about the standards achieved by school-leavers – but there was a growing frustration with uneven quality within the decentralized system, and it was this point that Jim Callaghan highlighted so strikingly.

Frankly, I don't believe these problems could have been resolved without a strong lead from government; and that's precisely what happened. It was Keith who, with his characteristic incisiveness, not only analysed and diagnosed these problems of the 1970s, but who also came up with the remedies; it was Keith who provided the theoretical underpinning on which we've been able to build. This is an opportunity for me to acknowledge my debt to him.

BS   You were a distinguished academic. You might have continued your career as a don. What prompted you to seek a career in politics?

JP   Well, I was very fortunate. I began teaching in Oxford when I was 24. I was elected to my Fellowship very young, and I remember the then bursar of the college writing me a letter after a few weeks, or months it may have been – very slow-moving, college life – saying he thought I'd be interested to know what my pension would be upon retirement and what the arrangements were and that kind of thing.

BS   And this was when you were only 24.

JP   Well, I was appointed to my Fellowship at 26. I was what was called a departmental demonstrator between 1969 and December 1971. I took up my Fellowship at the beginning of January 1972; one remembers these things exactly. That was the same year as I finished my doctorate. I only had two years of working on my doctorate at Cambridge full time before I was thrown into teaching, so it took a bit longer. I wouldn't want you to think that I was a slow worker or indolent. So I was then 26 – and in those days you went on until you were 67; I gave up tenure until the age of 67 to come into politics. And the letter said: Dear Patten, you have these pension arrangements and you get 33/80ths, you know, the complicated stuff that you're told. And PS. You retire on September 30 2013, which then seemed to me light years away. And I can remember thinking, good heavens above, am I really going to be doing this for all of my life? I always wanted to be an academic. I wasn't an active student politician at all at Cambridge. I wasn't active in the Union or one of the so-called Cambridge mafia with its distinguished exponents like Leon Brittan or Kenneth Clarke. I was never much involved and never got involved in the Union or seriously in the Cambridge University Conservative Association. I went to one meeting of the latter when I was there at the Cambridge Arms Hotel where I listened to William Rees-Mogg, whom I now greatly admire, talking about the need for the country to return to the gold standard. And I couldn't understand what on earth this was about and all these serious young men and young women – I thought, well, I shall go off and do other things. And I was really very interested in academic life. I always wanted to be a don. I enjoyed my ten years of teaching very much, wrote some books, finished my doctorate, taught a lot and built up the numbers of those studying geography at my college from an intake of about four or five a year to an intake of ten a year. And they all did reasonably well. They were a hard-working lot. They were *very* hard-working. At that stage Hertford was one of the first colleges to try to bring in people from schools that didn't normally send people to Oxford; there was a thing called the Hertford Scheme by which we gave unconditional places before A level, which was a brilliant idea of the people that designed it because for a while it enabled the college to cream off from high-performing comprehensive schools round the country whose children had never, ever, put in for Oxford because they were frightened of the exams. It was then very much still the third-term exam and all the rest of it. And so for a while we had absolutely brilliant people. My lot tended to be four out of ten from public school, six out of ten from state schools – most of them comprehensives – who never sent children before to Oxford. And a lot of them got firsts. There were years when two people from Essex comprehensives and two Etonians got firsts. And they all worked very hard and played very hard. I wasn't very much older than them, and I'm afraid I used to play with them a bit myself. I was a bachelor don living in college.

BS So by no means indolent, but a late developer in terms of your political interests?

JP Yes. And I got dragged in, quite willingly, to local politics after a while because it was after I got the famous letter from the bursar that I decided I would look around for something else. And one thing led to another and I was invited to put myself up to stand in the 1973 local elections in Oxford and I was elected for the North Ward of Oxford City which then included all of the university area down to the High Street in Oxford. It was a very bad year for the Conservatives. Mr Heath was in power and we were having the beginnings of our terrible trouble with the unions. There were three members elected for the Ward. Two Labour people got in, and then I got in by one vote over a Liberal and upon that one vote, I think, probably hung an awful lot. I suspect that if I hadn't got in I might have thought, 'Well, that was fun, but it was a bit like hard work,' and I might well not have gone on, because I wasn't at all fixed at that stage. But one thing led to another. I worked in the two (1972, 1974) elections for a very nice, very scholarly Member of Parliament for Oxford, Monty Woodhouse, a great Greek scholar at New College. He fought in the war in Greece and was a partisan hero, still happily alive. He was a junior minister in the Macmillan government. But he lost, unfortunately, in the 1974 October election. I'd been his driver, gopher, bag-carrier in both of the elections in the traditional way. And there was a vacancy. They wanted to get someone soon because apparently, although I've rather forgotten it, in 1975 people thought there might be quite an early general election. Wilson was looking rocky. He retired not long afterwards. And I'd been around just long enough to make a splash but not long enough to make enemies locally. I think that if I'd been waiting around for about another year I would have annoyed too many people. It's very hard to be selected in your own area. And I fought and won the 1979 election from another very nice, very distinguished, very scholarly Labour MP called Evan Luard, now dead, who was a Foreign Office minister in the Wilson government. He was a Fellow of St Anthony's College.

BS Could you describe your career as a Member of Parliament briefly, up until the point at which you became Secretary of State?

JP Back benches. Because I wasn't so up to speed politically, I didn't say very much around my first year. It was full of my contemporaries who had been long involved in politics. My old friend Chris Patten, whose friendship dates back before I came into politics; we're not related. William Waldegrave; a certain John Major, and others. We all came in in the 1979 intake, and for the first year or so I was very quiet, very much trying to catch up with my contemporaries who'd been much more involved in the practical hurly-burly of politics. I mean, Chris Patten had been Director of the Conservative Research Department, William Waldegrave had been Ted Heath's political secretary, and others of that sort. I then began to write a bit for the newspapers. I like writing, and I used to write for the *Telegraph* and *The Times,* and one day I was asked to write for the *Guardian*, and I did, and they were the sort of loyal but mildly disrespectful articles you'd expect from a youngish back-bencher – I came into the House when I was thirty-two. And shortly after that, I think because Mrs Thatcher had an eye to people who might be a nuisance, she called me round to No. 10 and invited me to join her government and sent me to the Northern Ireland Office.

BS Because she thought you might become a nuisance?

JP Well, I'm not quite sure why. [*BS and JP laugh*] It was either flattering or she confused me with Chris Patten or she thought I was going to be a nuisance. And I then found myself in Northern Ireland. And from then on I've had a fairly long time in government. I took no particular interest in education. I think I only spoke in one education debate, but that was a debate when a certain Neil Kinnock was their Education Spokesman and Chris Patten and myself teased him quite a bit during that debate.

BS That must have been quite fun?

JP Yes.

BS Can we turn to education policy?

JP Yes.

BS How important and how radical is the 1988 Education Reform Act?

JP I think very important. Just as radical as the 1944 settlement when seen with the other Acts that came afterwards, Brian. When seen with the 1992 Act and when seen with the 1993 Act, which we all know and love. And then to be seen with the Act which is going to reform teacher training, which is making very good progress in committee. I think if you take those together as a bundle of reforms – and I want to see no more mainstream legislation on education – I think extraordinarily radical; as profound and as far-reaching as the 1944 Act. The 1944 settlement was a creature of its time. It was concerned with bringing education to more people; people like me, because I benefited from a state education. You know, if it hadn't happened there wouldn't have been grammar schools – I wouldn't have gone to grammar school. It was concerned with bringing mass education up for all 15-year-olds and then to all 16-year-olds, and introducing grammar schools. It was concerned with institutions and organization – grammar, technical, secondary – and it was concerned with the new settlement with the churches. And that was all terribly radical for the mass education, but it was still very much concerned with form and organization, institution, the bodies involved. I think what the post-Baker revolution – and I happen to think that Kenneth Baker's Act is one of fundamental importance, and every credit to him – I think ever since then we've been more concerned with switching to outputs, what the education system produces. So, if you like, the 1944 Act was an institutional and organizational settlement bringing mass education and post-1988, the bundle of four Acts together, I think, make it very much more output-orientated, which is what I think we should be doing. The thinking that informs our ambitious programme of legislation lays stress on the interests of those who use and pay for the education system – pupils, students, parents, employers and tax-payers. The Education Acts of 1988, 1992 and 1993, together with the teacher training reforms currently before Parliament, form the basis of the new settlement of 1994.

BS   That's a large claim.

JP   A large claim, but one which I believe is justified by the breadth and scope of our reforms. Initially, they've not been uncontroversial; to use one of R. A. Butler's phrases, we've gathered in a whole barrowload of nettles. But I'm confident that our reforms will pay large dividends in raising standards of teaching and learning: it's on raising standards that the future of our country depends. I believe that children – and I hope I shan't be thought politically incorrect – need to be taught to work hard, to care, to be competitive. It's a question of educating and training our native talent as well as – better than – our competitors. And the pace at which we can pursue this aim doesn't just depend on what the nation can afford to spend on education, but on how effectively we use our available resources. Outputs are more important than inputs. Concentration on outputs is at the heart of the new settlement; the new, demanding, National Targets illustrate my belief that success must be judged not by faith, but by works. And this means a deliberate, an explicit shift of emphasis away from inputs – not just funding, but also forms of organization and teaching methods – to outputs – what pupils and students actually achieve. But having said that, there's one absolutely crucial set of inputs that sometimes gets neglected. I'm talking about the self-discipline, the competitive spirit, the determination that young people need to get the best out of their education – and the best out of themselves. It's these qualities – promoted by well-ordered schools and colleges – which will enable us to reach our targets. But it's been a sort of preoccupation with inputs of the more obvious kind – and with low achievers, indifferent schools and disaffected pupils – that has obscured some very significant achievements, particularly over the last ten years or so. For example, in 1950 only 10 per cent of young people received any full-time education post-16, and only one young person in 20 went on to higher education. These proportions grew fairly slowly over the next 30 years. By 1980 they had reached about 40 per cent and 1 in 8. And since then, progress has been dramatic. Now over 70 per cent of 16-year-olds continue full-time education, and the proportion gaining two A levels has nearly doubled – from 14 per cent to 26 per cent – with many more pursuing vocational qualifications. By 1992 the number gaining a degree had increased by 50 per cent, giving us the highest graduation rate in Europe; and with almost 1 in 3 young people now entering higher education, the rate for the present generation of students will be even higher. It has to be said that these are remarkable figures and reflect impressive work by teachers, lecturers and, of course, the students themselves. We've come a long way. Now, the national crusade to meet our targets means we've got to work even harder; we've got to aim even higher. Because our major international competitors, sometimes starting from a significantly higher base than us, have also been making great strides in recent years. We're well up with the leaders in participation by 16-year-olds, but we're still lagging behind in participation by the 16–18 age group as a whole – this is indicated by the latest international comparisons. So we can't afford to relax; we've still got to improve our efforts and drive up standards. And there are many important outstanding challenges. For example, illiteracy among young adults remains almost as high now as in 1982. A worrying number of schools are mediocre performers, even though we devote more of our GNP to state education than the Germans or the Japanese. These problems have yet to be grappled with.

BS   What would you identify as the particular strengths and weaknesses of the 1988 Act?

JP   I think it was a visionary attempt to make it possible for choice and diversity – which was the title of the White Paper that we produced in 1992 – to come about. I think that was it. Everything was introduced afterwards very fast. If there are any criticisms, it's that implementation was not perfect – I'm not telling you anything you don't know, Brian. However, if implementation hadn't happened rather quickly, would anything have happened at all? We had a very good debate in the House two weeks ago when we had the second reading of the Education Bill, and you'd find it useful to quote Angela Rumbold's words. She was much involved, and she said, I thought, very honestly and bravely, that there were problems. There are problems with all legislation, nothing's perfect. And she said there were particular problems with implementation, but she felt that if they hadn't gone on as it were pell mell – my words, not hers – nothing would have happened. Now let me read to you from *Parliamentary Debates* for 3 May 1994, and I shall present you with this. Angela was talking about testing:

> I am convinced that systems can be devised which will be satisfactory in terms of quality and understanding what is happening in schools without burdening schools further with great wodges of paper. [JP: *And you can say hear, hear to that*]

> I say that because I know perfectly well that the system that we introduced for testing and the curriculum in the days when I was Minister did burden teachers. I accept responsibility for that, and always have done. [JP: *That's quite true*] I always knew that, at some stage, we would have to rectify some of those institutions. But in order to drive through the measures that were so important for Britain's schools, we accepted some of the defects that were bound to occur. [JP: *In other words, she was talking about the classic dilemma of the reformer. Do you try to get everything right, or do you actually drive it on? And I think that's admirable*]

> In the same way, I am sure the Bill will bring such huge benefits to the schools and to the teaching profession that we must ensure that we do not overburden people in the process. I am sure that we shall make some mistakes, but that does not matter, because the principle behind the Bill is fundamentally correct for Britain's teaching profession

So I'm right with them. I won't hear all that much criticism even of the implementation. It's easy to criticize, but supposing we hadn't got going, supposing we'd waited and endlessly piloted, then we might actually not even be where we are today. So the Act – fine; the implementation – obvious problems. But we were trying to introduce a National Curriculum which, arguably, we should have had a hundred years earlier; trying to introduce testing, and all the rest of it.

BS   Conservative education policy prior to 1986. It doesn't feature large in the manifestos. What was going on, if anything, in your view?

JP   Well, not very much. It's always a matter of surprise to me that so little happened between 1979 and the 1986 Act, but I think you have to realize that it was happening against a background of a tradition that really the Department was concerned to distribute resources, ensure fair play, register schools – a very *laissez-faire* approach which meant that really the LEAs did it and governments didn't really have much of a view about standards – teaching standards, standards of examination results; literacy wasn't really thought to be an issue that government should be involved in. Actually, it all started in 1976 with Callaghan's Ruskin speech, which was then much watered down, allegedly by Shirley Williams, who was Secretary of State at the time. There was, I think, a very strong view among the civil servants, understandably. Only ministers are to blame; civil servants aren't to blame for anything because they just do as they're told; but there was a strong feeling that the relationship was right – you left it to the LEAs and they got on with it. So Callaghan didn't do much in the three years. He made, I thought, a brave and far-sighted speech. A *very* brave and far-sighted speech, but there was a lot of back-pedalling, and I don't think Shirley Williams carried it forward particularly vigorously, so the legends are. And then the Tories came in. Mrs Thatcher had been Secretary of State for Education. I think she'd been once bitten twice shy a bit by educa-tion. There were many other targets around, and it took a while before Keith Joseph could find the levers. It took him a very long time. He was actually trying to rethink, so I don't think he's had a fair crack of the whip. He was trying to rethink the whole way in which government looked at education, and that took him a long time against massive vested interests, I think; both inside the Department because they weren't used to working that way, and with the so-called educational establishment, whatever that is.

BS   I think Keith Joseph's reputation is being somewhat refurbished in latter years.

JP   Yes, I mean, I'm busily trying to refurbish it because I think he was a most cerebral man. And I don't think we would have got anywhere without him having gone through the horrors of all of that.

BS   It has been suggested that there's a kind of paradox involved in Conservative education policy, a kind of ambiguity, because on the one hand there's centralization of power over the curriculum *apropos* the 1988 Act; on the other hand diversity, variety in school-ing – LEA schools, GM schools, CTCs.

JP   Technical colleges.

BS   Technical colleges – parental choice, and there seems to be this paradox of free economy/strong state. Is that, do you feel, inten-tional in the legislation, or has it just happened?

JP   You'd have to ask Kenneth Baker. I don't know what his answer was to your colleague. Whether it was intentional or not, I think it's the right thing to have done, whether we stumbled on it or not; because why do we have the National Curriculum and why are we going through this difficult period with the implementation of testing, to put it mildly? The reason is to deliver a minimum entitlement, to borrow Emily Blatch's excellent phrase; a minimum entitlement for all our children to a decent education at a reasonable standard, wherever they come from and wherever geography has thrown them by chance. That, I think, is a proper thing for the state to do, and I don't think it's incompatible with, to borrow Kenneth Baker's phrase, trying to redistribute power from the hub to the rim of the wheel; which I think is a very good phrase of Kenneth's. Because what you're actually saying is, well, here are the standards, what we are really doing now is saying, over to you to carry out your teaching of your children up to these standards, but through a diversity of routes. Now, I don't think that's paradoxical. I think that's well matched. Incidentally, with twenty-twenty hindsight, I would have started our reforms of education with a 1980 reform of teacher training. I think that's where we should have started. But of course, you know, life's not like that, and we didn't think in those terms. And now, fifteen years later, we are doing it, and I think the Teacher Training Agency will be very important. Equally, and again I stumbled on this – and this is me rather than anyone else – when I introduced the 1992 performance tables against quite strong advice at the time from a lot of people saying 'This is dangerous. Why don't you pilot it? Why don't you shadow it? Bring it in over a period of years. The trade unions won't like it. Parents won't be able to understand it' and all that patronizing claptrap, which I think is terribly patronizing to parents – I loathe and despise that attitude. I went ahead and did it because there's a great drive in government under the Citizen's Charter, under the Prime Minister, to try to publish more information. So what I wanted to do was to publish more information and to make quite sure that we saw what was going on in our schools. What I hadn't realized – and I think this is happening quite rapidly – was just what a powerful lever, to think in those terms, the simple publication of information has been. Because I believe it's had an electrifying effect in a lot of schools and in a lot of local education authorities. And I have fairly clear evidence, anecdotal evidence, from what chief education officers have told me, and certainly from what is going on in our schools, that they've seen their relative standing and status and they don't like it in some cases and they want to work harder to put it right.

BS   Work harder to put it right for whom?

JP   Well, they may be putting it right for, you know, 'the school', in quotes, but it's actually putting it right for the children. And I think that by chance we stumbled on one of the most important post-war levers for levering up standards that we could have imagined – simply the publication of information. And we'll be doing more of it this autumn. It will be the third year this autumn; we'll be publishing taught time as well. The year after, the fourth year, I think we could validly begin to think in terms of indexes of how schools have done up and down. That's still to be decided. But I think those performance tables are extremely important.

BS   So the 1988 Act was a visionary Act which paved the way, so to speak, for choice and diversity, for the policies as spelt out in the White Paper of 1992?

JP   That's as I see it. And let me quote you a sentence from Butler's 1943 White Paper which might just as easily have appeared in the

1992 White Paper: 'It is just as important to achieve diversity as it is to ensure equality of educational opportunity.' But, as you know, Brian, that important message got somewhat neglected in the 1960s and 1970s. It's true that some diversity of provision survived; there were the church schools and other voluntary-aided schools, and of course those grammar schools that remained, but otherwise there was a depressing drift towards uniformity. And that was damaging, I think, because distinctive character and identity are powerful motivators for staff and pupils, and I want to give schools a much wider range of opportunities to develop their particular strengths. My first priority has been to encourage schools to specialize in technology, science and mathematics by becoming technology colleges. Of course, there were over 300 of the old technical schools in the late 1940s; twenty years on and their numbers had halved; and, in their original form, they've become extinct. And it was not because the concept of technical schools was misguided; these technical schools were victims of our failure to take technical and vocational education seriously. So in introducing the technology colleges initiative I've been very conscious of what happened to the old technical schools. We need to reverse the trend and start taking technical and vocational education seriously. And these technology colleges will extend parental and student choice by giving schools the chance to develop distinctive strengths while at the same time providing the National Curriculum. To become technology colleges, schools have to set targets for raising standards in technology, science and maths; they have to strengthen links with business by raising sponsorship and by appointing sponsor governors. Now that's the starting-point, and I hope to give other schools the opportunity to specialize in other subjects such as business, modern languages, sport, and so on. But providing diversity in schooling is of little value unless parents are given the opportunity to take advantage of it. The old, producer-driven regime tended to marginalize parents, whereas our reforms are putting them where they belong – right at the heart of the system. Parents are now better informed about the character and performance of schools; more open enrolment has removed artificial barriers to admission; parents can play a more active part in the management of the school through its governing body. And of course we've given parents the right to vote on whether their school should seek grant-maintained status. I believe self-government is the best way of running schools because it gives schools greater flexibility to respond to local needs and national initiatives, and to develop their distinctive strengths. But in this, as in other areas, parents should be given a choice. And I'm also extending choice for older pupils and students through the streamlining of the curriculum for 14- to 16-year-olds. This means that schools will have greater flexibility to offer a range of courses tailored to the strengths and interests of their pupils; and a wider variety of high quality vocational courses are being developed pre-16, designed to complement the GCSE. And this increasing flexibility for 14- to 16-year-olds leads naturally to the new, flexible, post-16 qualifications framework which is based on three distinct types of qualification – the well-established GCE A Level and AS Level; work-related National Vocational Qualifications; and the new GNVQs, the General National Vocational Qualifications. So it provides a menu of options which can be tailored to the aptitudes and abilities of the student. I'm not aiming to establish three rigid, separate pathways. There'll always be plenty of scope to mix and match different types of qualification. Each of these systems must be subject to rigorous quality assurance, and the new Code of Practice for GCSE qualifications is an important step in that direction. I'm working with the National Council for Vocational Qualifications and the awarding bodies to ensure that GNVQs and NVQs meet equally demanding quality standards.

BS   You hinted previously that this was the job you wanted.

JP   Yes, but I never thought it would be offered to me. I thought I'd end up, I don't know, as Secretary for Health, or something like that, Social Security, or whatever.

BS   Why did you want Education particularly?

JP   Because I've always had a lurking feeling that we were not doing as well as we could do as a country for the bottom 40 or 50 per cent by ability. I felt, and I do feel even more strongly now, that we do extremely well at university level. I wouldn't have dared promise when I was still a youngish Oxford don campaigning for the 1979 election – keen though I was to get into Parliament, I wouldn't have dared to promise to the electors that we would, if we had fifteen years, increase the participation rate of people in higher education from 1 in 8 in 1979 to 1 in 3 now. That would have struck me as quite impossible. When I went up to Cambridge in 1964 I was one of 7 per cent who then went up to university; now it's 30 per cent, and I think that's an extraordinary achievement, and one we must sustain. Butler, back in 1944, wouldn't have believed it possible, any more than I did, back in 1964, when I was just one of 7 per cent going up to university. And the fact that more students are going up to university doesn't mean more of the same – more young white men from privileged backgrounds; because the university students of today are drawn from a much wider social and ethnic spectrum. Nearly half are women. Mature students now make up a third of all full-time entrants. And a survey last year indicated that, for the first time, more than half of all first-year students came from social class C, D and E backgrounds. Equally, getting rid of the binary line between the universities and polytechnics has been a major step forward in promoting equal status between vocational and academic subjects. I'd always been convinced, as much as I'd thought about it – it wasn't all that deeply – that we'd never done anything to rectify what Prince Albert put his finger on in the 1857 National Conference on Education: which was our great instinctive love of academic qualifications and the academic path of, you know, Greats, Greek, Latin, ancient history, all the rest of it; and that we needed to do something about vocational education. And that's why during the last two years I was very pleased to get the chance to do something about that. And that we have done, by radically increasing the numbers of people going into further education – a 25 per cent increase over three years. It's astounding that we managed to find the money to do that. Norman Lamont was actually the person who made it possible, with Michael Portillo. To do that, of course, I had to decide what we should do about the pell-mell expansion of universities, and I felt it was time in any event that we had a pause to reassess where we'd got to, making quite sure there were no problems with quality. And I think most universities have welcomed this break, this sort of period of consolidation; but I consciously switched the money from higher education to further education. And more doesn't mean worse; in both further and higher education, systematic arrangements will ensure that quality and standards are assured, maintained, improved. As far as schools – well, I'd always felt that the top, the sort of people like me who were lucky and had that innate ability and good teachers, God-given, to handle A level, that was no problem – but I always felt, I still feel, that we're only slowly – and all international statistics show that to be right – getting to grips with those with lower ability.

BS   You took over from Ken Clarke.

JP   That's right.

BS   How would you assess the position when you took over?

JP   It was fine. There were no problems. We were obviously coming to the crunch point at some stage after I arrived, when the problems with the reforms were beginning to build up. See Angela Rumbold's prescient words. At some stage or another I was absolutely certain there would be a great row or a to-do, because eventually it was quite clear that the pressure was building up. It took me about nine months to realize that, but I was a new Secretary of State. And certainly there was no feeling in the Department from the most senior of officials that we were heading towards the great row that we had this time last year over testing. It wasn't really until Christmas last year that suddenly the signs began to come up that things were not going well. But I'd been responsible entirely since 1992. And I felt that Ken had driven on things very fast and very effectively, particularly, apart from setting FE colleges and sixth forms free from local authority control – and isn't it amazing now we have all our universities grant-maintained, all our colleges are grant-maintained, all our sixth-form colleges are grant-maintained. It's the way of the future. But you and I agree, although I know, Brian, you want to go even faster than we can presently go (see Sherratt, B., 1994 *Opting for Freedom: A Stronger Policy for Grant-maintained Schools*. London: Centre for Policy Studies). But I think Ken's lasting contribution, apart from beginning to get to grips with some of the problems that were facing us on the curriculum and testing, was to have set up OFSTED and the independent Inspectorate. And I think that's terrific. Our policy with regard to HMI was seen by some as tantamount to sacrilege. Of course, this body of men and women was set up many years before the 1870 Act, let alone the Board of Education: they were the eyes and ears of the Secretary of State. Generally speaking, they were people who'd achieved some distinction in the teaching profession. They were able to go into classrooms, report on exactly what they saw, and make their assessments on the basis of the nationwide experience they had from going into classrooms across the whole country. They still are. But the cycle of HMI inspections meant that out of 23,000 schools in the system, only 200 a year had a full inspection; at that rate it meant that a secondary school would get inspected once every forty years before Ken's reforms, and a primary school once every two hundred years. Now it's every school, as you know; in striking contrast, it's once every four years. And the old-style HMI reports concentrated mostly on what teachers were doing rather than on what pupils were achieving – on inputs rather than outputs. And when these reports were published – and they weren't even published until Keith took that bold decision some ten years ago – there was no way of ensuring that appropriate action was taken. In a few cases the report revealed such a public scandal that the local authority had to take action, but for the vast majority of reports – the 200 a year – however mediocre the performance that was revealed, those responsible could keep their heads down and wait for the fuss to die away. Nearly all of them did: publication was not enough. LEAs had their own inspection and advisory services, and a few undertook systematic inspection of their schools; fewer still published the results. They didn't fill the gap between the 200 and the 23,000. And it was the local authority reporting to the local authority. Ken Clarke changed all that. He put in place a system which would ensure that all schools were inspected with the rigour of the 200, that the standards schools achieved were set out in full, that they took any action necessary to improve performance, and that the governing body and senior management were accountable.

Nearly 1,000 secondary schools have already been inspected under the new system. They've prepared their action plans and sent them to parents. The inspection results with the performance table results – I should have brought those two together earlier – have together had that electrifying effect. Because I think the publication of information to the general public – who, of course, can understand these things – and the publication of inspection results and the feeling among schools that 'the inspectors are coming, we'd better find out; let's get hold of the framework documents; let's see what's going to happen, even if it's not for another two or three years', is having, I think, a galvanizing effect. Indeed, the OFSTED handbook for inspection is being used as a bible for school development and improvement. I believe we now have a revitalized inspection system which is proving its worth as an instrument for quality. I think that's a terrific monument to what Ken Clarke did.

BS   And performance table results?

JP   Publication of data on actual performance – on output rather than input – is a key feature. School and college performance tables are now a permanent feature on the new educational landscape, and they're already having a dramatic effect in informing parents and students in the choices they make, showing what can be achieved by the best and stimulating action to raise standards. The tables show that a few schools are achieving very poor standards. But I believe that the children in these schools, often from deprived areas, deserve better. So from this year, schools that fail will need to improve quickly or be taken over by Education Associations: these consist of small teams of experienced people whose task will be to turn the schools round. A crucial part of that – highlighted by the recent OFSTED report on 'Improving Schools' – will be to get teachers to raise their expectations of their pupils.

BS   How did you resolve the practical difficulties in terms of the implementation of the National Curriculum with assessment and testing? That must have been a real headache for you when you took over.

JP   Yes. As I say, we were beginning to get into a frame of mind before Christmas, I think – I hope I'm not speaking with hindsight, I can't remember now exactly when, before Christmas 1992 – when something had to be done. We were beginning to feel our way towards what should be done. Then there was the row about testing, the boycotts, and to a certain extent the pace was forced, to put it mildly, and we needed someone to go out with great integrity, highly respected with no known politics, to find the best way forward we could to reform the National Curriculum. That was Sir Ron Dearing and his reforms, as suggested – now out for consultation as I announced last Monday – were the result of that. But it's very hard for me to judge objectively, or to talk objectively, about a period that's so fresh. Certainly it was a major problem, but it is interesting that no one at the centre was really aware that these great problems were coming.

BS   And, I presume, you must be very pleased with the Dearing compromise, the Dearing solution?

JP   Yes, I've added my own twiddles to it; all children between 5 and 7 to have some British history; English to be given close attention in all subjects, whether it's geography or history; if you can't communicate and express yourself in English, then you can't function. We'll have to see what teacher-land makes of it over the next three months, but I think we have got the makings of a settlement now, which I hope will be in place by January next year, when the papers go out to all the schools so they know what they're doing for September 1995. There were a lot of problems, particularly coming from SEAC, much less from NCC – hardly at all from NCC – about the late delivery of materials, sudden changes to instructions, material not being delivered on time, very short notice, all of those things – and I learnt by having my fingers burnt by all of that. And the SCAA, as well as being involved in the process of reform, has been, I think, a pretty efficient body in terms of getting material out. And that's something which we must never lose sight of. So I think, five years from September 1995, up to the year 2000, should be a period of peace and quiet where we can concentrate on the outputs; on making sure that the test papers are rigorous enough; against a background of some stability, which I'm sure practising teachers would welcome.

BS   How would you characterize the distinctive ideas you brought with you when you assumed your present office?

JP   Well, I don't think I had any distinctive ideas, other than those to which I referred earlier, which was a feeling that we needed to do something about vocational education and to try to right the old binary line between the academic and the vocational. I feel very strongly that we need to do something about those people who've not been, perhaps, challenged enough – I don't use that word in the politically correct sense, I use it in the sense that they haven't been asked to work hard enough; they haven't had high enough expectations; like that marvellous report by OFSTED about inner-city school problems, about nine months ago or whenever it was, saying that they did not find major problems with resources or pupil–teacher ratios, but what they did find was substantial problems in teachers having low expectations. I believe that the one thing which will deliver children from the prison of circumstance and background, if they perceive it to be a prison, is a teacher or teachers who ask a lot of them; showing them that they can develop their imagination. But that's about as far as I can go. If I went any further than that – well, I couldn't, because I'd be making it up. Those are my gut feelings. I wasn't expecting to come here.

BS   Some would see the 1993 legislation as the planned, logical extension of the 1988 legislation, and subsequent legislation, whereas others see it as a planned, radical departure. How do you react to that?

JP   I think it's a logical extension of the 1988 legislation. It builds on it, trying to put into place those very important things which set up a proper funding mechanism for grant-maintained schools and a new mechanism for dealing with surplus school places which takes into account the fact that there are two sectors now – the LEA sector and the grant-maintained sector, ugly phrases – and also to set in train a whole range of policies to promote choice and diversity, which I think was the bridge to which the 1988 Act, which was a huge thing, couldn't quite get at the time. So I see it as building on. Certainly that's how I characterize it in my own mind.

Part Two: 6 June 1994

JP   That's a very nice tie, Brian.

BS   Austin Reed, Secretary of State. A birthday present from my wife.

JP   This is one that my daughter made me get in Jermyn Street from New and Lingwood. She's only seven, so she's allowed to make her father look peculiar.

BS   Not at all. The teddy bears are very subtle; I wouldn't mind one like that myself.

JP   New and Lingwood.

BS   We were talking about the National Curriculum, Secretary of State. How do you respond to those who say that the National Curriculum, as envisaged by Kenneth Baker, was something of a mistake; in fact, they might say that you had to pick up the pieces?

JP   All of us carry on in the seamless robe of government from where our predecessors left off; and I'm a great admirer of Ken Baker. I worked closely with him twice in my professional life as a minister. First, when I was Minister of State for Housing, Urban Affairs and Construction, when he was Secretary of State for the Environment. Second, when he was Home Secretary and I was Minister of State in the Home Department. So I've worked very closely with him. I didn't work with him during that particular period – 1988. I think Ken was trying to make up for a 100-year-old short-fall. We should have had a National Curriculum at the turn of the century or earlier. I believe, myself, that his motif of 'broad and balanced' was right; and I would argue that we still have a broad and balanced curriculum; albeit that it's slimmed down and albeit that there's perhaps a bit more concentration on the basics at the core which highlighted that. What happened to the National Curriculum is that – and only ministers are responsible, no one else is to blame, so if anybody doesn't like anything that I have done that's my fault, I can't blame anyone else – but none the less ministers listened to enthusiastic teachers and enthusiastic educational experts who said that this, that and the other must be in the National Curriculum; so if you like, it was a gold-plated kitchen sink into which everything went, and I think we found out all too painfully, and I got some of the sharper end of it, that the National Curriculum was over-crowded, over-elaborate, over-prescriptive. I think we have managed to split it down in such a way as will give us, from September 1995, a five-year period in which there will be no further changes.

BS In retrospect, might you have preferred it had there not been a National Curriculum, and that you might have introduced the slimmed-down version yourself?

JP I'm no good at hindsight. I think we are where we are. I think we should have had a concentration on the core basic skills and I think we should have had a National Curriculum – I have always believed in a National Curriculum, just like I have always believed that we should have concentated much more on vocational education, as Prince Albert exorted us to do back in the 1850s. Our reforms are all about raising standards, and the National Curriculum has a key part to play in that. It is the National Curriculum, perhaps, which would have most surprised Butler, but I've yet to meet a teacher who doesn't think there should be one. I believe now is the time for setting key standards and for setting out the fundamentals of what should be taught in our schools. It's hardly surprising that Butler and Churchill could see no role for central government in the curriculum. Fifty years ago people tended to be less mobile, looked for work locally; even after the war their expectations were more modest. Schools could meet local needs more easily without letting their pupils down. But all that's changed. All pupils are entitled to a good grounding in the basics; if we don't give them that, then they're going to be lost in the literate, numerate, technological world of today: all teachers need to know what the highest standards amount to, so that all our schools can aspire to them. It was the post-war phobia about discussing the content of teaching at the national level that prevented schools from exploring what the highest stan-dards might mean. And all our pupils need to be stretched, to be encouraged to achieve higher standards, because investment for the future depends on a versatile, better qualified, more confident people. And that's what the National Curriculum can produce: it can raise expectations by setting demanding standards. It estab-lishes a curricular entitlement for all pupils; it provides the means –

including through national testing – to establish whether those standards are being met, and, if they're not, to sound the alarm. OFSTED, the independent school's Inspectorate, is clear that since it was introduced – five years ago – the National Curriculum has already raised expectations. And the review now being taken forward will strip out unnecessary bureaucracy and release teachers' energies to pursue higher standards.

BS   The corporate act of worship seems to be causing some problems – or rather some headteachers might see it causing some problems – or you may see it as some heads causing you problems. How do you now approach the whole business of a corporate act of worship, in that some heads seem to be saying that it won't work?

JP   It's the law of the land – it's not a J. Patten production. Parliament decided in 1944 – the Butler Act which is so often praised to the skies – that there should be a daily act of worship. This was reinforced during the passage of the Baker Act in 1987–88. The provision of the 1988 Baker Act, which says that there must be the daily act of worship of – I forget the exact words – predominantly Christian character, was put through the House of Commons with a huge majority. But, wait for it – it was on a free vote – 372 voted in favour and 101 voted against (these figures are in my mind because I was addressing the National Association of Headteachers last Thursday), and all parties went to the division lobby – it was an all-party vote in favour of this; so it was a free vote of the whole House of Commons, like you have a free vote over fox-hunting, or a free vote over abortion, or hanging – so if headteachers don't like it, it's the will of Parliament, not the will of this Secretary of State with his own interests in religion. That having been said, the Prime Minister, as he pointed out in his interview in the *Sunday Express* yesterday, and reported on page 3 of the *Sunday Express*, is very strongly in favour of a morning assembly with a religious element to it, as I am – I think it is a period in which the whole school gets together, or at least the whole tutor group or the whole class (however it's arranged), and I think that if headteachers don't like it they are of course quite entitled to campaign to change the law, but meanwhile they should obey the law. (Sorry to go on so long, but there are two other points.) OFSTED – the Inspectorate – tell me that in their 1992–93 study into this RE issue, they looked at something like 130 Primary Schools (I can remember these figures again because I was briefed for them – I still just remember them from last Thursday) and 100 per cent were carrying out their duties properly. They visited 188 secondary schools but found that in 40 per cent the law was not being observed, and in a number of other schools there were tensions and difficulties. Now I'm not saying that any headteacher or deputy headteacher, particularly if he or she is not a

Christian, should have to take part in religious worship, but there are lots of other teachers in the schools. There should be thirteen and a half thousand RE teachers in our schools at the moment, but about half of them are absent without leave, not teaching RE, although the most recent survey showed that there were nil vacancies, or near to nil vacancies, for RE teachers – we've got thirteen and a half thousand with an RE speciality, but only half of them are actually teaching RE – some of them may have been promoted, maybe heads, maybe deputies, or whatever it is, but an awful lot are not teaching it, so that they could certainly be used; and of course heads could also turn to the Standing Advisory Councils for Religious Education (SACRE), and can turn indeed to local churches, and in the case of Jews and Muslims and others ...

BS   Yes, I have three tame priests who come in on a regular basis.

JP   Very useful.

BS   Very useful, yes. Can we turn to something which, as you know, is rather dear to my heart – the whole GM issue? How do you see the GM policy and its future implementation?

JP   Well, let me look. I keep a card on my desk, so as of 6 June we've got 1,122 'yes' ballots – yet we have rejected some, we've rejected 79 – but overall we've got about 1,000 either operating or they've published their proposals and they're about to start. We're bound by our election manifesto – parental choice drives the process. It continues to be a very successful process. Once a ballot is taken, in seven out of ten cases parents vote 'yes'. The numbers have reduced in recent months – in terms of the numbers of ballots overall – but although the numbers of ballots are fewer, wherever ballots happen seven out of ten vote 'yes'. There are various explanations for why the process is not going even more quickly than it's going now, although I will eat my academic hat garnished if by the time of the next general election we haven't got more than half of England's secondary schools grant-maintained. Even on the present rate of growth, that seems a very likely projection – that's half of the 4,000. That's an 'irreversible change', to use the language of socialism. Why has it not gone even faster? There are various explanations that have been put forward. One is that the government is not going through a period of unparalleled popularity in the early part of 1994, and therefore people aren't so inclined to do things that they know the government want. And indeed, it was very interesting in mining areas during the height of that business over pit closures – we suddenly lost a number of ballots in mining areas, and it is thought to be a kind of walk-out, a protest vote against the government. The second reason is that there are among secondary schools – who have provided the burden of grant-maintained schools so far – that there are among secondary schools a cohort or a group of natural GM schools driven by heads and governors who want to be independent – some with a tradition of grammar school background, but by no means all, as you know from your own experience, and as I know from schools like Small Heath or whatever else; there are schools with no background of independence, no direct- grant background or grammar school background at all; but this is a group of people who want to be independent, and we are gathering those up. But there are a lot more who, to use your expression, Brian, prefer the educational dependency culture. Or thirdly, that we are hoist on the success of our own local management of schools policy. Most people say, 'Oh heavens – like in Buckinghamshire or West Sussex – we've got £90–£95 out of every £100; it's much cosier to stay with the LEA.' So those are the reasons which have been adduced to me – I'm too much in the thick of it all to know which reasons are correct. What I am satisfied with is that we have got more than 1,100 'yes' votes today, whereas we had a couple of hundred GM schools, as you know, Brian, at the time of the last general election only two years ago.

BS   I can fully appreciate why you want to stay with parental choice in terms of GM ballots, but why was it necessary to legislate for annual consideration by governors?

JP   Because we believed – I believed – that there were in some parts of the country – and we had sound evidence for this – chairmen of governors who were refusing to let the issue be considered at all in the school governing bodies, and so we thought it right that it should be formally on the agenda every year, and that due notice should be given. I think governors should have the right to discuss these things properly, and properly consider them.

BS   Was it ever the government's intention, do you think, that the majority of schools, or the majority of secondary schools, should become GM? It doesn't necessarily seem to be there in Ken Baker's mind, but he does say that it certainly was in Margaret Thatcher's mind – that she was anxious to see all schools GM.

JP   Well, it certainly is my view and the Prime Minister's view that we regard grant-maintained as the natural model. As I said – I hope I haven't said something risky – I'd eat my academic hat garnished (I hope I have lost it if I fail) if we don't have a majority of our secondary schools in two and a half years' time, or whenever the next general election comes, because the pace of change is such that statistically it's the most likely thing to happen. The Prime Minister and myself regard grant-maintained as the natural model, but we also believe in choice – we're Tories – and freedom of choice. I don't know what Margaret Thatcher's view was, I never discussed it with her.

BS   She was very impressed with the idea, on hearing of it, apparently, and said, 'Yes, we must have all schools out as quickly as possible.' And that rather filled Ken Baker with a degree of apprehension, I think, because at the time, of course, there wasn't a single GM school.

JP   Well, we didn't legislate.

BS   Can we talk about the FAS, the Funding Agency for Schools.

JP   Yes, of course.

BS   Some would see it – and I'm not necessarily one of them – as a bureaucratic intrusion into the provision of education, in some respects almost replacing LEAs where GM schools were concerned; replacing the bureaucracy from which they were freed when they opted out. Now, obviously you don't see it that way: how do you see it?

JP   I see the Funding Agency for Schools as a light touch body; minimal interference; acting as a conduit for state funds for grant-maintained schools; ensuring the money is properly spent; dealing also, very importantly, with the extension of the most popular grant-maintained schools; looking very hard at the provision of new schools – where I would wish, myself, that the majority of new schools that have to be built will be grant-maintained or in the voluntary aided sector. (I know VA is not part of their remit.) There are those who say, 'Oh, you have just created a super LEA.' If I had been in that business I would have gone down the track of having regional representation, you know – South-Eastern Region, South-Western Region, North-Eastern Region, or whatever. For the Funding Agency for Schools I've been stalwart against that. I believe that the FAS is doing a necessary bureaucratic task. After all, if they weren't doing it, civil servants from my Department would have to do it. Someone's got to do it. Someone has to pay the cheques, and I know this of Sir Christopher Benson, the Chairman, and a number of his colleagues – and you think of Sir Robert Balchin, Mr Stanley Kalms, the Chairman of Dixons, the great retailers – I mean, these are people who believe in delegation and light touchery; that's why they're on the Board. You can see why if there's any gossip I have appointed the High Master of Manchester Grammar School to be the Chairman of the Teacher Training Agency – it's in this morning's papers – Geoffrey Parker. One of your brethren, Brian.

BS   Yes, indeed.

JP   One of your brethren: I hope the world is pleased with that. He's retiring from Manchester at the end of this term.

BS   Why does the FAS have to have functions beyond funding? It's called the Funding Agency, and yet it will have other functions.

JP   It's got functions to do with the planning of the schools – whether some should be shut down if there are many surplus places, whether new schools should be started up, whether there should be reorganization. We favour a mixed economy – we've got a mixed economy – while we have parental choice about grant-maintained status we're going to have different versions of the balance between maintained and grant-maintained schools in different parts of the country. That means there has to be an element of planning, and I would prefer to see people coming to the Funding Agency saying, 'We want to start up a new school.' Someone has to do the job.

BS   Promoters.

JP   Yes, well absolutely, positively promoters – we want to see lots of them as well. I shall be making an announcement in two or three weeks' time about the new system that we are going to have for promoters, and I think that will go down pretty well. But schools can't start up in a vacuum, someone has to judge whether they are good proposals, whether they are needed, whether the promoters are useful – I prefer that to be done by the FAS than my people here.

BS   And it will have, according to the White Paper, an evolutionary role, which is a mysterious way of putting it perhaps, and I am interested in how it might evolve.

JP   Well, at the moment it will be funding the 1,000 or so grant-maintained schools, and it will be bringing the Common Funding Formula in; it will be looking at the starting up of new schools; it will be looking at the expansion of grant-maintained schools; and in the areas where it's got the major planning function it will be a very major player in promoting educational change in terms of saying, 'Well, we would like this, and more schools have got to come in this area because it's an area of growth on the South coast – we'll look for promoters to start these new schools.' I can see the charm of a totally hands-off system, except in the end that means that every decision would have to come to my desk via civil servants – I don't think one can do it any other way, but just someone there taking the decisions.

BS   What about the future role, then, of LEAs? We've already touched on how LMS is working so well it might appear perhaps to some that there's little point in going for GM, and yet LEAs still basically run the schools. What about the future?

JP   Well, some LEAs – I mean in three areas, I think Hillingdon, Brent and, I've forgotten, one other – in the terms of the 1993 Act the FAS will be in total charge because more than 75 per cent of the places in the secondary sector are grant-maintained; so in those areas the LEA has a more residual role. No one has to have an LEA, a Local Education Authority, any more after the 1993 Act. I think in one or two areas they're looking at putting some of the functions of the LEA together with some of the functions of the Social Services Department and, where there are Housing Authorities, Housing as well, with a kind of all-singing, all-dancing service providing a sort of role. So I think we will find LEAs mutating, changing, diminishing; but again, we've always had a multi-layered, multi-faceted local authority system in this country; and I guess it's consistent with the freedom of choice approach – choice and diversity – that there shouldn't be one single pattern for how this developed. I mean, clearly a number of LEAs are desperately keen not to give up any power at all: I'm often accused, as Kenneth Baker was, as John MacGregor was, as Ken Clarke was, of centralizing power in the centre; but all I'm busily trying to do is to bring power into the hub and then redistribute it to the rim of the wheel – that's how I see it both conceptually, practically and politically. So we're removing power, giving opportunity to local people, as you do, Brian, to run your own school, and that I think is a very good system. If I was a chief education officer, I would be proud of the fact that my schools were running at such a high level of delegation that it was no longer necessary for me to be in existence any more. But I guess there aren't many people like me as chief officers of local education authorities.

BS   What have you been seeking to achieve, Secretary of State, in your policies on teacher training and higher education – the Teacher Training Agency which you have just touched on? The current policy appears, as with all new policies, to be attracting a degree of criticism.

JP   Sure – well most new policies do. There are always vested interests. There are quite clearly a lot of vested interests in higher education institutions in this country as far as teacher training is concerned. I think many of them have taken rather a patronizing approach towards schools; I think many of them have been rather high-handed in the way in which they've expected schools to take on trainee teachers and actually not paid an adequate sum of recompense to the schools themselves. If there are groups of schools – there are groups in Birmingham, there are groups around Bullers Wood in Chislehurst – who want to run their own teacher training themselves (post-graduate teacher training, that is), I think that's a very good thing: we have now got about 250 young people being trained. You only have to go to those schools to find, so I am told (I haven't actually been, but Emily Blatch and Robin Squire have both been to groups of these schools), to see the real enthusiasm that there is there. And in the case of the consortium in Kent, they're using a higher education institution to give them services they don't want to provide themselves – in this case it's the University of Cambridge – the University of Cambridge has to go to the schools to deliver the service. I think this is absolutely right. If you've got a tip-top higher education institution in a university department – fine. If it's not doing so well – and there are one or two rather dozy and doubtful ones around – then after the passage of the Act, should Parliament decide – and they have announced Geoffrey Parker's appointment today, funnily enough, and by coincidence on the day you happen to come here, and I hope that the teaching world welcome the fact that a national class headmaster has been appointed – we haven't appointed a vice-chancellor or a business man or a redundant politician; we've appointed someone at the height of his powers to do this – I think that should Parliament decide that the TTA should be set up, one of its first tasks of course, with OFSTED, will be to look at all people providing teacher training, whether it's schools or higher education institutions. They will not hesitate, I am sure, to recommend changes if they think that some of these courses are not actually up to the mark. It's a very popular profession – teaching – 29,000 new entrants last autumn into teaching (probably slightly too many – we've got no problem on the supply side). I am just worried that the worst, and it's unfair to parody the whole teacher-training world with the 1960s' tag – a lot were very good ones – but the worst are providing still too much theory, not enough practice.

BS   Absolutely. Can I ask you a very general question? Why, in your view, are Conservative policies on education superior to the alternatives which have been canvassed over the past fifteen years?

JP   Well, I don't want to sound too dismissive of the alternatives: let me deal with the alternatives first. I won't be particularly dismissive about the Liberal party – they are very confused; I mean they won't, for example, come clean as to what they really would do with grant-maintained schools if they were in power, but they've come forward and they've said that they want to spend a penny more – the product of a penny income tax on education; so that's fine – it's a high-spending approach. It hasn't done them much good – the MORI pole that was produced in *The Times* the week before last by Peter Riddle which pointed out how different topics had done since 1992, shows that for the Liberal party in three areas it's lost ground since 1992, and one of those three areas is education. But anyway, they are a high-spending party; they'll spend more money. The Labour party – even the most charitable Labour party people that I meet privately will say that they're not quite sure what their policy is; and amazingly enough, whereas the Labour party has already overtaken us in every single area except defence, where we just cling on to our lead as the most competent party, in only one area has the Labour party actually fallen back since the 1992 general election, and it is in education; and in fact we have improved our position since 1992 (despite all the horrors I went through last year with testing); so I don't think they have got an alternative education policy. It's very stuck to the NUT. They're driven by the unions. I think our policy is better because it concentrates on outputs – not inputs. The whole of the post-war world in education has talked about the inputs – how many teachers, the teacher/pupil ratio, how much heads – with respect – are paid or not paid, school buildings, numbers of books. Well actually we've got rather a good record: we are spending half as much again (if you worry about inputs) than we were in 1979: teachers are being paid 56 per cent more than they were in real terms in 1979 (that's the average teacher): we are spending half as much again I think – 40 per cent rather – on books than we were in 1979. But I'm interested in the outputs, and that's why I think our policies are better, because we're concentrating on what comes out the other end. I'm not satisfied with the fact that we've now got a record graduation rate, or that we've got record numbers of 16-year-olds staying in full-time education – it's moved from about 40 per cent to about 70 per cent since 1979. What I'm really worried about and concerned about is what comes out the other end, as you are as a headmaster – the number of children with A to Cs; the number of people with good grades at A level; and I think our performance tables probably (as I think I said the last time we spoke, Brian) are the single most important post-war innovation – more important than spending money, more important than any of the Acts of Parliament I've been involved in; because by exposing performance you drive up standards. So I think we've got an open, output-driven system, as opposed to the Labour and Liberal parties, which are input-driven, and particularly in the case of the Labour party, in hock to the producer lobby – again, with respect to your profession.

BS   Perhaps I can ask you what might seem a rather impertinent question?

JP   Carry on, I love them.

BS   John, what's it like being Secretary of State? What kind of a job is it?

JP   I said when I came here that I wanted to make education more interesting, more debated nationally, because I don't think the British have an education culture like the French do or the Germans do, and I certainly, I think, have succeeded in making it more interesting; although not always in ways that I found particularly comfortable, particularly last year in the row over the National Curriculum and testing. It's extremely hard work, like all cabinet jobs are: it's high-profile, in any event, because everyone's been at school, many people have got children at school, there are 24,000 schools.

BS   Everyone's an expert.

JP   Everyone's an expert, everyone's got a view. Twenty thousand primary schools, etc., 470,000 teachers of different shapes and sizes: so I found it in my first two years quite the most demanding job I've ever had, but also quite the most rewarding job, because I think we've got an enormous battle on our hands to catch up with our worldwide competitors, to work harder, to leap over the French, the Germans, the Japanese, the tiger economies of the Far East. And, therefore, there are some times I feel a bit like a foot soldier in the Second Battle of the Somme. You know, in a shell hole sometimes (as I was last year over testing); sometimes trudging through the mud towards the wire. I think the battle's well worth fighting, because, in the end, if by the time of the next general election we've got an output-driven, higher-performing education system, with standards genuinely going up – and I've tried to anchor standards with the new codes of practice on the Examination Boards – that's a battle worth fighting. So I find it exhilarating.

BS   And what kind of Secretary of State are you? We hear of past Secretaries of State, having different styles in terms of working with their ministers, working with their civil servants and so on – how do you work?

JP   Well, you must ask others to judge me. But how do I work in terms of a description of my style? It's trying to be as corporate as possible. You happen to be here on a Monday. Well, every morning of the week I have what's colloquially known here as 'morning prayers' – my kind of daily assembly in the Department; and that's when I meet every day with all the ministers, and my Special Adviser, and my Private Secretary, and the Press Secretary, and the Permanent Secretary, Sir Tim Lankester; but on Mondays it's even wider than that, and I get all the Deputy Secretaries in as well, and we talk about the week's business. Monday morning is the most important meeting of the week – we went on for nearly an hour this morning, discussing problems that we've got in front of us. And I try to delegate as much as possible; and I try to give each of my ministers individual things and tasks to do. Like Lady Blatch, for example – her job is keeping the House of Lords calm, getting legislation through the House of Lords, which she is brilliant at; but she's also done much of the detailed work on the National Curriculum reform package – the departmental end of it – with extraordinary vigour until two and three in the morning; going through it line by line, just checking that everything was acceptable to us; and I couldn't do without her – she's the most elegant and stylish engine room that any Secretary of State could imagine. Or just take one other example – I won't go round the whole team – Eric Forth. When he came here with me two years ago, we looked at two areas of policy – truancy and special educational needs – and I gave him both of those, and he has produced all that excellent work on truancy and the truancy watch campaign and all the rest of it, which is real and happening in 76 (I think) local authority areas. And he's produced the Special Educational Needs (SEN) Code of Practice. Well, that's a jolly good thing to have on your record, to have done those things. I try to give people, each individual, things to do.

BS   You're a former don, and well used to the cut and thrust of intellectual debate. Do you run your meetings in that kind of way? Are you tough on them intellectually, so to speak?

JP   Well, I am good friends with all my ministers, so we tend to get on very well, and we don't have to spend too long talking because we know each other's minds. That may be dangerous. With officials, with the very top officials, certainly, we have a very free and easy relationship; very informal. It's jackets off, as you and I are now, most of the time. But I'm very careful with officials lower down. They don't often see ministers and you don't want to frighten the pants off them by engaging in too tough debate: so what I do try to do is, I have very large meetings with a lot of junior officials – the junior officials actually do a lot of the work – and some of the bright young HEOs (Higher Executive Officers or Higher Executive Officers Direct, who are sort of university high-flyers) – I like them to come into meetings and see what's going on and listen, because then they can understand how quickly business has to be done. I talk to staff – I've had a meeting here in the Department where I've spoken to junior staff about what it's like to be Secretary of State. I think it's very important. There is a feeling in which the DES in its old guise over there in Elizabeth House was a bit suspect – South of the river, out by itself, on a limb, part of 'the Education Establishment' (whatever that is) – the representatives of the teaching profession on earth rather than a government Department. I think a lot of that was very unfair, although I think some previous Secretaries of State have actually said that quite publicly.

BS   Kenneth Baker has implied it, I think.

JP   I think one or two others have also said that. But it's been a move – we have moved to a new building, the Inspectorate's now independent, there's been a massive move at the top of the office. A new Permanent Secretary, new Deputy Secretaries, new Under-Secretaries; great changes have happened, and certainly the Department of Education seems to me like any other Whitehall Department I've worked in (and I have worked in four others), and I think morale is really pretty good.

BS   It's obviously a tremendously demanding job. So how do you – if you do have any free time at all – how to do you relax?

JP   Well, if you look me up in *Who's Who*, where you have that silly thing about recreation.

BS   I have.

JP   There you'll see 'talking with my wife and daughter' and that is very much my form of relaxation – I mean they are very much soul mates of mine. My wife is in just as demanding a job as me: she's a director of a number of Public Companies; a major job in the City; director of companies like the Ladbrook Group. So she leads a very intensive life, and when I go off to visit schools in Stockport or Biggleswade she's as likely to be getting on a plane to Boston or to Monte Carlo, as she was the week before last. So we try for the weekends to reserve a day. And there's our talkative and amusing daughter who, needless to say, I love, who is seven – she'll be eight next Friday – and we try to spend a lot of time with each other at the weekends. But we shift our family up from Oxfordshire, from our country home there, just outside Oxford, every Sunday night – we did last night. And then my daughter's at a London school; my wife works in London; I work in London; and so we try never to be apart; and they are, I think, the best form of relaxation. So I'm not apart from them as many politicians are from their wives and families. And, you know, we have breakfasts in the mornings and I shall see them all tonight: so that's my kind of major pleasure. It would be foolish to say that anything else other than family or work is really important, because there isn't the time. It's a seven-day-a-week job. You never know when the telephone's going to ring. I've got what I think is a pretty good garden in Oxfordshire – I'm something of a gardener, and we live near the Thames and I have a pond and stream and waterside plants; I'm quite interested in bamboos, and I grow various sorts of bamboos by the side of my little pond and stream – it is a natural pond. I'm interested in old British cars: I've got a couple of old Bristols which are hand-made aluminium jobs, one from 1954 and one from 1969 (it is its twenty-fifth birthday this year). Our family are three, and we have two Burmese cats. They are very much part of our life, and they travel as well backwards and forwards. We used to have two Burmese cats, and as a sort of joke (although it's sort of easy to get, because the name is Patten) we called one General (Patten), and the other Willow (Patten). But unfortunately General had to be put down because he got an infectious blood disease, poor thing; and so we got another one, which I wanted to call Knitting (Patten), but I wasn't allowed to by my 7-year-old daughter, who thought that was frivolous. So that's our life. And we try and travel as much as we can. We try to take one weekend off in about six; we go to France normally, the three of us, and get away completely and leave Emily in charge, which she does wonderfully well.

BS   And what of your political ambitions for the future?

JP   Oh, serve in the present job that I am in for as long as possible. I've got no ambitions – I've said so publicly on a number of occasions – to be Prime Minister or do anything other than be involved particularly in social policy – I am very interest in social and domestic policy. But it's never too good to have too many ambitions.

BS   But when the muse of history takes out her sieve and looks at John Patten's period of office as Secretary of State for Education, what assessments do you think might be made then?

JP   I have no idea at all. I expect she will say – it depends on how wide the bore of her sieve is – I expect she will say it was a bit tumultuous; and he led with his chin a bit too much there; and he might not have been as diplomatic as he could have been over here; but my word, he made education something of national interest; he made people for the first time ever aware of what went on in our schools, through the performance tables and the regular school inspections, and he helped us begin the long process of catching up with our competitors. And if she's as generous as that I will be pleased.

CHAPTER 8

Gillian Shephard

WITH BRIAN SHERRATT

Gillian Shephard was born in 1940 and educated at North Walsham Girls' High School and St Hilda's College, Oxford, where she read modern languages. Between 1963 and 1975 she worked as an Education Officer and as a Schools Inspector in Norfolk. Subsequently, she worked for two years with Anglia TV. She spent many years as a member of Norfolk County Council and has served as Chairman of its Education Committee. She has been member for Norwich South West since 1987, and held a number of junior ministerial positions before being appointed in 1992 as Secretary of State for Employment, in 1993 as Minister of Agriculture, and in 1994 as Secretary of State for Education. More recently she has overseen the amalgamation of the Departments of Employment and of Education.

Part One: 10 October 1994

BS   Could we begin, Secretary of State, by looking at how you developed your own ideas on education? Could you tell me something of your own experiences of school? Perhaps there were some teachers who influenced you particularly?

GS   My school experience was that I attended a very small rural primary school and then a rather small girls' grammar school, also in a rural area. After that I went to Oxford.

BS   Where you read modern languages.

GS   Yes. So, if anything, I am conscious of the limitations of the state system, although I was fortunate enough to have good teachers. I am very conscious now of having been to schools which were extremely small, where I would probably have greatly benefited from having had much stiffer competition early in my school career. I am also conscious of the limitations of the curriculum provided by a small girls' grammar school. For example, there was only one modern language offered, there was only one classical language offered. It was the fault of no one. The teachers were marvellous. Nevertheless the size, I think, with hindsight, was possibly restricting.

BS   So do you favour large schools?

GS   I certainly don't feel that it is easy for schools at the smaller end of the spectrum now to deliver the National Curriculum.

BS   Were there any particular teachers whom you recall with affection who might have influenced you particularly?

GS   Almost all my teachers, I think. In particular, the headmistress of our primary school, who was the most gifted and enthusiastic teacher. She had the gift of making everything interesting to children because she herself was enthusiastic about natural history, about local history, about language, everything. Certainly, many of my teachers at secondary school I recall with great affection and gratitude because they put so much time and effort into all of us. French teachers, the Latin teacher who also taught us music, English, history teachers. You couldn't have had a more dedicated set of teachers, and it does give me a certain view of the potential role of teachers in the way they influence children.

BS   Before you came into politics you were in education yourself. You were an LEA officer and inspector. What did you do before you became an officer and inspector?

GS   I taught. I worked in the careers service. I did a job as adviser for community provision – village halls, playing fields, that kind of provision in the further education sector. I taught in further education. I lectured for the extra-mural board, the WEA. I did a tremendous number of voluntary things – helped set up a rural life museum in Norfolk, ran the United Nations Association. I ran a vast range of things in my spare time. I was, as you say, an adviser/inspector. One of the things I did was to set up a primary French scheme in the County of Norfolk. Alas, it was abolished but it was very good and got great plaudits from HMI, I recall. Then when I left that I worked for a television company as a production assistant to one of the directors who was also a programme presenter, so that I had a very interesting insight into an extremely commercial world.

BS   What was the attraction of politics?

GS   Well, because, when I first started in local government, it seemed to me that the balance of decision-taking, of power if you like, lay with the officers. After local government reorganization that changed; power lay with the political side of local government. I'm well aware that many people in urban and metropolitan local government had been used to dealing with politics for many decades. In shire counties, however, the advent of politics coincided, I believe, with the 1974 reorganization. It seemed to me then that the interesting place to be was where the political decisions were being made. Once the opportunity presented itself I took it. Of course, when you get involved in local government, if you get involved in running health authorities, which I was also doing at local level, then eventually you start asking yourself questions about where the big decisions are taken, which is in Westminster and Whitehall. It was curiosity and interest that drew me to seek election as a Member of Parliament.

BS   Can we now turn to the Education Reform Act 1988? How important, how radical is the 1988 Act?

GS   Very radical indeed in terms of what it sought to establish. I'm on record as having said frequently that the French had a national curriculum for more or less two hundred years before we did and that I had always felt that the devolved pattern of education provision in Britain was something that held us back. The fact that the 1944 Act, excellent though it was, didn't insist on the teaching of anything except RE and PE – both essential of course – meant that within the law it would have been possible for teachers and governors to get away with very eccentric curricula. I think that the introduction of the National Curriculum was one of the most important reforms that you could begin to see. But obviously there were other developments such as GM schools, for example; the way school governing bodies were given more responsibility with local management of schools; the involvement of, and insistence on, information for parents. These were all reforms that were long overdue, and it took a Conservative government to bring them in.

BS   With hindsight, are there any weaknesses in the 1988 legislation?

GS   I think if there is a weakness it is that people expected all this change to be absorbed rather quickly and with very little pain, as one always does. Politicians travel hopefully. They have to. You always feel there isn't time. If you look back and think that what we were trying to do took the French two hundred years and the Germans a hundred years, then it isn't surprising that there was a certain amount of turbulence in education while the reforms were going through and while we've been attempting to get them absorbed into the education system. But I believe this is rather a good fault, if one can put it that way. Because you have to have enthusiasm. You have to have drive, which certainly many of my predecessors – notably Ken Baker – had in order to get the changes punched home. Now is the time for us to absorb this and to get it all working, well bedded in.

BS   Up until about 1986 there was nothing much at all on education in the manifestos.

GS   One is always accused of this ...

BS   I'm not accusing you of anything, Secretary of State ...

GS   ... no, no, no, no. Sorry. It is true. This point is always made. However, the interesting thing is that Mark Carlisle in the 1980 Act reintroduced the emphasis on parental choice. The 1981 Act was an epoch-making Act in terms of education for special needs, bringing about all the Warnock reforms. So it's curious that we've allowed these points to be made when in fact there were two very big steps in the early 1980s. However, I know that accusations have been levelled at the Conservative party for not putting education at the top of the agenda, and that it was only with the 1988 reforms that we did. All one can say is that there were two important steps at the beginning of the 1980s and of course an enormous amount of preparatory work to get the huge reforms of 1988 and the subsequent Act going.

BS   How would you characterize the Conservative policy on education between 1988 and 1992? What were the underlying intentions?

GS   To raise and establish standards which could be applied with more rigour; to involve parents more and to increase choice and diversity in the state sector. But also to make sure that the choice of independent schooling remained there and writ large. These are very broad aims, but you can actually see now – with the introduction of testing, with the publication of performance tables, with the codification of parents' entitlement – all these things now working through. If you look at what is on the ground – GM schools, LEA schools, CTCs, technology colleges – the whole range is much richer now than ever it was. I think that is very exciting.

BS   There's a sense in which there's a paradox, perhaps, in the 1988 legislation. A free economy/strong state paradox, in that the legislation did create diversity and choice with the introduction of GM schools, CTCs alongside existing LEA and independent schools, and, furthermore, devolved budgets to state schools, creating greater autonomy – and yet the curriculum appears to have been prescribed from the centre. So there appears to be a paradox there. Perhaps the paradox is heightened by the fact that independent schools have not been required to follow this prescribed curriculum. Do you agree that there is this paradoxical element in the 1988 legislation?

GS   No I don't agree that it is a paradox. I think if you're going to allow more variety in provision then what you must have is a certainty that you are delivering what children need, and that is why you have got to have a strong framework of the curriculum, of testing, of performance tables within which the diversity can flourish, and that is what I see happening. I'm sure it hasn't felt like it while the National Curriculum was being introduced, because it has been difficult. As I said, it would have been anyway. But if you're going to have a diversity of provision then you must have certainty about what is being provided.

BS   An argument from some heads in the GM sector might be, for example, that if the government has permitted schools to become autonomous, self-managing and self-governing, then why cannot GM schools also organize the curriculum for themselves? After all, the curriculum is essentially the proper business of schools.

GS   I personally feel that parents should have the entitlement to believe that wherever their children are being educated they are going to get the same menu. I think some GM heads, and indeed heads in the maintained sector, chafe under the load of bureaucracy that's been engendered by the National Curriculum. If we can get that right, and indeed if we can refine and make less onerous the demands of the National Curriculum, so that schools have some free time with which to develop their own strengths – and we're well on the way to doing that – then I think there might be less criticism. I believe that schools have felt very over-loaded in terms of the requirements of the changes. If they then feel that they've been listened to, that the curriculum load has been lightened, that they have a bit of time – which is what's been asked for, and indeed what's been promised – to organize and pursue their own strengths and enthusiasms, then I believe the atmosphere will be very different. And in fact more and more independent schools are now following the National Curriculum.

BS   The five former Secretaries of State we've spoken to all identified Keith Joseph as the cerebral force behind the 1988 legislation. Would you agree with that? You also mentioned Kenneth Baker as pushing through the National Curriculum reforms. Would you like to say something about your predecessors?

GS   I agree with my colleagues that Keith Joseph was certainly the force behind the education policy that we now have. But I must say I think the sheer strength, determination and bounciness of Kenneth Baker in pushing the stuff through the Commons was essential to get the whole thing up and running. I agree with many critics that we probably tried to go too fast and we have had, therefore, to refine and redefine subsequently. But I don't see anything wrong with that. I think that the whole thing needed a very determined push, and Ken Baker was most certainly the one to give it.

BS   What ideas on policy-making are distinctive of your own? What are you bringing with you to the Department for Education?

GS   I'm bringing with me a chronological attitude, if I can put it that way. What I mean is that at this stage, and for my time here, we've got to do a lot of listening, we have got to devote a fair amount of time to consolidation, to stability, to getting the reforms thoroughly bedded in and refined where we need to, so that they can actually flower. That is a rather dull thing to say, because of course it's always more fun to say, 'I want to turn this or that upside down'. But as far as schools are concerned, I believe we want a period of consolidation and stability, and I believe that's what teachers think too. I'm certain the public think so.

However, the interesting thing about the job is that it is so many-faceted. While we are certainly ready for stability in the school sector, in the HE sector I believe we do need to look carefully now where we are, to take stock and also to see what needs to be done to respond to the changes which have been taking place in the sector. The whole thing has expanded enormously. We have the influence of the new universities on the traditional universities. We need to look at what they are providing. One vice-chancellor actually said to me, 'We really need to look at what a degree is, what we mean by a degree now,' and it's that fundamental sort of question that we are approaching in the HE review. The time is right, certainly, for that.

We are also seeing more and more demands for very convincing vocational education. Now I have always chafed against the notion that somehow academic education is for the clever and vocational education is for the dim. Doctors, after all, have been trained vocationally, so have lawyers, and I don't think they would take kindly to being described as dim. And there are a lot of attitudes all round this in this country which one would seek to expose at the very least. There's a lot of thinking going on and there's a lot more work needs to be done again on the effectiveness and the currency of NVQs, GNVQs. It's being tackled with a will, but that side of the work has got to have due emphasis paid to it now, and we need to be certain of where we are going. So that's another push during my time.

Education in the early years is something that I think is very important – we are doing work on that in the Department. It depends of course on resources, timing, and so on, but there's a great deal of interest in it, and I am keen to tackle that whole area while not of course seeking to reduce the diverse provision that already exists.

I am extremely enthusiastic about English, the use of English, the correct use of comprehensible English. I believe that we have not only a tool that everybody has to be empowered to use, but also a heritage of national and international importance that we musn't waste. I've a great range of things that I want to do, but legislation, I think, is out.

BS   I think many heads will be pleased to hear that. If the photographs tell the truth, you were obviously delighted when you were appointed Secretary of State for Education. Why did you want the job?

GS   In the Cabinet the reality is that you accept what the Prime Minister asks you to do or you resign – this is actually the reality. I have enjoyed the other two cabinet jobs that I have done enormously.

Indeed in Agriculture it could be said that the background that I had and the constituency interest that I had were a great help in the job. Equally, in this job in Education I have a rather antique but nevertheless relevant professional background, which I hope will enable me to make a sound contribution. But of course it also has to be said that education, in my view, is one of the most important issues at any time in a country's history – not just now, but at any time: it is about our future; it is about our competitiveness; it is about our cultural inheritance. It's about all our young people, and our children – all their aspirations and their parents' aspirations. I don't think you could have a more important agenda than that.

BS   Absolutely. Can we look at the 1993 legislation? Some commentators regard the 1993 Act as the logical extension of the 1988 legislation, whereas others see it as a kind of radical departure from it. Some see it as a package, whereas others see it as full of ambiguities and contradictions. How do you understand the 1993 legislation?

GS   Well I don't think that one can say that it's full of ambiguities. I think if you set standards, and you set out publicly expressed expectations for schools, then you certainly do have to have a framework for dealing with those that fail, and that was one of the measures introduced in the 1993 Act. It probably was also time (twelve years later) that we looked again at the provision for Special Educational Needs, to see how what we had put in place was working, and that was another point. And then of course there was the question of an improved planning framework for school places. Now there, because we have made such a case of parental wishes and parental choice, we had to empower ourselves to cope with dealing with parental demands for popular schools, and that again is what the 1993 Act set out to do.

BS   It set up the Funding Agency for Schools.

GS   Yes. Which was the next logical step to take forward on how to cope with growing numbers of GM schools, and that had to be done, and I believe it proceeded logically out of the establishment of GM schools *per se*. Clearly you have to have an alternative mechanism, albeit a 'light weight' and 'light touch' mechanism for coping with the administrative repercussions of a large sector of GM schools.

BS   Yes. Initially there were some GM heads who perhaps thought that, having opted out of an LEA, they were now being opted in to another kind of bureaucracy.

GS   Yes, I think many of those heads, however, if they had queries on personnel, on employment law, on pensions, on funding matters generally, will feel glad that they've got something a bit less cumbersome than the whole DfE to deal with. I went to the FAS last week, and I was delighted to find that everybody I met was feeling that they were establishing good personal relationships with heads in the

GM sector, exactly as one would wish – everybody was saying that, and that is exactly what we want. We don't want a huge thing. It certainly isn't a duplicate DfE or a duplicate massive LEA – not at all, and that is not at all the way in which I perceive it to be working. I was impressed.

BS   Yes. I had reservations to begin with, but I have changed r y view, I must say.

GS   Yes. You can't tell, can you? You find that you need them. We don't want the FAS to be bigger than it needs to be, but the personal relationships and the helpfulness are the thing – GM schools occasionally need that sort of support (not all the time, but occasionally).

BS   Can we turn to the whole GM issue in particular, and look at the policy and its future implementation? Was it ever the intention that all schools should ultimately become GM, do you think?

GS   I certainly think that some of my predecessors hoped that the natural state would be that all schools opted out of LEA control. So far, of course, that isn't the case, although as I speak we've got 1,007 opted out, 51 in the pipeline, and many more enquiries; and the distinct feeling in my own mind is that in some LEA areas it would only take one to go to have a domino effect and many to go. We know some of the triggers. People are interested in nursery, people are interested in sixth form, and there are a number of other triggers. Yes, I do think that some of my predecessors hoped that this would be the case, and I have to say to you that with reorganization of local government on the stocks, who can say whether that might not end up being the case anyway? I certainly think that we are seeing signs of Special Educational Needs schools wanting to move in that direction as the proposals for local government review see the light of day. We shall see. I am concerned to help as many schools as possible to become self-governing, partly because I think this independence is tremendously healthy, partly because it's so clear that GM schools are providing a marvellously good education, are very closely in touch with the parents, and are working well within their communities: partly because there are all kinds of less tangible, more-difficult-to-describe benefits that are spin-offs. I think that the involvement of the community in the running of GM schools is a wonderful thing, and I don't know that any of us predicted that that would be how it was. I perceive in those running GM schools a terrific spirit of entrepreneurialism, of 'Well, let's have a bash at this, let's approach this person, let's see if we can do it this way.' In other words, a freeing up of all the enthusiasm, the expertise and ability that is there in people but which needs to be unshackled. And I see that as a most tremendous side-benefit which nobody could have foreseen, but it is there.

BS   I agree with you entirely. That being the case, however, why is it that there aren't more GM schools?

GS   I think when you see the development of something new like this it is bound to proceed in surges and plateaux: I think this is life, this is how it is. In the first tranche we probably saw people who were already chafing and dying to go it alone, and this gave them that opportunity. We now come to those who may need a little bit more persuasion, or who want to see for themselves how it's going before they take the plunge, and of course one could not do better in those sorts of places than to get them along to successful GM schools, where I believe they would be immediately convinced.

BS   Do you think the critical mass has been met – 1,007 – in the unlikely event of a Labour government? Do you think there are sufficient GM schools to ensure their continuance?

GS   The Parliament has a further two and a half years to run. In that time I expect there to be many, many more GM schools. But GM parents are already letting their muscle be felt. They are already saying, 'We are not having any return to what we had before. We like what we have'; and I think any group of politicians, whatever party they were in, would give themselves cause for thought if they were faced with two million parents spread right across the country, and of course there will be many more.

BS   Indeed. Perhaps I could ask you a general question. Why, in your view, Secretary of State, are Conservative policies on education superior to the alternatives which have been canvassed over the last fifteen years?

GS   Well, what are the alternatives, one asks oneself. I don't believe that the Labour party has had any kind of coherent education policy over the last fifteen years. Indeed it's very difficult to perceive that they have any now. They do seem to oppose vehemently all the changes to do with standards, the changes to do with accountability to parents, with self-government, with the new curriculum, with the exams, with the testing, with performance tables – they have opposed all of these. Only, a couple of years after each event they come creeping up behind. So I don't see the Labour party having any kind of alternative agenda. It is the Conservative party that has set the pace throughout, and we intend to go on doing so, and I truly believe that our message about standards – and that certainly is going to be one of my main messages – our message about standards really strikes a chord with what everybody wants.

    As far as the Liberal Democrats are concerned, again, it is very difficult to see what they have contributed to the debate. They say they want more spending on education. Well, everybody is always happy with that, but what they don't say is what they would spend it on. They do seem to be totally against GM schools. What they are *for*, it is very difficult to say. I just think that the Conservative party has taken control of the agenda and is pursuing it.

BS   How important will education be as an electoral issue, do you judge?

GS   I hope that it will be very important, because, of course, I believe that we have the right policies and we can demonstrate that we have pursued them steadfastly and with success throughout the last fifteen years. So I hope that it will be an important agenda item. And given the large numbers of parents in the country, and the large numbers of children at school (eight million or so), I believe that it will be.

BS   Can you tell me something about the job itself – the office of Secretary of State for Education? What's it like being Secretary of State, and what kind of job is it? What kind of Secretary of State are you? How do you do business with the civil servants?

GS   Well, this is my third cabinet job, and I've been in five departments overall. Each department is very different. In this job I find that there is an enormous amount of enthusiasm in the Department for the policies that are being pursued by the government. But of course it is either the GM sector, if you are talking about schools, or LEAs who are carrying out the policies, so the interesting thing here in contrast with my last job, which was in Agriculture, is that you are often at arm's length from a number of things that you are doing. A number of agencies have been set up as well, of course, so you aren't so 'hands on'. In Agriculture you are literally running the administration of grants and the administration of policy for the industry throughout the country, so it is terrifically 'hands on'. So, for example, is Social Security, where I had my first ministerial post; so is Customs and Excise, where I had my next one. So, if anything, I find it more 'hands off' than some of my earlier tasks. But what is welcome is the enormous range of people that you have to deal with – teachers, people in HE and FE. The range is great and you are working across the board, from children with special needs (and all the imaginative and caring work that goes into that), to young people at the very top of the ability spectrum. I met recently those who had won awards in the international maths, chemistry and physics olympiads. Young people who will be at the cutting edge of university teaching, of research, some of the top thinkers in our country, so that you get the whole range. I also greatly welcome, really, the emphasis on parents, because parents' aspirations are something that we must take careful account of. All parents want their children to do better than they did, and I believe that to seek to meet the aspirations of parents for their children is a tremendously worthwhile objective, and one that you can seek to realize in this Department.

BS   Ken Clarke told me that he found the way in which civil servants operate within this Department rather different to the way in which he experienced in others. I think he says something to the effect that he had to impose himself somewhat. Is it different here?

GS   No, I don't think so. I've found that wherever I've been.

BS   That you've had to impose yourself?

GS   Absolutely. If you mean business, you've got to bang the table, and that's what I've found everywhere.

BS   How do you cope with the pressures of the job, Secretary of State? (Maybe you don't experience them.) From *Who's Who* I understand you are interested in music and gardening and France. How do you cope with the immense pressures of the job?

GS   I am helped in this job because I do feel that I've got a background of knowledge on which I can rest – it is out of date, but I understand the currency. This helps to cope with the sort of daily or weekly crises that occur that are part of the stock in trade if you're in charge of a department. I find the work in the constituency a tremendous relief and support. Norfolk is a long way from London – not necessarily physically, but in every other way – and the preoccupations in the constituency, which I take very seriously, are, in a sense, a rest from the work that you do in charge of a department. I really have found, although I know I've moved fast between Departments, I do find it a help to have been in a number of them. Experience does help – it may not be long, but it is rather varied. [*GS chuckles*]

BS   I don't suppose you have any free time at all, but if you ever do, how do you fill it?

GS   Well, if I do have any free time I certainly do gardening if I possibly can. I'm a great walker, as they will tell you in the Department. I try to walk in the morning – three miles a day is what I try to do when we're here.

BS   You walk to the Department?

GS   Yes, I do. I like swimming. I get a lot of joy from my family. My parents live very close to us at home. I've got two step-sons, and I am very close to my cousins, who farm, and so we've got a big, rich life at home which is completely separate from work, and I think that's very important. I do actually rather enjoy cooking as well.

BS   And ambitions for the future?

GS   Well, quite frankly, I've moved about so fast that what I would like, and I hope I shall be allowed, is to remain here to realize the ambitions that I've sketched out: namely to get everybody facing the same direction, to consolidate, to stabilize, but to pursue the HE review, to continue to emphasize standards, to work on the under-fives, and to make a determined assault on the use of English. Really, I think that's quite a big agenda, and, as I said, it doesn't require legislation, thank goodness. But those are the things I want to achieve in my time here, and I do hope I shall be given the time to do that.

BS   Effectively you have answered my last question. But since I've asked every one else who has held your office, I must also ask you. When the muse of history takes out her sieve, how will Gillian Shephard be judged?

GS   Who can say, for a start, because you can't tell what tomorrow will bring, let alone anything else, but I hope people will have seen that I've grasped what I perceive to be the need of the moment, which is to stabilize and consolidate work in schools. But also to take forward the government's rigorous approach on vocational and higher education, and have a strong emphasis on language. I am, after all, a linguist, and I hope, if resources allow, to do some work on early years education.

BS   Thank you very much indeed, Secretary of State.

GS   Thank you very much.

Part Two: 21 March 1996

BS   Secretary of State, may I begin by saying how very pleased and grateful I am that you have managed to find the opportunity to see me at such a very busy time and at what must be a particularly harrowing time for you with the Dunblane tragedy.

GS   Yes, the Dunblane tragedy, of course, coming on top of the murder of Philip Lawrence, has focused everybody's eye on the vulnerability of children and teachers. Both events were appalling. The Dunblane tragedy was unprecedented, and we are all doing as much as we can both to maintain teachers' confidence, but also to support the enquiry into the Dunblane event.

BS   Of course it is not really possible to legislate for that sort of deranged and entirely unpredictable kind of act.

GS   No it isn't. Of course, you can't prevent a deranged individual from acting. What you can do is to make sure that as many sensible precautions are taken as possible to protect schools, pupils and teachers.

BS   When we spoke in October 1994 you had been Secretary of State for 83 days. What has it been like since then? Obviously there have been many developments; a great deal has happened; you've obviously been very busy and also very high-profile. What has it been like for you personally?

GS   Well, it's been very busy. It has also been very exciting. It must be one of the most interesting jobs to have in government, and the merger of the Education Department with the Employment Department was so much in line with my own thinking about the place of education within the country's economic development that the merger was entirely welcome to me, and it's been enjoyable, busy and stimulating.

BS   Can we talk, then, about the merger of the two Departments? Why was that done, and how was it done?

GS   The Prime Minister rightly saw that education and training and employment are for the individual a continuum, and he felt that it would be useful if the machinery of government reflected that. I believe that a very productive cross-fertilization has resulted, and that we are still only at the beginning.

BS   What has it meant in terms of structure? You have been Secretary of State for Employment; you became Secretary of State for Education, and now, since 5 July 1995, you have a massive Department. What has it meant in terms of restructuring and the allocation of responsibilities to civil servants who would previously have been working either in the DfE or Employment?

GS   Yes, curiously quite a number of people have as it happens worked in both Departments. What we have tried to do in terms of the structure is to make the most of the merger by, for example, looking at all qualifications together or looking at training and education issues for everyone between 14 and 19 rather than separating them out as in the past. You can imagine the bonus that the merger has been – for example, the development of Careers Education and Guidance – how good it has been to look at literacy and numeracy across the board with TECs now involved. So, there is only good coming out of it.

BS   The Department for Employment presumably had an entirely different in-house culture to the DfE. Virtually every Secretary of State for Education we have spoken to talks about the unique culture of the DES and, later, the DfE. To what extent is the new Department of Education and Employment influenced by either culture?

GS   Yes, there is a very different culture, and you would expect it to be so, because education has always been run by others, not by government, and therefore the Department for Education had a policy role, a regulatory role, but not a hands-on role. That has changed a little over the years, but that has been its role, whereas of course the Employment Department has always had a hands-on role: it runs the Employment Service; it runs training schemes; it has an active role in the regions, and therefore you can immediately see that the two heritages of the Departments fit them to play different roles. Therefore, there has had to be some adjustment, yes, for both sides.

BS   Has it been dramatic?

GS   I wouldn't say it had been dramatic, but it won't have been entirely comfortable for everyone.

BS   How would you characterize the adjustment?

GS   I would hope that it has provided a catalyst for each of the former

Departments to give of their best. It certainly resulted in new ways of thinking.

BS   Has it increased your work-load very obviously?

GS   Yes, it has doubled it.

BS   How do you manage to cope with that?

GS   With some difficulty. [*GS chuckles*]

BS   You would like forty-eight hours in the day, I suspect.

GS   Yes, it would be very useful.

BS   You're the most influential woman in British politics today. I think that's fact and not flattery. I would be very interested to know what you consider to be the advantages and disadvantages of being a woman in the Cabinet. Do senior women politicians manage differently to their male colleagues?

GS   I think it would be better if there were more women in senior positions in British politics, in British business and in British management generally, and of course we shall get there eventually. I do believe women manage differently from men. I think women's management style – which is characterized by communication, by team-working, by an attention to detail – is appropriate in today's world, and will be more appropriate in tomorrow's world, because that is certainly the view of large employers, and certainly the way that things are going. However, men managers are usually very good at seeing the broad picture quickly and are very good at confrontation, which is sometimes necessary. I think you need the skills of both, and I also think that each needs to acquire the skills of the other, if possible.

BS   That's really very interesting, because when Kenneth Clarke became Education Secretary he spoke to me about the 'devil' being in the 'detail' of the National Curriculum, and I think he found it rather a frustration to have to deal with that mass of detail, although of course that is precisely what he did. It also appears that Kenneth Baker, whom you greatly admire, was particularly good at painting the large picture, the architectural framework of the education reforms, with a big brush.

GS   That really is marvellously put.

BS   Do you think that there is some truth in that?

GS   I think that successive Secretaries of State have had different strengths to bring, and as I know I have said before, Ken Baker had both the vision and the *force* to push through legislation – really at what seemed to be against the grain at the time, but which has now come to be with the grain – no question about that – and I think he was absolutely remarkable, I must say. And really rather popular with schools. They didn't always like the policy, but I think they had to admire the verve with which he approached it.

BS   You are seen by some journalists as a prospective leader of your party. Obviously there's no vacancy at present. You're also seen as 'a safe pair of hands'. Do you see yourself as 'a safe pair of hands', and do you see yourself as perhaps one day the leader of the Conservative party?

GS   Well, I don't speculate on hypothetical situations.

BS   And I'm not entirely surprised to hear you say that. [*GS and BS laugh*]

GS   As far as I'm concerned, the Prime Minister will lead the party up to the election and beyond. I think people tend to see women as safe pairs of hands ...

BS   ... is that somewhat patronizing?

GS   I think it is, yes. I think that the description is designed to describe people as only being a safe pair of hands, and not lending to them other attributes. I hope that I have attributes in addition to having a safe pair of hands, but I have to say that having a safe pair of hands – if I have – is quite useful too.

BS   Do you agree that you have?

GS   No, I certainly wouldn't tempt fate by saying that! [*GS and BS laugh*]

BS   In which aspects of policy do see yourself making a particular mark? What is Gillian Shephard's contribution to the development of education policy since she became Secretary of State?

GS   Well, I came to the Department with a number of objectives: the introduction of full-scale nursery education; a thorough and fundamental review of higher education; an emphasis on the importance of vocational education, and, overall, a very strong emphasis on standards. I am delighted to have been in the position to have introduced a qualification for headteachers. I think the ability of a headteacher is without doubt the most influential factor in improving standards in everything in schools. There's no question about that. The merger of course brings other opportunities, and certainly enriches the chances we have of improving vocational education.

BS   Why did you introduce vouchers for nursery education?

GS   We wanted to put parents at the centre of the system. For far too long people have been emphasizing the interest of the 'institution', and indeed the debate surrounding the introduction of vouchers shows that we haven't got very far along the road of separating out the interests of providers from those of the customer, which is very regrettable. The debate over nursery vouchers has certainly focused attention on that. It is quite clear that the Opposition and many local education authorities are still utterly absorbed by the interest of providers in institutions. Now the world has moved on entirely from that in every other respect, in every other sphere, and why not education? And, therefore, this introduction of vouchers is seminal, it's very important.

BS   How would you characterize the objections to the introduction of vouchers?

GS   As institutionalized.

BS   Do you hope to extend the notion of vouchers beyond the nursery sector?

GS   Well, we have certainly been attracted by the idea of learning credits for the post-16s, and we've looked at an independent study that has been done on those and have put out the findings of that study for consultation, because that is another area where we could consider this kind of approach. It's very much more complex because we wouldn't be starting from scratch, as we are with nursery vouchers, but nevertheless it could work.

BS   Do you want to see that happening during your time at the DfEE?

GS   Well, the thing's gone out for consultation at the moment. One is never quite clear how much time one has. [*GS chuckles*]

BS   ... which is another story.

GS   Yes.

BS   How do you view the contribution that Sir Ron Dearing has made and the Dearing Reviews? Have those Reviews achieved the objectives you were aiming for?

GS   Yes. The first one that I had contact with was of course the curriculum review, or curriculum and testing review, where Sir Ron was able to propose, for example, the revision of the National Curriculum and also some very sensible new emphases on the basics, for example, in primary schools, and I found those entirely valuable. I believe they have achieved the purposes we wished.

BS   And the 16 to 19 review?

GS   As far as the 16 to 19 review is concerned, I wanted to examine that whole area because although we have introduced GNVQs we are very far from having a parity of esteem between vocational and academic routes. There have been criticisms that the A level route is too narrow and too narrowing, or not rigorous enough. Then there is of course the NVQ route. It seemed to me right to look at the whole area, but what is essential is that the rigour is retained in A level. Indeed that A level is retained. But that we give the opportunity to broaden what can be offered at the same time. But rigour is all-important – we cannot leave it.

BS   Some might be inclined to say that you have been more of a friend to the LEAs than some of your predecessors, and I believe you see LEAs as having a very important role to play in terms of school improvement strategies arising out of OFSTED reports and action plans.

GS   Well, it does rather depend on the LEA. I mean, some have allowed schools to get to the stage of failing, and of this fact being discovered by OFSTED, which seems to me to be reprehensible and incomprehensible. Others are using the OFSTED exercise in order to prevent their schools from failing, and are putting in preventive measures. As far as they're concerned this is very good for driving up standards. What is clear is that the role of LEAs is changing, they are becoming enablers because of LMS, because of grant-maintained. The whole thing is changing; there is an evolution; there is still a role for them to play, but there is, I have to say, quite a disparity in the standards of different LEAs.

BS   Is it an important role they still have to play?

GS   Well, it certainly is important at this stage, but I think that it is evolving and is diminishing.

BS   Will it diminish to the point where there's no longer a role for them?

GS   Well, I'm not sure. But there's no question that the finance role of LEAs is diminishing all the time. As schools get more independence they are getting more capable of running their own affairs, and there is no doubt that running their own affairs frees up such enterprise and such initiative that we are looking at ways of extending that financial independence for schools across the board.

BS   GM schools have acted as a spur on the performance of some LEAs, haven't they?

GS   Yes. The successes of the GM programme so far are not limited to GM schools, because one of the major achievements is the impact they have had on LEA performance. Grant-maintained status gave schools a choice either to remain in their traditional relationship with their LEA, if that's what parents wanted, or to become self-governing. Now it's that choice that has begun to transform the relationship between schools and LEAs. The relationship was already changing, of course, and would in any event have changed further as a result of the local management of schools (LMS). Legislation over the past ten years has given all schools far more power to call the shots, and I think that's exactly as it should be. But credit where credit is due. Some LEAs now accept that it's not their job to control schools, and they've worked hard to change their ways in terms of supporting schools with the services schools want rather than dictating to them what to do. Even the Association of Metropolitan Authorities seem to accept that LEAs don't wish to return to a pre-LMS system in which schools had no choice over where they could buy goods and services and had to endure long delays waiting for council suppliers to deliver goods. Well, in some areas at least those days are mostly gone, but I don't for a minute believe that LEAs would have moved so far or so fast without the GM spur. The key to making any supplier responsive is to give the customer a choice. That is what GM status does. LEAs knew that if they did not shape up, they would lose their schools.

BS   So LEAs have shaped up?

GS   Schools are now subject to less central control and interference. They enjoy more delegation and flexibility. And although not all of them may be prepared to admit it, schools in the LEA sector have a great deal to thank GM schools for, because they now enjoy many of the freedoms which in the early days went with GM status. So that apparent conversion of some LEAs has been quite swift and quite successful, but there are several LEAs which are still not delegating enough to their schools and many that are still ensuring that their schools are virtually forced to use them as suppliers, despite the appearance of choice.

BS   So has the difference between grant-maintained and LEA-maintained schools narrowed so far that there's now not much point in trying to become GM?

GS   Not at all. LMS is *not* the same as GM, and, to be quite frank, never can be. LMS can never equal GM. There are still plenty of strong reasons why schools should want to become grant-maintained.

BS   And what are those reasons?

GS   Well, the first reason is to get the power to spend money better for the benefit of pupils. This means controlling 100 per cent of the budget, including the element previously spent on LEA central services. Now, because GM schools have the power to match every last pound of their budget to their own priorities, it has made them eagle-eyed in scrutinizing how their budget is calculated in the first place. Currently, funding for most GM schools is based on calculating what the school would have received had it stayed with its LEA, and I believe that – for the present at least – this remains right. I know that many GM heads and governors feel strongly that it provides too much scope for LEAs to manipulate budgets to the disadvantage of GM schools. I take these concerns very seriously, and so does the Funding Agency for Schools. Any doubts about the accuracy of LEA data and dice-loading are investigated thoroughly.

BS   So you're not an enthusiast for a national funding formula?

GS   I can appreciate why the principle of a national formula is so attractive, but putting it into practice would involve major changes. Any change can produce losers as well as winners. And one of the immutable rules of politics, as of life, is that losers shout louder than winners. So we must proceed with care and examine the options thoroughly.

BS   But GM status for schools isn't only about funding.

GS   No, it's about much more than money. It's about flexibility and freedom. It's about giving schools the power to decide how they want to develop to meet the needs of their pupils and their communities. This point is often misrepresented, as though the government had some hidden agenda to pressurize GM schools to introduce radical changes from day one, preferably so that they would all become grammar schools. That is nonsense. GM status suits all types of schools. Some schools became GM to preserve the comprehensive nature of the school, and if a school is happy with its present character, that's fine. Diversity is strength, and it is the very diversity of the GM schools which produces much of their success.

BS   I know that there are some primary schools with ambitions to provide nursery facilities and several comprehensive schools wanting to develop sixth forms.

GS   Many primary schools, large and small, want to add a nursery class. Going GM gives them freedom to propose such changes. In the past year, we have approved nearly twenty proposals for new nurseries in GM schools, and there are more in the pipeline. Nursery vouchers should encourage further expansion. And in the secondary sector, GM status gives schools freedom to propose setting up new sixth forms. Seven out of ten GM secondary schools already have sixth forms compared with just over half of LEA secondary schools. Many are achieving excellent standards, as their A-level results show. Thirty-eight new GM sixth forms have been approved since 1991–92, twenty-six in the last two years alone.

BS   And some GM schools have specialized in technology or languages.

GS   Yes. GM schools were in the forefront of the specialist schools programme, which helps schools develop distinctive strengths in particular subjects. There are now over 140 schools in the programme, both technology colleges and language colleges. Nearly 50 are GM. Reports from the first tranche of technology colleges – 40 of which are GM – show that good progress is being made against their targets for raising standards.

If a school wants to specialize in a particular subject, it may want to make corresponding changes in its admissions policy. That is one reason why I'm proposing to give GM schools more control over their admission arrangements. You'll know all about that, and my plans for a new Circular which removes swathes of central government prescription. The consultation period on these proposals has now ended, and I was pleased that so many expressed support for our deregulation proposals.

Of course, many schools would like to develop what they offer in a range of ways, but need capital funding before they can do so. Next year's GM capital programme will be 6 per cent higher than this year's, which was itself an increase of 13 per cent. As for allocation, the Funding Agency is moving towards a more strategic approach. As well as specific support for essential projects, it includes greater emphasis on formula funding, which is planned to increase by 10 per cent next year. But it will never be possible for this or any other government to fund by grant every worthwhile capital project. So we have been trying to find new ways of helping schools to realize their ambitions. The Bill currently before Parliament will allow GM schools to borrow commercially. The popular Seed Money Scheme, the Public Finance Initiative and the new rules on asset disposal will all put GM schools even more firmly into the driving seat.

So, in all these ways we're seeking to give schools opportunities. Schools are best placed to judge how they should develop to meet local needs. That has to be within some national framework which can balance conflicting interests. But within those limits, I want the national controls to be as light and flexible as possible. I want schools to feel that it is for them to shape their future. Without needing to keep seeking permission. Without having to jump through endless hoops.

BS   You've spoken about the benefits of GM status, firstly in terms of greater control by a school of its budget and secondly in terms of a GM school having more power to determine its own future.

GS   Yes, but there's a third benefit, which is the most important of all. That is the sense of ownership. It's difficult to explain this effect to people who haven't experienced it. You can't necessarily point to specific things about a school which could not have been done if it had not gone GM. None the less, many GM schools say that the most profound effect of going GM is not what it does for your budgets or your buildings. It's about the change in atmosphere. It's about what happens when the people concerned with the school – staff, governors, pupils, parents – feel: 'This is a new beginning. This is now our show. We are now in charge. We are responsible for the success or failure of this enterprise, which is to do the best we can for the children in our care. We cannot pass the buck to anyone else. And we are determined that we are going to make a success of it.'

The greater control which GM schools have over their budgets and their future development merely gives them opportunities. But if opportunities are not taken, the education of the children will not benefit. The pride of ownership and the sense of responsibility are what cause schools to take those opportunities in a way they would not previously have done. That is why self-government can be so powerful. Rather than waiting for someone else to tell them what to do, it encourages schools to say to themselves: 'We could do that. Let's do it. Now.'

BS   But does this mean that GM schools are somehow less accountable? There are certainly those who would try to claim that grant-maintained status means that schools are not accountable in the way they perceive LEA schools to be.

GS   No. This sense of self-determination does not, of course, mean that GM schools do not have to account for what they do. Yes, I agree it is true that critics often say that GM schools are unaccountable.

That's nonsense. GM schools account in so many ways: through their governors – many of whom are parents living in the school's own community – through OFSTED inspection reports, through annual reports and parents' meetings, through performance tables, through financial returns and accounts to the FAS, through publication of audited accounts, and so on. GM schools should be proud of their accountability, which is rooted in their commitment to serving their local community and, above all, the pupils in that local community whom they educate.

BS   And then of course there's the suggestion made by critics of the GM policy that GM schools are cut off from other schools in the area and that their teachers become professionally isolated.

GS   Well, self-determination doesn't mean that GM schools are isolated – that's just another favourite canard. Opponents certainly try to make GM schools isolated, in the hope of creating a self-fulfilling prophecy. But I've been told many times that going GM has widened the school's horizons. Previously the world beyond the LEA's borders was treated as alien territory. Now teachers in GM schools are part of a national network which gives them access to a much wider range of educational dialogue and experience. The GM sector is now well-supported by a range of organizations, national and local. GM schools have the Grant-Maintained Schools Advisory Committee, which does an excellent job in creating links and representing the interests of GM schools and teachers. Then there's the Grant-Maintained Schools Foundation, which gives vital help to schools on the way to becoming grant-maintained, and the Grant-Maintained Schools Centre. So no school need fear that by going GM it will be left to fend for itself with no help or support. The difference is that GM schools can choose what help they want, when they want it, and who they want it from, rather than having to put up with interference masquerading as help – from one monopoly supplier and master.

BS   Perhaps we can return to GM schools later, if we have the time?

GS   Yes, of course.

BS   Who is actually shaping policy on education at the moment? I ask this because I read in *The Times* this morning about the Prime Minister's speech yesterday [20 March 1996] to the Social Market Foundation in which he proposed to extend selection – and you were referring to the suggestion by critics of GM schools of a hidden agenda just a moment ago – from grant-maintained schools to church schools, local authority comprehensives and specialist schools. Mr Blair attacked the Prime Minister for wanting to turn the clock back and effectively reintroduce the 11-plus. I gather you're not the keenest supporter of selective education, are you?

GS   Well, you shouldn't believe all you read in newspapers, I have to say.

What is so splendid about this job is that its importance is fully recognized by the Prime Minister with all that that means. It means that there is a support for this Department, an interest in everything that we do, an active engagement in the discussion of policy which not all colleagues have the benefit of in other Departments. And I have of course been in five Departments, so that I am in a position to make comparisons.

BS   And not all Secretaries of State have had the support of their Prime Minister.

GS   The point to emphasize is that the Prime Minister and I come from similar social backgrounds. Very different in terms of environment, but similar social backgrounds which have given us very similar attitudes towards the importance of education as an enabler and a ladder for children. Which means that we start from the same position, without having to describe it to one another. And therefore we are *determined* that our education policy is going to be the best we can possibly provide in the interests of all those children, all those people, who need ladders – that's where we start from, and we are absolutely united in that. As far as splits are concerned, I should forget them! There aren't any. It's always a dramatic story for the newspapers. There have been quite a lot of flights of fancy recently, but that's just what they are.

BS   Well that's clear enough. You and John Major agree on selection. The majority of schools in this land are of course comprehensives with non-selective intakes. Would you advocate that comprehensive schools look seriously at a selective intake?

GS   I would advocate that schools look at anything which they feel helps raise standards and helps them to develop a specialism, perhaps, to build on their own strengths and to accede to parental wishes. And in all those cases, to have a partially selective entry, or indeed fully selective entry, may be the answer. And we are indeed currently completing consultation on pushing up the 10 to 15 per cent that schools can select without having to publish statutory proposals, as you know. And I really think that schools are very well placed to make these kinds of decisions themselves. But there is no doubt that selection is popular with parents. That's emerged from an ATL survey, as well as from MORI polls and so on.

BS   So it's a vote winner too?

GS   I would think so. But the criterion always has to be: does it mean that the school will deliver a better education? And if it does, then it's got to be taken seriously.

BS   What influence would you say that Margaret Thatcher had – she was Secretary of State for Education and Science from 1970 to 1974 – what influence do you think she had in the formulation of Conservative education policy in the pre-1988 and post-1988 periods?

GS   I can't know that, but what one must not overlook is the importance of the education reforms that came in before the 1988 Act. For example, the Assisted Places Scheme was introduced early on ...

BS   ... by Mark Carlisle ...

GS   Yes, there was the 1981 so-called Warnock Act. There was the legislation to restore the opportunity to LEAs to have grammar schools, there was an increase in parental choice with open enrolment, and there was also a requirement that parents should have more information. So there was a tremendous lot going on before the big reform acts of the mid and late 1980s, and I would suggest that, with Keith Joseph, Mrs Thatcher was very enthusiastic about the aspects of freedom and choice that characterized those 1980s Acts.

BS   What do you now see as the policy of the Labour party on education? I asked you about this last time, but things have moved on.

GS   Yes, they have. It is unfortunate that the Labour party, which in the past has been able to pride itself on education policy, has now got into a position where its policy is divided, muddled and chaotic. It is not possible to know where they stand on selection, given that they appear to support it for some members of their front bench, but appear to want to get rid of it for others. We don't know where they stand on grant-maintained schools. They are using weasel words, but it is quite clear that, if they dared, they would want to abolish grant-maintained schools. They are giving the impression on the one hand that they want to have diversity, but when they have the chance to vote for it, as in nursery provision, for example, or grant-maintained borrowing, they vote against it. What is it all about? Extremely difficult, very unclear.

BS   In the event of a Labour victory, do you think they would abolish GM schools?

GS   Yes, certainly. I think that they would be under marching orders from their parliamentary party, and of course from their friends in town halls up and down the country who have certainly proved they aren't friends of grant-maintained schools.

BS   So the tail would be wagging the dog?

GS   I would say so, yes.

BS   What about the Liberal Democrats? Is their policy more coherent?

GS   I'm not sure what it is, but what we do know is that it would be more expensive. [BS laughs loudly] That's all I have to say on that.

BS   At the Birmingham Conference last September, which you attended with John Major when he spoke about his twelve-point plan, he appeared to be refurbishing the GM policy. What's been happening on the GM front?

GS   Well, I'm delighted that we are still getting a steady stream of schools going GM. That is splendid. We are also finding that GM schools now understand that their future would be under threat in the event of a Labour victory. They now understand that their freedoms would be swept away and that their difference would be swept away. I'm delighted by the developments in nursery. I'm delighted by the continued enthusiasm. We have had a lot of support for the GM borrowing powers. We certainly intend to produce more proposals to help GM schools in the quite near future, because we believe in the contribution that they have made to diversity, and above all to standards.

BS   Of course GM schools feature in HMCI's list of good and improving schools in his recent annual report.

GS   Yes. No less than 29 per cent of the 70 schools listed were GM, compared with only about 15 per cent of the schools inspected. And in the last list of 32 schools judged to be outstandingly successful, an astonishing 44 per cent – nearly half – were GM. I think that's terrific – a real tribute to the success of the GM sector. And of course the good news goes on. In the National Curriculum assessments, a greater proportion of pupils in GM schools achieved higher levels than in LEA schools at each Key Stage and in every subject. At GCSE, nearly half the pupils in GM schools achieved five good passes compared with 39 per cent in LEA schools. And of course GM schools have better attendance rates and less truancy.

BS   Of course the cynics will say that GM schools are only getting these results because they're mostly located in the more middle-class areas.

GS   Well of course none of us would try to pretend that a school's performance isn't influenced by the pupils it recruits. But equally, we all know, cynics included, that there are many GM schools in difficult areas, contending with more than their fair share of social problems. And it's in the nature of GM schools that they don't seek to shuffle off responsibility on to the pupils, or the parents, or the government, or anyone else. They take responsibility for providing their pupils with the best education they can produce. And our studies suggest that it is in the urban areas in particular that GM schools have made most progress in raising standards year on year. Of course, I'm not suggesting for one moment that GM status is a kind of magic wand. It doesn't turn poor schools into star performers overnight, but it can release more energy and determination and inspire more vision than people ever suspected they had. I'm confident that the benefits in terms of what pupils in GM schools are able to achieve will become more apparent with each passing year.

BS   Recently my friend Chris Woodhead, Her Majesty's Chief Inspector, has been criticized for expressing his views on the future of local education authorities in a paper he wrote for *Politeia*, the right-wing think-tank. He's been accused by CLEA [the Council for Local Education Authorities] of compromising his independence and entering the party political arena. Do you feel that OFSTED has somehow been politicized of late?

GS   I don't see that OFSTED is political at all. But it is pretty outspoken about standards in education. That is what I want to hear. That is why they are there, and why we pay them. We want a realistic view. We want tough action; for example, the new code on inspecting good and bad teaching which has just been announced, and which we first brought forward at the Prime Minister's Birmingham speech in September. OFSTED, in a way, are one of the single most important features of the government's reforms, because they tell us what is happening, they're giving us an enormous amount of information. They provide a check, and they can show us the way in which to put things right, make them better. They couldn't be more important. I'm very, very enthusiastic about OFSTED.

BS   Vice chancellors have grown increasingly unhappy about the squeeze on funding for higher education, while at the same time it was suggested that prospective undergraduates might have had to have put down a hefty deposit – £300. What are your reactions to this state of affairs in higher education?

GS   Well, it is the case that there has been a reduction in capital funding for higher education which we expect institutions to make up by access to the Private Finance Initiative. We are currently, with them, examining ways in which private finance can help them make up that reduction. We are also looking in detail at the effects of the budget on what is happening in universities. I think that their proposals for a 'hefty deposit', as you call it, were entirely unnecessary, divisive, and really basically not acceptable. But what we do need is the fundamental look that we are now having in the Higher Education Committee of Enquiry. Because the sector has expanded so fast; because we have brought together polytechnics and universities; because the pace of change in employment patterns in technology is so great; because there is a globalization of knowledge – because of all those things, higher education needs just as fundamental an examination as it had under Robbins 35 years ago. And I am delighted to have set up that Committee of Enquiry. I regard that as a major achievement in my time here.

BS   How do you see it developing?

GS   Well, that of course is the purpose of the Committee of Enquiry. I hope that it will have a big emphasis on quality. One thing we cannot afford to lose is any ounce of credibility in the quality of what's produced – what does a degree mean? Does it mean what it used to mean? That is so essential. It will need also to look very carefully at the interaction of research and teaching. Research too is essential for its own sake and also for the sake of the development of the economy.

BS   Teacher training is obviously of crucial importance. Yet teacher training has been criticized by teachers who have been through it;

it's been criticized by politicians as well. To what extent has the policy on teacher training been developed during your time as Secretary of State?

GS Well, we have made sure that the TTA is instituting a fundamental review of what is going on. OFSTED can inspect teacher training institutions.

BS And it has already done so.

GS Yes, and the reports are published. As a result we expect perhaps a diminution in the number of institutions offering training. We have also asked them to look carefully at the way in which primary teachers are trained to teach the basics, which is very important. They're developing the headteacher qualification, of course. And I have also asked them to do a fundamental review of the £400,000,000 we are currently spending on INSET. I am not satisfied that that money is being spent to the best effect. I think there is a reinvention of the wheel. I think there is duplication, and they are examining that as well. So rather a lot has gone on in teacher training in my time here.

BS Do you support the notion of teacher training taking place essentially in a school or schools, as opposed to in a university department?

GS Well, there is a place for both. We mustn't forget that one of the criticisms that has been made of teachers by OFSTED is that they aren't sufficiently acquainted with the subjects they're teaching. Therefore, to be certain that people are well equipped with knowledge is very important. But then of course you come to the skills; they have to be just as important. It's a balance, isn't it? There's no point in being a brilliant historian if you can't impart it. Equally, you can impart things brilliantly, but if you don't have the knowledge it's rather a waste. So both things are important. But I do think that good, solid experience in a school is very, very important from all kinds of points of view.

BS I agree that the knowledge base is critical – how can you teach anything if you don't know it? I would have thought that the standard first degree would have provided that knowledge base. What I was thinking of more particularly was what happens after graduation. Do you think the actual teacher training, as opposed to subject training, should be located in schools – do you think there is still a place for educational theory as traditionally taught by the university departments of education?

GS I certainly think that the balance is switching, and probably rightly, to skills and competencies in the classroom. I am sure that is right. I think that education theory, of course, is important as background, but it's not much help on a wet and windy Friday afternoon with class 4B.

Index